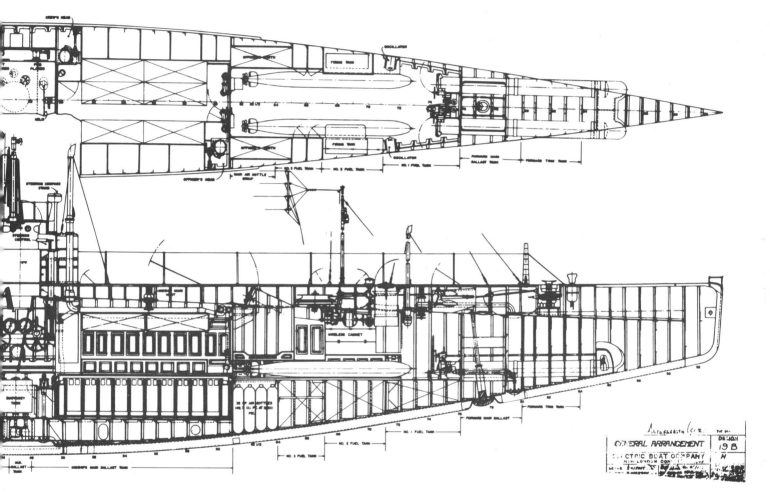

HMCS/M CC2, Electric Boat Company drawing. – author's collection

C A N A D A'S
SUBMARINERS

— 1914 — 1923 —

THE
BOSTON
MILLS
PRESS

E55 and other boats of the Harwich flotilla, 1918.
– RN Submarine Museum

CANADA'S
SUBMARINERS
—— 1914 — 1923 ——

Dave Perkins
Foreword by Vice-Admiral James C. Wood, CMM, CD.

This book is dedicated to all Canadian submariners, past, present and future. It is a part of the history they are still making and one of which they can be justly proud.

Canadian Cataloguing in Publication Data

Perkins, David, 1936–
  Canada's submariners: 1914-1923

Includes bibliographical references.
ISBN 1-55046-014-5

1. Submarine boats – Canada – History. 2. Canada.
Royal Canadian Navy – Submarine forces – History.
3. Great Britain. Royal Navy – Submarine forces –
History. 4. World War, 1914-1918 – Navy operations –
Submarine.   I. Title.

V859.C3P47 1989   359.3′257′0971   C89-094944-1

Published by:
THE BOSTON MILLS PRESS
132 Main Street
Erin, Ontario N0B 1T0
(519) 833-2407   Fax: (519) 833-2195

American Association
for State and Local History
Award of Merit

Winners of the
Heritage Canada
Communications Award

Design by John Denison
Cover by Gill Stead
Edited by Noel Hudson
Typography by Lexigraf, Tottenham
Printed by Ampersand, Guelph

The publisher wishes to acknowledge the financial assistance and encouragement
of The Canada Council, the Ontario Arts Council and the Office of the Secretary
of State.

Contents

Vice-Admiral James C. Wood, CMM, CD

FOREWORD

by Vice-Admiral James C. Wood, CMM, CD

    David Perkins has done a masterful job in sorting out the hearsay, rumours and myths about Canada's early experience in submarines. His detailed research in this volume has resulted in a highly readable book that will appeal not only to those who have served in submarines, but to all Canadians. He has captured the essence, the sounds, the smell of these undersea craft and the spirit of the small band of Canadians who served in them. This book is the story of people who gave their best, sometimes their lives, to convince Canada that there was a place in its navy for submarines. That they failed was not for want of effort and dedication, but because a central government and unimaginative naval leadership could not grasp the significant role that these strange vessels could and would play in naval warfare.

    The first faltering, almost bizarre steps taken to acquire HMC Submarines *CC1* and *CC2* for "McBride's Navy" would be mirrored decades later when Canada again took steps to acquire submarines for its navy. No doubt, in his next volume, Dave Perkins will unravel the tale of this era. The submarines and their equipment will surely be different, but the case for them in Canada will again be pressed by dedicated, courageous individuals who put their careers on the line in search for support and recognition of these unique, uncomfortable but magnificent machines.

    The current submarine debate which is raging in Canada today will perhaps, one day, provide material for a final volume which will record the success or failure of today's submarine proponents in pressing their case for a lasting and meaningful place for submarines in Canada's naval structure. Surely we cannot fail!

H1 *and* H3 *alongside at St. John's with* HMCS Canada *astern, circa 15-20 June 1915.*
    – F. Gordon Bradley collection

PREFACE

To say that I have been captured by my subject would be an understatement. I have been completely captivated. Submarines, and most of all submariners, are fascinating subjects, as I well know from my own experiences.

In the beginning I simply set out to document and describe the operation of Allied submarines in Canadian waters during World War II. I knew there must have been some kind of activity because I'd been shown photographs taken sometime in 1944 depicting British submarines docked at Halifax. When I made inquiries locally I met with such a lack of information that I was spurred into finding out for myself, to satisfy both my own curiosity and that of others who encouraged me to pursue the topic. And so it all began.

That I have been able to trace this story back to its very beginnings in 1914 and to fill this account with such detail is due to the help I have had from a large number of interested individuals and institutions. First and foremost among these is Gus Britton at the Royal Navy Submarine Museum in Gosport, England. I could not have succeeded without his advice, encouragement, guidance and co-operation, nor without the help of his "buffs."

I am also indebted to the staff at the Public Record Office, Kew, for their patient assistance, and to the Keeper of the Photographic Collection, Imperial War Museum, Lambeth, for his help in finding some really great pictures.

Thanks, too, to Dr. Alec Douglas at the Directorate of History, National Defence Headquarters, Ottawa, and to all his very able staff members both past and present. Marilyn Smith at the Maritime Command Museum and Graham McBride at the Museum of the Atlantic, in Halifax, also rendered assistance far beyond the normal call of duty.

Thanks are due to the helpful staff at the Public Archives of Canada in Ottawa, the Province of British Columbia Archives and Vancouver City Archives. My gratitude is extended to the Province of Nova Scotia, Department of Culture, Recreation and Fitness for their financial assistance and the encouragement they provided.

To all the wonderful contributors, and especially the ex-submariners in Britain, Newfoundland and the rest of Canada who have provided so much of the "real stuff" for my story, goes a very special thank you. I would surely have foundered without the recollections of the many wives and friends, officers and men, who answered my pleas for help so openly and generously. To that intrepid researcher into World War I submarine matters, Brian Head, my special thanks for his help and understanding.

I would like to take the opportunity here to acknowledge the generous co-operation of Lieutenant-Commander Colin Maitland-Dougall, RN, (Ret'd), who let me loose among his family's papers, records and photographs to find out for myself.

Thanks, too, to Mr. and Mrs. J.B. Lansdell, who were so helpful in providing me with details of the life of Mrs. Lansdell's father, John Grant Edwards. As you read this story you will realize just how important the co-operation of these individuals has been to me.

The support I have received from my wife and children has been beyond measure. Their co-operation and understanding have made this a very rewarding and pleasurable experience. Thanks gang, I really do appreciate all your sacrifices.

J. David Perkins
Dartmouth, Nova Scotia
January 1989

INTRODUCTION

That a group of young Canadian naval officers should be found fighting their country's enemies overseas during the First World War is not unexpected. The Royal Canadian Navy had of necessity remained closely connected to Britain's Royal Navy since its inception ten years before the war began, and a number of junior RCN officers could always be found in the gunrooms and wardrooms of the Imperial fleet.

That several thousand sailors from Canada and Newfoundland were to be found in the ranks of the Royal Navy, where they too answered the call of the Empire, is not surprising either. Canada had far more volunteers than it could ever make use of and for part of the war the Royal Navy actually maintained a recruiting station in eastern Canada.

That Canada should acquire and operate two submarines of her own and that a group of Canadian officers should serve aboard British submarines, however, is surprising.

A war like World War I had never been fought before. None previous had been so far-reaching, so technologically advanced, so deadly, nor, as the "war to end all wars," so disappointing in its failure to live up to expectations. It was an enormous undertaking conducted on a vast scale involving millions of people. Many new concepts were introduced into the arsenals that equipped both sides, including electronics, the internal-combustion engine, powered flight, and the submarine.

At the beginning of the war neither Britain nor Germany had any tried-and-true idea of how to exploit the capabilities of the submarine, and a great deal of experimentation took place during the course of the conflict. Both countries were forced by circumstances to use the new weapon in different ways, and they perfected their methods as the war progressed.

The submarine of the Great War demanded tremendous physical and mental effort from her crew. At that stage in the development of submarine technology, man and his machine were much more interdependent than they are today, when highly developed electronics have taken over much of the routine work previously performed by the men themselves. In 1914-18 very little machinery could be made to function without human assistance. The submarine sailor had to possess a detailed working knowledge of his machine so as to make it perform to its fullest potential.

The wartime submariner was a new breed in the world's navies. Well disciplined and imbued with a superb team spirit, the submariner was tough yet resilient, knowledge-able about his equipment, at one with his environment and confident in his resolve — attributes not always found in other sailors of the time.

To the captain of a warship, then as now, the greatest challenge ever encountered is that of engaging the enemy to the best of his ship's ability. All else has to be subordinated to this ideal. Only after the enemy has been engaged can the struggle for survival begin, usually at a time when the opponent's determination for the destruction of his antagonist is at its greatest intensity. It was not unusual for tiny submarines to pit themselves against mammoth battleships at ranges of less than half a mile, in total disregard for the calculated odds of survival, or to lie among uncharted minefields off an enemy shore for days on end, waiting, watching and reporting where a careless move would blow the entire crew to eternity. To achieve success in this type of warfare the captains had to have determination and a very steady nerve supported by a sense of defiance almost bordering on contempt, as well as complete technical mastery of their vessels. Needless to say, their personalities varied greatly, and this translated itself into success and failure in sometimes very dramatic fashion.

For the submariners there were the added risks of being at sea in all weather and under all warlike situations in vessels that were neither real ships nor, by modern standards, real submarines. The early submarine's seakeeping ability was mediocre at the best of times, while her dived performance was only marginally better. As a consequence, the casualty rolls on both sides contain many instances of "Lost at sea from unknown causes."

During the Great War the moral strength of the crew was always assumed and seldom questioned. The physiological effects of fatigue, prolonged tension, stress and the more mundane problems brought on through lack of sunlight, breathing contaminated air and eating a bad diet were almost never taken into account until it was too late to reverse the situation, and good men had to be put on the invalid list and their services lost, usually for a long time. That more men did not fall prey to a variety of mental and physical disorders is a tribute to the robust constitutions and the high level of human endurance to be found in the men of that era.

The demoralizing effects of long periods of separation from home and loved ones was another factor that was not appreciated until near the end of the war. Ships were shifted from one part of the world to another for long periods of time with almost no warning and often without any consideration given to the effect on families and marriages. Separation from home and loved ones was a fact of life that had to be lived with as best one could. Even had they been so allowed, most dependants simply could not have afforded to follow their menfolk.

Morale in the British Submarine Service remained high throughout the war, despite its suffering the highest casualty rate in the Royal Navy. The men possessed a pride of service conceived in hardship, born of technical professionalism, and nurtured by their own endurance and the sacrifices of their comrades. Although the submariners would have been the first to deny it, they were, in the literal sense, foremost among the unsung heroes of the war at sea. For obvious reasons submarine operations were kept secret throughout the course of the war. Their exploits were seldom mentioned in the papers and journals of the day, except where it was useful for the sake of propaganda. Even when their deeds were recounted, the boats and their crew members remained nameless. While the family of a man in the Grand Fleet could read all about the happenings concerning individual ships — albeit often deliberately contrived for the sake of public morale — very little was allowed pertaining to the activities of the submarines or submariners. The men themselves took a perverse pride in their anonymity, but it must have been hard on their families and dependants in an age when the daily paper was the most important news media and played a very active part in inter-community affairs.

This was the service into which these Canadians, mostly very young and some at the beginning of long naval careers, placed themselves voluntarily and without reservation. They had little thought other than getting as deeply involved in the war as was possible, for that was their professional calling. Their story begins as the war itself began and follows their adventures from Canada's West Coast, to Montreal, the East Coast, to the shores of Britain and the war-torn waters of the North Sea, the Mediterranean, the North Atlantic and the Irish Sea.

1 DAYS OF CRISIS

When an anarchist assassin's bullets took the lives of the Archduke Franz Joseph of Austria and his wife, Sophie, on a street in the Bosnian town of Sarajevo on the Sunday afternoon of June 28, 1914, little did the perpetrators realize just how far-reaching and devastating would be the results of those two pistol shots.

To most of the people of Canada it was a dramatically entertaining incident reported in their newspapers as having happened in a town with an almost unpronounceable name in the faraway Austrian-dominated Balkans. For the journalists of the sensationalist popular press, the incident provided a golden opportunity to break out of the summer doldrums and the reporting of unhappy national economic trends. In the more responsible papers and journals it created columns of speculation as to what might happen in Europe, and particularly in the Balkans. Those who followed the situation were well aware that there existed all the ingredients for another Balkan war. To the diplomats and politicians of Europe, however, the murder of the heir to the powerful Hapsburg throne presaged the realization of their worst nightmares. They knew that the events that had been set in motion that day could only result in a war involving the great powers of Europe — a heavily armed, delicately poised Europe with global diplomatic, trade and military alliances.

In British Columbia the summer of 1914 had been long, sunny and reasonably prosperous. Like most Canadians in the days before electronic communications, the citizen-settlers of the West Coast for the most part concerned themselves with parochial affairs, although a deepening country-wide depression was beginning to make itself felt, drawing their attention to matters beyond their province's borders. As national expansion slowed, so trade slackened, jobs became harder to find, property values slumped. Some businesses had already been forced to close their doors. To add to their disquietude the situation in Europe, starting with the news from Sarajevo, appeared to be going from bad to worse.

For the predominantly immigrant British population of the province, the European situation did not arouse a deep concern. The violent events and diplomatic wrangles that began making the headlines almost daily were happening half a world away, in places most had never heard of. In any case, no one doubted that the combined military forces of Great Britain, with the greatest navy in the world, and her allies, France and Russia, with the largest armies in the world, would be more than sufficient to deal with any challenge emanating from a crumbling Austro-Hungarian Empire, an upstart Germany or a wavering Italy. There would surely be no need to embroil the peaceful settlers and traders of the Mother Country's distant colonies.

The citizens of British Columbia, as elsewhere in western Canada, were too isolated from world events to be able to form a realistic appreciation of the dangerous situation that was developing in Europe during July and early August 1914. Eastern Canada, with closer commercial ties to Britain and western Europe, was much more concerned about the escalating crisis. While the disintegration of relationships between the German-led Triple Alliance and the Triple Entente, headed by France, accelerated into what would become the First World War, British Columbians went about their business content in the safety afforded them by sheer distance and the protection of Britannia's sure shield.

Richard McBride, the Premier of British Columbia, viewed the smouldering European crisis from a somewhat different perspective. Two points were of particular concern to the premier and his cabinet. The first was the German naval presence in the Pacific, which might cause problems if given the right circumstances, the other that in the event of war Japan would be obliged to honour its commitment to become an active military ally of Britain by virtue of the treaty signed between the two powers in 1902.

The problem posed by the German warships was one of immediate concern to McBride and urgently required attention, while the ascendancy of Japanese maritime strength and what its objectives might ultimately be was more of a long-term problem. Should there be a war, both issues would be of critical importance to his government, and the people of British Columbia could be expected to demand answers and assurances from their elected leaders. As he saw it, these problems could only be resolved by a substantial Canadian military presence, both at sea on the Pacific Ocean and on land at strategic points along the West Coast. In July 1914, however, only a shadow of the defensive measures that McBride and many others considered necessary existed, nor had he been able to convince the Dominion government in Ottawa to provide for them.

Four years before there had been some hope for the establishment of a meaningful naval presence when the Naval Service Act was passed by Sir Wilfrid Laurier's Liberal government. Under the Act, which received royal assent on May 4, 1910, the Dominion of Canada undertook to provide for its own naval defence. In the event of a declaration of war by Britain, Canada's naval forces would be placed at the disposal of the British Admiralty. This lodged responsibility for the protection of Canada's shores with the Admiralty as part of the overall strategic plan. A Department of the Naval Service was created and a Canadian-born retired Royal Navy officer, Charles E. Kingsmill, was given the position of Director of the Naval Service. He held the rank of vice-admiral.

A small, balanced fleet of one scout and five light cruisers supported by five large sea-going destroyers was envisioned. All of these vessels were to be built in Canadian shipyards, even though high Canadian wages for labour made this the most expensive option and much of the sophisticated equipment would have to be imported. In the interim, two obsolescent British cruisers were to be purchased to provide training and experience, while the dockyards at Halifax and Esquimalt would be reactivated and a college for training naval officers established.

With the collapse of the Liberal government on September 21, 1911, most of these plans went by the board as Robert Laird Borden, the Conservative Prime Minister, put the Naval Service Act in limbo while his government worked out their own maritime defence strategy. In December 1912 he introduced the Naval Aid Bill whereby the Government of Canada would give the British Admiralty $35 million to pay for three Dreadnoughts in return for British consideration of Canadian needs for protection at sea. It was even suggested that the Dreadnoughts could be built in Canada, an idea that intrigued the First Lord of the Admiralty, Winston Churchill. At that time there were no slips big enough to handle such large warships, but it was anticipated that the new Vickers yard under construction near Montreal would have the required capacity.

The proposal met with strong opposition from the Liberals and from the Quebec nationalists, who were ably represented by Henri Bourassa and his paper "Le Devoir." After a bitter debate lasting 23 weeks and the imposition of closure, the contentious bill survived passage of the House. Its chances of surviving the Liberal-dominated Senate, however, were very poor, and in May 1913 the Upper House not unexpectedly rejected the bill. Borden, faced with an ever-worsening economic depression, took little further interest in maritime defence matters. Canadian naval development was left in a vacuum.

However, some of the main features of the original plan had been put into effect, including the acquisition of the two training cruisers. Both ships arrived during 1910, HMCS *Niobe* at Halifax in October and HMCS *Rainbow* at Esquimalt in November. The arrival of the ships allowed recruiting to begin and a modest start was made to manning the ships with Canadian sailors in place of the British crews who were on loan until a changeover could be effected. The dockyards at Halifax and Esquimalt were reactivated and the Royal Naval College of Canada opened in the old naval hospital building in Halifax dockyard during January 1911.

Neither the Liberal nor the Conservative governments had formulated, nor indeed even seriously considered, a separate defence policy for the West Coast. This would not become a reality until 1930. In July 1914 McBride's most urgent concern was how to provide a defence against the possibility of raids by marauding German warships along the British Columbia coast. This was a very real possibility, for modern engineering had made the world a much smaller place than most people realized, drawing every corner of the globe into the reach of the contestants. As the crisis in Europe intensified, so the press in Canada extolled the dangers and the populace of the exposed coastal communities and settlements of British Columbia suddenly became painfully aware of their vulnerability.

The warships that were of such concern to Richard McBride were units of a German cruiser squadron based in China, at Tsingtau on the Yellow Sea, on the other side of the Pacific Ocean. Known as the East Asiatic Squadron, it was commanded by the very capable Vice-Admiral Maximillian Count von Spee. His ships were fairly modern, manned by regular service personnel, including two of the Admiral's sons, and had a reputation for excellence in gunnery and a high standard of military efficiency. The big guns of the squadron were carried by the sister armoured cruisers SMS *Schanhorst* and *Gneisenau*. Completed in 1907, each of the 12,781-ton ships was armed with eight 8.2-inch and six 5.9-inch guns. Their vital areas were protected by 6 inches of armour and a 2-inch-thick armoured deck. The light, unarmoured cruisers SMS *Leipzig*, 3,756 tons, *Nurnberg*, 3,390 tons, and *Emden*, 3,664 tons, mounting ten 4.1-inch guns apiece, made up the balance of Von Spee's forces. With clean bottoms and tight boilers, all of these ships could attain speeds of 23 knots or better. When war was declared the two armoured cruisers and *Nurnberg* were together at Ponape in the Caroline Islands, *Emden* was at Tsingtau, while *Leipzig* was in Mexican waters at Mazatlan.

The Royal Navy had no less than three squadrons of warships on station in the Western Pacific positioned to counter any moves by Von Spee's five ships. On the China Station there were two armoured cruisers, HMS *Minotaur* and *Hampshire*, two light cruisers, *Newcastle* and *Yarmouth*, as well as the pre-Dreadnought 10-inch-gunned battleship *Triumph* in reserve at Hong Kong, all under Vice-Admiral Sir Martyn Jerram. Rear-Admiral Sir Richard Pierse had one pre-Dreadnought battleship, HMS *Swiftsure* (sister ship to *Triumph*), the light cruiser *Dartmouth* and the *Fox*, an obsolescent cruiser, under his command in the East Indies. In Australian waters Rear-Admiral Sir George

Patey flew his flag in the modern 12-inch-gunned battlecruiser HMAS *Australia* and commanded two new Australian light cruisers, the *Melbourne* and *Sydney*, and two older cruisers, HMNZS *Encounter* and HMAS *Pioneer*. These ships had the support of a well-developed network of fuel depots, bases and dockyards stretching from Australia to Singapore and China. On paper this was a formidable force, but later events were to demonstrate its deficiencies in a dramatic fashion.

In the not unlikely event of a declaration of war against Germany by Japan, the naval forces of the relatively new and powerful Imperial Japanese Navy would be added to those of the Royal Navy. Von Spee would then be faced with an overwhelming superiority of numbers and firepower, all bent on the destruction of his cruisers and the capture of their only repair base, for it was no secret that Japan coveted Germany's colony on the Chinese mainland and would besiege it at the first opportunity.

With all of this naval might available to defend British interests in the Pacific, including the Canadian West Coast, against only one German squadron that stood but little chance of reinforcement, it seems questionable as to whether or not there was any real need for local defences on the British Columbia coast. The reality as McBride saw it was that the British put little actual value on the coastal communities of his province; it mattered little to them if the Germans raided his shores. Such raids would be only of a nuisance value in the long run and may even expedite the eventual destruction of the enemy by British forces. The British commanders considered it most unlikely that the Germans would bother McBride's constituents, and later events were to prove they were quite correct in their assessment.

The ships available to the commanders of that era were very different from those of even a decade before. The modern British and German cruisers, those completed around 1906 and later, were particularly good examples. Fine sea-boats, well armed, fast, reasonably habitable, and mechanically reliable, they were limited in their effectiveness only by the logistical problems of obtaining the necessary fuel, ammunition and stores, and the limitations imposed by a lack of long-range communication. Many of these ships were powered by turbines and all were capable of making sustained high-speed runs. The primary fuel for the manually stoked boilers of the warships of 1914 was coal, upon which fuel-oil was sprayed to obtain extra heat when high speed was called for. The 4,800-ton British Bristol-class of 1910, a fairly typical light cruiser, carried 1,350 tons of coal augmented by 1,250 tons of oil. This gave an operating range of about 5,000 nautical miles at 16 knots. At their full speed of 26 knots, however, fuel consumption more than doubled.

Coaling ship was a frequent operation and, except for major bases where some mechanized equipment was available, it was accomplished by slinging the stuff aboard in sacks and baskets, a filthy, all-hands evolution that went on until it was finished. Coaling ship at sea was very difficult and could only be carried out in calm weather when the collier and warship could come alongside one another. Because this process required the co-operation of the weather, it could never be relied upon. The highly complex evolution of coaling while under way would be developed during the war but was not generally practised in 1914.

Best-quality steam coal was needed for the warships of the Royal Navy and this was stockpiled at strategic points around the world, wherever Britain's warships might be likely to go. The supply of coal was of critical importance and the Admiralty employed a fleet of colliers to keep up with the insatiable demands of the world's largest fleet at war.

By 1914 some type of primitive short-wave radio, or "wireless set" as it was then known, was fitted aboard most warships, along with its attendant aerial array strung between high masts. Messages were tapped out in Morse code using telegraph-type hand keys and sent out by means of vacuum-tube transmitters. With a reliable range of only 200 to 400 miles, wireless was more of value in the tactical than in the strategic sense. Signals sent from these early transmitters were fairly easy to intercept, thereby advertising a ship's presence in a particular area. Although there was no means of measuring the range, a rough bearing could be obtained, different nationalities distinguished by the pitch of the signal and call signs recognized. Long-range communications had to rely on the telegraph system with its vulnerable wires. For ships operating far from home this meant putting in at Allied or neutral ports having a telegraph-equipped embassy or commercial telegraph office where they could exchange coded messages with their home base. Where possible, wireless relay stations were established, but even then the transmission of an important message and receipt of the reply could take hours, or even days, depending on atmospheric conditions and message traffic priorities.

Germany possessed a number of colonies in the Pacific Islands and had made arrangements for caches of supplies and fuel to be stored at isolated anchorages well in advance of the commencement of hostilities. In addition, a small fleet of loaded colliers had been collected at Tsingtau for dispatch to pre-assigned German-occupied ports in order to sustain a prolonged cruiser campaign. To reinforce the naval squadron in its role of commerce disruption and destruction, several large passenger liners in service in the region were ordered to rendezvous with the warships a few days before the declaration of war, to be fitted out as armed merchant cruisers (AMC). One of these AMCs, the 16,000-ton *Prinz Eitel Friedrich*, was already at Tsingtau being fitted out when war was declared. A second, the Russian *Rjasan*, was captured by the *Emden* on August 4, armed, and re-commissioned as the *Cormoran* on the 7th. The German commander could also count on assistance from a highly developed intelligence system with agents in every neutral country. Realizing that secure communications would be impossible once war was declared, the German Admiralty had relieved Von Spee of the necessity of communicating with Germany and gave him a completely free reign in how he conducted his operations, the one overriding consideration being that he was not to allow his ships to be bottled up at Tsingtau.

The East Asiatic Squadron had a vast area in which to cruise and no one could predict where or how they would conduct their operations. Considering the forces pitted against the Germans, particularly if Japan entered the fray, it was probable that sooner or later the Pacific Islands would be denied them. From there it was believed Von Spee would most likely make for the South Atlantic and the vitally important Allied shipping routes to and from the River Plate. Here he could link up with three other German light cruisers, SMS *Konigsberg*, which was in East African waters, and the *Dresden* and *Karlsruhe*, stationed in the Caribbean.

On the west coast of the Americas there was little of military interest to Von Spee, as almost the entire coast would be neutral. The only British possession of any real importance was British Columbia. Here were coal stocks, thriving fishing and lumber industries, and shipping facilities of all kinds. Whether or not the Germans would risk a raid was beside the point; the *Leipzig* was certainly in a position to do so, and if they chose to mount one, there was pathetically little that the Dominion of Canada or the Province of British Columbia could do about it.

To counter this possible threat the Royal Canadian Navy possessed only one warship, the 23-year-old, 3,400-ton light cruiser *Rainbow*, the training ship for the Pacific contingent of the fledgling RCN. A member of the numerous Apollo class, she had first commissioned in 1892. *Rainbow*'s only protection was a 1¼-2 inch armoured deck, and she was fitted with a pair of obsolete 6-inch and six 4.7-inch quick-firing guns. The old ship's five boilers and twin reciprocating engines were long past being able to sustain her designed speed of 20 knots for any length of time. She was manned by a reduced regular crew consisting mostly of Royal Navy personnel on loan, most of her Canadian complement having deserted when the Conservatives came to power. In the event of a war it was intended that her complement would be filled out with new recruits and the partly trained men of the recently created Royal Naval Canadian Volunteer Reserve. There were also two British sloops, HMS *Shearwater* and *Algerine*, based at Esquimalt, which were of no fighting value whatever. Both sloops were cruising in the same waters off the Pacific Coast of Mexico as the German cruiser SMS *Liepzig* when war was declared.

Ashore at Esquimalt and Victoria were two batteries of obsolete 6-inch guns on disappearing mountings at Forts Rodd Hill and McCaulay, and a pair of newly installed but incomplete 9.2-inch guns with only primitive fire-control equipment in a redoubt on Signal Hill. In a shed in the dockyard were a number of harbour-defence submarine mines left behind by the British when they evacuated the base in 1906. As would be discovered later, when they were most needed, there was no one left who knew how to prepare or lay them. Whether or not he had any faith in the Royal Navy coming to his rescue, McBride felt he had good reason to be uneasy about the material state of the RCN and the condition of the local defences.

The question of Japan's rise as a naval power in the Pacific had plagued the West Coast ever since her navy demonstrated its capabilities during the Russo-Japanese war of 1904-05. Despite the Anglo-Japanese treaty of 1902 the "Orientals" were not to be trusted so far as the predominantly white Anglo-Saxon population of British Columbia was concerned. The immigration of large numbers of Japanese to labour on the railways, in the mines and at the lumber camps during the first decade of the century had created a situation that was ripe for exploitation by the bigoted white community of the day. Reinforcement of the thousands of Japanese in the province by units of the powerful Japanese fleet conjured up visions of the "good people" of the coastal cities and towns being murdered in their beds by the "yellow peril."

In 1907 this anti-Japanese sentiment had given rise to riots in the streets of Vancouver. Cooler and wiser heads, however, examined the allegations closely and could see no threat, whether real or implied, in the growing Japanese community, but on the whole found their advice and counsel being ignored.

The Colonial Defence Committee, a subcommittee of the Committee of Imperial Defence, had made a study of the Canadian West Coast situation in 1909-10 and concluded that with the Anglo-Japanese treaty in effect no special defence precautions beyond those already in place were really necessary. In the unlikely eventuality of the treaty breaking down, it was concluded that the West Coast could expect only light raids by unarmoured cruisers and that Vancouver and Prince Rupert should be armed accordingly with 6-inch guns. The Canadian government readily went along with the findings of the committee: Wilfrid Laurier and his cabinet could not perceive of any real threat to the West Coast communities. In 1912 these provisions were re-examined by the Admiralty, who recommended the establishment of a major naval base at Vancouver to support a local defence flotilla of four torpedo boats and three submarines. The depot at Esquimalt had been condemned by the Admiralty years before as being too exposed for use as a primary base. It was also considered that in the event the treaty did break down, or expired and was not renewed, Vancouver should serve as a base for a much stronger naval force.

The work of procuring and siting the guns at Vancouver and Prince Rupert, the purchase or building of the torpedo boats and submarines, and the building of a base at

Vancouver were never taken in hand. Esquimalt, by virtue of the obsolete shore batteries already sited there, became the focus of defence for the entire area. In 1911 the mounting of the two disassembled 9.2-inch guns that had cluttered the road to Signal Hill since being abandoned by the British when they vacated the base in 1906 was resumed under the auspices of the Minister for the Militia, Colonel Sam Hughes. If this one token to the defence of the entire West Coast was acceptable to the government in Ottawa, it was of little concrete value to the provincial and community leaders of the coastal towns and settlements of British Columbia who, in that eleventh hour of July 1914, began to realize that they and their livelihoods were virtually unprotected while the great powers of the world were hurtling inexorably towards the calamity of a World War.

Iquique *(CC1) and* Antofagasta *(CC2) alongside in Seattle, August 1914.* – PAC 113254

2 McBRIDE'S NAVY

Realizing that the federal government was unlikely to take a lead in the naval defence of the West Coast beyond what was represented by the batteries at Esquimalt and the obsolescent *Rainbow*, McBride let it be known that he and the provincial government were prepared to take action of their own. As the crisis deepened, the Militia forces and the Royal Naval Canadian Volunteer Reserve were encouraged to organize, seek recruits and prepare for mobilization. While this was in progress the marine defences of British Columbia were about to be offered assistance from a completely unexpected source.

Unannounced and without prior communication with anyone in Victoria, James Venn Paterson, an American shipbuilding entrepreneur of Scottish origin, boarded a steamer at Seattle, Washington, for the five-hour run to Victoria. He arrived in the provincial capital on Monday, July 27, carrying in his mind a business deal that he felt would be of benefit to both himself and to the people of British Columbia.

James Paterson was president of the Seattle Construction and Drydock Company. He had two brand-new submarines to sell and was looking for a buyer. In arriving at his decision to make this overture to the Canadians, Paterson does not appear to have consulted with anyone else, nor was any other authority aware of his intentions. His activities that day are obscure, but it is probable he met with Captain W.H. Logan, surveyor to the London Salvage Association, to whom he described his intention of disposing of the submarines. Logan, who knew Paterson, was well aware of the existence of the two boats. He was a frequent visitor to Seattle and it was his business to be acquainted with the activities of the shipyards there. No further inquiries were attempted at that time and Paterson went about his business in Victoria, and later at Vancouver, somewhat surprised at the complacency displayed by the Canadians in the face of the threat of a serious war.

Paterson had good reason to want to sell the submarines, for they had recently been rejected by their original buyers, the government of Chile. Named *Iquique* and *Antofagasta*, after two of that country's coastal communities, they were known in the shipyard as Chilean submarine torpedo boats Nos. 1 and 2, or simply *C1* and *C2*. Laid down almost three years before, *C1* had been launched in June and *C2* in December 1913, and had only run their sea trials during July 1914. The hulls had been fabricated by Paterson's company according to specifications and drawings supplied by the Electric Boat Company of New Jersey, American owners of the Holland Boat Company patents, and the vessels were completed using parts and equipment supplied by Electric Boat and their subcontractors in the East.

Captain Charles Plaza, senior officer of the Chilean Naval Commission at Seattle, had refused to accept the submarines after diving and endurance trials carried out in Bellingham Bay. His public reasons, explained in full in the July 26 edition of the Seattle *Sunday Times*, were that the boats were unable to operate according to design specifications while carrying the stores load as specified in the contract. During the trial runs, when the boats were fully loaded as desired by the Chilean authorities (grossly overloaded according to Paterson and Electric Boat), they had been unable to make the designed speed, attain the designed range of operation, were sluggish in rising to the surface and difficult to control underwater. By Chilean standards this rendered the subs both unsafe and unacceptable.

In a report sent to England dated July 25, Captain Plaza also communicated his findings to Sir Philip Watts, principal naval advisor to the Chilean government. The Chilean authorities could find no particular fault with the way in which the boats were assembled, but rather blamed the Electric Boat Company for providing a design that did not fulfill the contract requirements. Paterson was of the opinion there might have been other reasons. He was convinced the Chilean government lacked the means with which to pay for the two submarines, although later examination would show they had already remitted $714,000 of the $818,000 price agreed to. At the same time Chile was having two 14-inch-gunned battleships, the *Almirante Latorre* and the *Almirante Cochrane*, and six large 31-knot destroyers built in Britain. It was his contention that they had defaulted on payments for these as well. Whether they were in financial straits or the submarines had really behaved as badly as claimed, Chile had failed to make payments on them for almost a year and was technically in default of the contract. When the Chilean government suspended its payments to Electric Boat, they in turn ceased making progress payments to the builder, which left Paterson considerably out of pocket.

Despite this, there was no reason why the Chilean authorities could not have come to an arrangement with Electric Boat, paid whatever balance was agreed to and taken full legal possession of the submarines. In the meantime, Captain Plaza and his crews had remained in Seattle attending to the boats, which had tied-up at Paterson's shipyard after the unsuccessful completion of their trials.

On July 28 Austria declared war on Serbia. On that same date the British Admiralty sent out a warning telegram to all commands ordering a preliminary state of alert, the mobilization of reserve forces, and advising that war with Germany and her allies appeared to be imminent. With the Austrian declaration of war the populace of Canada suddenly became aware that Great Britain and her Dominions were about to become embroiled in a war against Europe's mightiest military alliance. Britain's declaration, if and when she made one — and there was little doubt that she would — would automatically include all of the Dominions and colonies in her great Empire.

Paterson was again in Victoria, on Thursday, July 29, and was present at a meeting of about half a dozen influential local businessmen held that afternoon at the Union Club, an exclusive gentlemen's establishment. During the conversation it was suggested that warships might be purchased from Chile. As that country was already committed in an ongoing dispute with Argentina, it was concluded they would be unlikely to part with any. At this point Paterson and Logan brought up the matter of the two submarines lying at Seattle and Paterson confirmed they were for sale. Although his offer was considered with interest, no one was prepared to suggest a deal nor did Paterson divulge a price. Later that same day he returned to Seattle, still pondering Canadian reserve in the face of certain disaster.

Knowing that McBride would be sympathetic to their suggestions, Captain

Logan, and perhaps others who had attended the Union Club meeting, approached the Premier with the news of the availability of the two submarines. This was not the first time submarines had been suggested to the Premier and he almost certainly had a fair idea of the value of that type of craft. McBride would have been aware of the Admiralty reports which proposed the stationing of submarines at Vancouver and had been approached as recently as early July by an individual offering four (apparently fictitious) submarines for sale, these recently completed for a South American government. Although he would have preferred a cruiser or some destroyers, none of these were being offered, so the submarines had to be seriously considered as being the only readily available option.

During the rest of the day the matter was discussed, but no positive moves appear to have been made until Saturday, the 1st. There is evidence to suggest, however, that McBride telephoned or telegraphed Vice-Admiral Kingsmill on the 29th warning him of the possibilities, for Kingsmill was actively seeking submarine-trained personnel in Ontario on the 30th. By that time the Premier was convinced of the desirability of obtaining the two boats but was doubtful as to how such a proposition would sit with the politicians in Ottawa.

At the time, the Hon. Martin Burrell, Minister for Agriculture and Member for Yale-Cariboo, was on holiday in the provincial capital and staying with the Hon. G.H. Barnard, Member for Victoria. That morning McBride telephoned Harry Barnard and asked him to arrange a meeting between Messrs. Burrell and Logan. This was duly accomplished. The three men met in Barnard's office a short while afterwards, at which time Logan apprised Burrell of their ideas for buying the submarines. Wanting a professional opinion, the three men went to the dockyard to discuss the matter with the acting Senior Naval Officer, Esquimalt, Lieutenant Henry Byng Pilcher, RN. Although Commander Walter Hose, RCN, held the appointment of SNO Esquimalt, he was also in command of the *Rainbow* and was fully involved in getting his ship to sea. Pilcher informed Logan, Barnard and Burrell that he thought the submarines would make a valuable addition to local naval defences. At this time Logan informed the others that he felt the boats could be had for about $375,000 apiece. Burrell, although receptive to the idea, would make no commitment on the part of the government. Over the weekend McBride held further discussions regarding the boats and finally scheduled a meeting of all concerned to be held in the dockyard at 3 p.m. on Monday, August 3.

By Monday morning it was obvious that a declaration of war was probably only hours away. To emphasize the urgency of the situation, the German cruiser *Leipzig*, and possibly *Nurnberg* as well, had been reported heading north. The old *Rainbow*, without a complete crew or the proper ammunition aboard, went to sea to provide what protection she could to British shipping. If anything was to be done about the submarines, it had to be done quickly, for once a declaration was in effect the United States would invoke her neutrality laws restricting the sale of warships or other weapons to a belligerent power.

Even before the formal 3 p.m. meeting, McBride, Burrell, Logan and Barnard got together to discuss the purchase. During their conversation the matter of the price once again came up and Logan offered to telephone Seattle to verify that the boats were still available and confirm the amount that Paterson wanted. In his first talk with Paterson, Logan was assured the submarines were still for sale but could not get a firm price and was asked to phone back later in the day. Paterson, in the meantime, contacted the Electric Boat Company in New Jersey, who in fact held the original contract and actually owned the boats, and negotiated a selling price with them. He later claimed that Electric Boat wanted $600,000 each and that he talked them down to $555,000 per boat, to which he added an additional $20,000 each to cover his expenses. Later in the day Logan again called Seattle and asked the price, to which Paterson replied, ". . . $575,000 each or $1,150,000 for the two submarines." Logan, who had a pretty shrewd idea of the true value of the vessels, was somewhat taken aback at this and asked Burrell to confirm what he'd heard. This he did and received the same answer, $1,150,000 for the two. Paterson would not negotiate, that was his price, take it or leave it. The Canadians were left with no option but to pay up. The boats were needed and needed quickly, and if that was the price, then that was what they would have to pay. McBride agreed to advance the money, but he would need time to work out the details of how this was to be done.

While in conversation with Paterson it was agreed that he would undertake to move the boats to a point in neutral waters near the international boundary, where he would be met by the Canadian deputation who would make the payment and take over the boats. It was arranged that Logan would go to Seattle in the morning to co-ordinate preparations and act as intermediary. In the meantime a message was drafted, coded, and telegraphed to Naval Service Headquarters informing Vice-Admiral Kingsmill of the pending purchase:

Esquimalt B.C., Aug. 3, 1914

Naval, Ottawa Ont.

Two submarines actually completed for the Chilean government Seattle, estimated cost $1,150,000 could probably purchase; ready for action, torpedoes on board. Chilean government cannot take possession. I consider most important acquire immediately. Burrell concurs. Provincial government will advance money pending remittance.

Esquimalt Yard

At Seattle Paterson was preparing to move the *Iquique* and *Antofagasta* on the strength of the telephone conversation. He did, however, take the time to send a telegram to Logan specifying that he wanted to be paid by "government cheques signed by the proper authority upon delivery as agreed." As it was a Monday and the Chilean crews were working in and around the boats, Paterson had to be careful not to arouse their suspicions. There would be no problem in having his own workmen going aboard, and by this means he had the boats surreptitiously prepared for sea. As well, he hired the trials officer, a retired USN submarine officer, Lieutenant-Commander S.B. Smith, and two 9-man crews to steam the boats out of American waters that night. Late that afternoon Logan's reply arrived:

Victoria B.C., Aug. 3, 1914

J.V. Paterson
    Seattle Construction and Drydock Company,
    Seattle

Awaiting Federal decision. Don't move until you hear further from me tonight. Apparently everything alright.

(Signed) Logan.

This was going to cause Paterson some difficulties, for he would have to delay the move until the following night. His first concern was how to keep the 18 hired crewmen quiet for 24 hours. They had not been told where it was they were being hired to take the boats. He decided to tell them nothing and hope for the best. His shipyard workers were not aware of what was going on either; Paterson reasoned that at least some of them must have been suspicious because of the nature of the work they'd been asked to do. All through the next day these and other problems had to be carefully handled so as to keep the Chileans in the dark.

On the 4th Captain Logan, accompanied by Sub-Lieutenant T.A. Brown, RNCVR, boarded the steamer for Seattle, where they arrived at about 2 p.m. to meet with Paterson and assist with the transfer of the submarines. At the time there was concern about espionage and the American seaports were thought to be full of German spies and saboteurs, hence one reason for Brown's presence. Another was that he had been charged with finding out if there were any submariners among the crews who might be willing to enter Canadian service and reporting these to McBride. Dressed in scruffy civilian clothing borrowed from a cook, he attempted to blend into the background wherever Logan went, keeping an eye out for eavesdroppers and suspicious characters and ensuring that no German sympathizers were included in the passage crews. Paterson later commented that, "He looked like a first-class hobo." Early that morning the shipyard workers returned aboard the boats, opened up the hatches, cleared away all appearances of preparing for sea and carried on with their work as usual.

Before leaving Victoria, McBride had provided Logan with suitable credentials and asked him to recruit as many submarine-trained Americans as he could. During the afternoon he went to Bremmerton Naval Yard, where he met with the Commandant, Captain Blamer, and discussed the possibilities of recruiting time-expired men, or those on extended furlough, for service in Canada. Blamer, however, refused to assist in any way and left Logan to his own devices. Undeterred by this unsympathetic reception, Logan interviewed a number of candidates, two of whom sent telegrams to Washington requesting their discharges, but they were refused. Logan had better luck in the Bremmerton repair shops, where he was able to recruit three men by offering them very high rates of pay. Ultimately only one of these was retained in Canadian service, the other two returning to Seattle after being interviewed at Esquimalt.

At Esquimalt and Ottawa arrangements for the acquisition of the boats were in progress, accompanied by an urgent exchange of messages. The first came from McBride after he'd been warned that a declaration of war was imminent. It was addressed to NSHQ and read:

> Can get submarines over immediately. Urgently suggest to do this before declaration of war, after which builders fear international complications. Shall not act without authority.

Ottawa in turn sent a telegram off to the Admiralty seeking advice. This read:

> Am informed two submarines ready for delivery Seattle, ordered by Chile. Chile unable to take possession. Government desires information as to Admiralty opinion of capabilities of Chilean submarines at Seattle. Understand skilled British ratings in crews. Do you advise purchase?

This message was sent twice so as to assure its arrival and to emphasize Ottawa's concern.

Meanwhile, the Premier was engaged in getting the necessary cheque for over a million dollars ready for dispatch to the rendezvous the next morning. This was drawn on the Canadian Bank of Commerce by the Province of British Columbia and signed by Richard McBride. When it was ready the Premier sent the cheque to Lieutenant Pilcher at the Naval dockyard by the hand of a Mr. Ryan, an employee at the Parliament Buildings who was known and trusted by McBride. With war very much in everyone's thoughts and work going on at a near panic pace, he could find no one else he could trust without a long and involved explanation.

Lieutenant Pilcher, in the meantime, had sought out a retired British naval officer living in the area who had reported for duty some days previously and had accepted a temporary lieutenant's commission in the RCN. His name was Bertram E. Jones and he had served in submarines from 1907 until as recently as 1912, when he had been captain of the Royal Navy submarine *C28*. He had only left the RN 18 months before, at which time he immigrated to the West Coast. Fortunately for the Naval Service of Canada, the well-qualified Lieutenant Jones, who was only 28 years old, was available to undertake the job of inspecting and accepting, or rejecting, the submarines. To assist with the inspection Chief Artificer Engineer Reginald H. Wood, who held the position of Chief Engineer, Esquimalt, was seconded to the deputation. Lieutenant Jones would carry the cheque.

The next telegram of importance was sent to J.V. Paterson at Seattle, stating, "Have got money." It was signed, "McBride and Pilcher." This was what Paterson had been waiting for, now he could complete his subterfuge. That evening he re-embarked his two passage crews and once again made ready to sail. Some of the dockyard workers asked what was happening and he informed them that in order to economize time they were going out to the trial grounds to prepare for some trials to be conducted on the morrow. The men were satisfied with his explanation.

Meanwhile, Sub-Lieutenant Brown had reported back to McBride and he in turn dispatched an interesting telegram to Ottawa dated 7 p.m., August 4:

Following message from submarine agent. Saw crews, will volunteer, satisfactory in every respect. Have been warned that should leave before midnight. Owners telegram received payment delivery. Message ends. Instructions requested.

Presumably the willingness to volunteer was intended to mean the crews were prepared to make the passage to Esquimalt and then return to the USA, not join the RCN.

As evening wore into night a light fog settled over Seattle harbour, creating an ideal cover for the illicit departure of the submarines. Paterson had no intention of seeking government permission to sell the submarines or to transport them out of American waters. As soon as it was dark the crews slipped aboard, Logan accompanied Paterson in *Antofagasta* and Brown went aboard the *Iquique*. Shortly after 10 p.m. the lines were let go and the boats, without lights, got under way on their silent electric motors. Once off West Point and well clear of the harbour, the submarines' diesel engines were started and worked up to full speed. Their destination was a position five miles south of Trial Island, outside the US three-mile limit but still eight miles inside the Canada-USA boundary.

While this was taking place McBride was sending another coded telegram to NSHQ, Ottawa:

August 4, 1914

After consultation with Burrell and naval officers have advanced to-night one million and fifty thousand dollars [a serious clerical discrepancy occurred here which would cause a lot of trouble for McBride later on, the price should have read "one million, one hundred and fifty thousand dollars"] to Lieut. Pilcher, senior naval officer, in command for purchase two modern submarines lying Seattle harbour and built for Chile. All arrangements complete for their arrival Esquimalt tomorrow morning unless untoward incident occurs. Congratulate Canada if this operation successful on acquisition of such useful adjunct defence of country.

R. McBride

At 11 p.m. Greenwich time, the Royal Navy was ordered to "commence hostilities against Germany" and an hour later Great Britain formally declared war on Germany. The ill-prepared, undermanned and poorly equipped Royal Canadian Navy was now, technically at least, at war for the first time in history.

At faraway Whitehall the odd Canadian request for information and advice regarding the two Chilean submarines received immediate and serious consideration, which was surprising considering the circumstances. Fortunately for all concerned Sir Phillip Watts was immediately available. He was intimately familiar with the design of the two submarines and had a good opinion of their worth, despite the report he'd received from Captain Plaza. After consultation the Admiralty replied to Ottawa as follows:

> 6:50 a.m.
> London, August 5, 1914
> Your message Chilean submarines is recommend purchase by Canadian Government if they can be manned by Canada (or Canadians).
>
> Admiralty

By the time this telegram was received at Esquimalt the two vessels were making their way through Puget Sound. Forts Mamostown, Casey and Wilson were passed without incident between 2 and 3 a.m., and by first light on the morning of August 5 they had reached the rendezvous off Trial Island and were on the lookout for the tug *Salvor* with the Canadian deputation aboard. There was no sign of the tug, but the subs were in plain view of any awake passengers or alert crewmen aboard a Seattle-bound passenger steamer, the *Iroquois*. To allay suspicion Paterson altered course parallel to the international boundary, so as to be observed inside American territorial waters. A short time later, around 5 a.m., they sighted the *Salvor*. The three vessels closed one another and stopped while the principals gathered aboard *Antofagasta*. Paterson was anxious to get his cheque and clear off, but Lieutenant Jones had other ideas and asked that he might be allowed to inspect the boats first. Although Paterson was reluctant to spend time doing this, it was a reasonable, if unexpected, request. He was hardly in a position to refuse and grudgingly gave his consent.

Jones and Wood, taking Smith along as guide, then proceeded to make as thorough an inspection as they could under the circumstances. To Paterson's surprise this included the opening up of the battery tanks in both boats — Lieutenant Jones knew what he was about. Two hours later Jones returned on deck, approached Paterson and exclaimed that he was completely satisfied and that in his opinion they seemed to be very fine boats indeed, if not somewhat elaborately equipped. Addressing Paterson almost formally, he then asked, "May I take possession of the boats?" Paterson replied, "Certainly," whereupon Jones produced the cheque and handed it to him asking for a receipt. This surprised Paterson, who considered possession of two submarines to be receipt enough for anyone, but he decided to humour the officer and agreed. There being no other paper available, Jones took an old letter out of his pocket (which was in fact McBride's letter introducing Mr. Ryan to Lieutenant Pilcher), filled in the appropriate wording on the back and handed it to Paterson to sign, which he did with cold and shivering fingers. The Province of British Columbia was now the proud owner of two brand-new warships. All hands were mustered aboard, white ensigns were hoisted and three rousing cheers were given for the King, after which the submarines and their attendant tug got under way for Canadian waters and Esquimalt.

The reception the two boats received when approaching Esquimalt was something less than friendly. The examination steamer at the harbour entrance took them to be German ships and headed for shore with her whistle screeching, its lanyard lashed to the rail. This aroused the interest of a battery of light guns manned by the Army and set up to overlook the harbour approaches. The sergeant in charge prepared to engage but waited for orders to fire from his commander, Major Agnew, who was in an observation post some distance away. Aboard the boats Logan suddenly realized what was happening, the small ensigns at the mastheads had not been recognized and he raced through the compartments looking for a large flag to fly. All he could find was a white tablecloth, which he took to the bridge and waved at the gunners and others who had gathered on the shore. Major Agnew, who had only been briefed about the arrival of the boats a short time before, telephoned an explanation through to his battery commander. Most other observers mistook the tablecloth for a white ensign, which immediately calmed the sudden panic. Shortly afterward, around 8 a.m., the boats went alongside in the dockyard to be greeted by the Premier and the acting SNO, Esquimalt.

A discussion took place at dockside and McBride was given a full report of the takeover by Lieutenant Jones and Mr. Wood. The Premier was satisfied in most respects but dismayed to discover that there were no torpedoes on board. When questioned about this Paterson brusquely replied, "We are not an ordnance factory. We are producing the ships but not the ordnance or ammunition." McBride also found out that there were no skilled crewmen aboard willing to enlist, as he'd hoped. Having the opportunity to talk to Paterson personally, he questioned him about the fairness of the amount he'd been asked to pay. The shipbuilder defended his price, claiming that he could have asked more had he gone along with the Electric Boat Company's original quotation. When the conversation ended, Paterson, Captain Logan and Smith, the trials captain, went into Victoria to find some breakfast, after which Paterson went to a bank to cash his cheque and to conduct some banking transactions. The manner in which he did this, coupled to the clerical error misquoting the price of the boats in the message to Ottawa the day before, would provide the Opposition with sufficient reason to demand an inquiry into the whole purchase deal early the following year. The outcome of this inquiry, conducted by Sir Charles Davidson, would serve to completely exonerate Richard McBride and the others connected with the purchase of any wrongdoing while at the same time exposing James Paterson as a profiteering, but not dishonest, businessman.

United States President Wilson lost no time in declaring that country's neutrality and immediately set about defining the position of his administration so far as providing armaments was concerned. Among other things it was forbidden to arm ships for the purpose of war on behalf of a belligerent power, not that this would necessarily have stopped the sale of the completed but unarmed boats, but it would have made such a transaction immeasurably more complicated. Legislation passed early the following year would serve to make such a sale completely impossible. On the chance that the errant submarines were still within American territorial waters, the Cruiser *Milwaukee* was dispatched to round them up, but she was destined to return to Bremerton empty-handed.

Once they realized what had taken place, the Chilean government registered a strong protest with the American government that would eventually result in an inquiry into the deal made between Paterson and the Electric Boat Company. The only useful result of this inquiry was that Paterson was obliged to pay up the full amount owing to Electric Boat. This cost him a further $29,962.50.

The Chileans, although reimbursed by Electric Boat, were now without any submarines. They also lost, at least temporarily, the ships under construction in England. The British government bought (appropriated with payment would have been closer to the truth) the two battleships (the nearly completed *Almirante Latorre* became HMS *Canada*, the incomplete *Almirante Cochrane* finished up as the aircraft carrier HMS *Eagle*) while four of the destroyers found their way into the RN as the Faulknor class. In 1917 Britain ceded six American-built H-class submarines to Chile, while in 1920 that country's government bought back the *Almirante Latorre* and the three surviving destroyers.

On returning to his office the Premier was handed a decoded telegram dispatched from NSHQ at 11:20 a.m. Ottawa time, which read: "Prepare to purchase submarines. Telegraph price." To this McBride replied at noon Victoria time with a terse message of his own: "Have prepared, purchased submarines." Later in the day a more conciliatory communication was received from the Prime Minister:

Ottawa, 5 August

Yesterday morning we communicated with the Admiralty as to advisability of securing two submarines mentioned, and as to feasibility of manning them, as without crew they would be useless. They advise purchase provided crews could be secured. As this has been accomplished we appreciate most warmly your action which will greatly tend to increase security on the Pacific coast, and send hearty thanks. Please advise us of their arrival.

Signed: Robert Borden

With the submarines had come a multitude of problems that had to be solved before they could put to sea as effective warships. Not least of these was the question of what to call them, while another was where to find the officers and men to man them. A third was the matter of torpedoes; there were no 18-inch weapons on the West Coast. Once again McBride called on the services of the doughty Captain Logan, and he was asked to see what he could do with respect to finding some. After an exchange of telegrams with his confidential contacts at Seattle, he determined that there would be no help forthcoming from American naval sources. He did learn, however, that the Chileans had two Whitehead torpedoes fitted with practise heads that might be available. For the second time in two days he journeyed to Seattle. Locating the torpedoes, he attempted to inspect them, only to find they were well guarded by the Chileans. He was told that he would have to deal with Captain Plaza. Finding the head of the Chilean naval delegation at home, Logan discussed the matter of the torpedoes with him and eventually persuaded Plaza to relax his security. He also made arrangements to acquire the gyroscopes, primers and detonators (the latter two were needed for converting the practice heads into warheads), which were held at Paterson's offices. Returning to the shed where they were kept, Logan prepared the weapons for transport, hired a fast power-launch, and engaged a pilot to spirit him and his charges back to Canadian waters by way of Deception Pass, thus avoiding the American forts.

While Logan was making his surreptitious arrangements under the noses of an alerted American navy, the Deputy Minister of Naval Affairs had openly telegraphed the Seattle Construction and Drydock authorities asking them to supply torpedoes. The USN soon found out about the request and established a close watch on the company's premises. Logan was now faced with having to break into the shipbuilder's offices to steal the missing gyroscopes and other parts without being caught for stealing weapons from a neutral country. Despite these complications and the high cost of doing it, he was willing to proceed with the liberation of the torpedoes but thought it wise to consult with McBride before taking the final steps. McBride, having already determined that suitable torpedoes were available at Halifax, called off the deal and instructed Logan to remain at

CC2 running on the surface shortly after arrival, August 1914. – Maitland-Dougall family collection

CC2 at Victoria, BC, in the winter of 1914. – Maritime Museum of the Atlantic

Seattle, arrange for the shipment of the spare parts for the subs and to stand by for another assignment, one not connected with the submarines.

An unfortunate personnel problem caused a slowing down of the preparation of the two boats when their first Canadian captain, Lieutenant Jones, had to take on other duties. During the hectic days prior to the declaration of war and immediately afterward, the acting SNO Esquimalt had literally worked himself into a state of nervous collapse. McBride, who declared himself commander-in-chief of the Pacific Coast on August 6, ordered the SNO to go on leave and temporarily appointed Bertram Jones in his stead, pending the arrival of a suitable relief. Before his departure, Lieutenant Pilcher telegraphed Ottawa informing NSHQ that the boats would be named *Paterson* and *McBride*, after the two men responsible for their acquisition, provided Ottawa approved. Ottawa, however, did not approve; NSHQ had other ideas. By the authority of an order in council dated August 7, 1914, the Dominion government purchased the boats on behalf of the Naval Service of Canada, which commissioned them into the RCN, naming them HMC Submarines *C1* and *C2*, and placed them at the disposal of the Admiralty. The Royal Canadian Navy had acquired its first submarines, and with them its first diesel engines.

The authorities on the West Coast had no expertise in the construction of any kind of warship, including submarines, and as a consequence were entirely at the mercy of the likes of James Paterson when it came to making such a purchase. Despite Paterson's claims to the contrary, the boats were overpriced for what they were and their design had already been superceded by two classes of USN submarine, both of which had been laid down and completed, some in adjoining slips, during the same three-year period in which the Chilean boats were being built. Other serious deficiencies directly attributable to Electric Boat and the Seattle Drydock and Construction Company would become apparent in time. Nevertheless, the boats were available and were made effectively operational, and it's to the credit of the officers and men who manned them and engineering support given ashore at Esquimalt that they were a success.

What kind of submarines had British Columbia foisted onto the Naval Service of Canada through its home-style defence procurement action? The two submarines were examples of the classic Holland patented designs as developed by the Electric Boat Company in a continuous succession of improved classes. Direct descendants of the Holland-class designs provided to Vickers for the Royal Navy in 1901, they were contemporaneous with the British D class of 1911. Compared to the British submarines, however, they were obsolete in both concept and equipment.

The two boats were nearly identical, the biggest difference being that *C1*, built to design 19E, had four 18-inch torpedo tubes forward, arranged two above two, while *C2*, to design 19B, had only two tubes forward, one on each side of the bow at internal deck level. Both had a single tube in the stern, a Chilean modification. As a result of the arrangement of the bow tubes, *C1* had a bluff bow shape and was 144 feet 6 inches in length, while *C2* was given a long tapering bow, making her 151 feet 6 inches long. Both boats measured 15 feet on the beam, and their normal surface draft was 11 feet, while both displaced 313 tons surfaced and 421 tons dived. Surprisingly they were built to submerge to 200 feet, an unusually deep diving depth for that period. The hulls were generally circular in section and shaped like a cigar, being wide amidships and tapering towards the bow and the stern. These were single-hull boats and all tanks were inside the pressure hull.

A light steel casing covered the upper hull, giving the little boats a reasonable seakeeping capability. Amidships the tall bronze conning tower, periscope shears and battery ventilation exhaust trunks were protected by a low bronze-plated fin structure that also served as the bridge platform. Small extensions at either side in front of the tower hatch gave a little additional deck space, and a chest-high canvas dodger could be rigged on light stanchions around the front of the bridge to provide some protection from the weather. In the middle of the bridge stood a cast-bronze steering stand containing the magnetic compass, an electric steering control and electric engine order telegraph. This stand had a pressure-tight lid which had to be secured before diving. As originally built, the wireless aerial was strung between collapsible forward and after masts. This was later reduced to a single pole stepped ahead of the fin.

Internally the boats were divided into four main compartments. The forward torpedo tube and stowage compartment contained the tube rear ends, bowcap operating mechanism, provision for reload torpedoes (to be laid flat on the deck in both boats), officers' accommodations, including built-in wooden bunks and cupboards, and the wireless set. Below the deck were three fuel tanks as well as five high-pressure compressed air bottle groups stowed together in one well.

The forward battery compartment was the next aft and it contained half of the main battery in a tank below deck. The tank was lead lined, held 60 cells secured in place by wax-impregnated hardwood battens and was covered by wooden panels, a layer of thick acid-resistant cloth and then a tightly wedged planked deck. The space above deck provided accommodation for the crew and was designed to take nine pipe-framed canvas-bottomed bunks, sufficient for half the crew. Only two of these appear to have been provided and the hands either slung hammocks or slept on the deck. Along the sides were lockers for personal gear and two enclosed heads (water closets), that forward being for the officers, the one aft for the hands.

The next compartment consisted of the command position and after battery spaces combined. The command space itself was only 6 feet deep and spanned the full 15-foot beam. In the centre of the forward bulkhead was the helm controlled by a conventional wheel, to its left the low-pressure air venting and blowing panel for operating the main tanks, and to the right the water-tight bulkhead door leading forward. Along the port side were the two planesmen's positions and the large handwheels for controlling the angle of the fore and aft hydroplanes, or "bow rudders and main diving gear," as they were then called. On the starboard side forward was the trim pump and water distribution mainfold, while aft of this were the large levers for opening and shutting the Kingston valves that allowed seawater into and out of the ballast tanks. Immediately behind and above the helmsman's position was the hatch leading into the conning tower. Aft of this the main periscope entered the compartment from the hull above. It was provided with electric hoisting gear, and when lowered its bottom rested on the command space deck.

The conning tower was oval in section and had a clear height of 6 feet above the narrow deck that ringed its interior. Around the top of the tower were five glass bull's-eye ports giving an all-around view. The upper hatch leading to the bridge platform above was in the front of the top of the tower, in the centre was a small periscope used for navigation and keeping a lookout, while immediately behind that was the inlet for a ventilation pipe that ran up to the top of the periscope fairwater. This was fitted with flap valves at bottom and top, and it was used as an air-induction pipe to allow the diesels to be run with the upper tower hatch shut when on the surface. This was done in bad weather to keep high seas out of the boat. There was also a compass image reflector, telegraphs and an electric steering controller in the tower, and it was fitted for use as an escape chamber.

Below the command space was a small compartment containing the buoyancy, or amidships trim, tank, the auxiliary ballast tanks to port and starboard, the fresh-water tank, and the low-pressure air reservoir and high-pressure air reducer and cross

Forward compartment, CC2. – Maritime Command Museum

CC-boat control room. – Maritime Museum of BC

CC-boat starboard main switchboard. – Maritime Museum of BC

connection to the high-pressure air main line. The six Kingston valves and their operating rodding were also located in this compartment.

Aft of the command space was the after battery compartment, with the second half of the main battery in a tank under the deck identical to that forward. Along both sides of the space above were ranged the main-motor control, battery charging, and auxiliary power-distribution panels. On the port side immediately aft of the after-planes there was a small, electric galley range and a deep sink. On the opposite side were lockers for rations and mess traps. Down the centre of the wood-planked deck was a portable mess table with folding ends measuring 12 feet long by 4 feet 6 inches wide, which was flanked by backless seat lockers. As well as being the main-motor control space, this area also served as the cafeteria and provided sleeping accommodations for six men, four on the table and two in hammocks overhead.

The next, and last, compartment consisted of the engine room and machinery space combined. The two main engines were in fact German-designed MAN diesels manufactured in the USA under licence. Disposed to port and starboard in the conventional way, these were direct driving, reversible, bast-injected, two-cycle, six-cylinder diesel engines of primitive design, even by 1914 standards, and were to prove a constant headache to the engineering staff. Fuel and lubricating oil tanks were situated under the engines. Aft of these were the main-motors, or generators, depending on how they were being used, while on the shafting joining the engines and motors were manually operated clutches. On the surface the diesels were clutched directly to the shafts to drive the propellers, the de-energized motors spinning without effect. When dived, the engines were unclutched from the shafts and the motors, taking their power from the main battery, drove the propellers. To charge the batteries the motors were unclutched from the shaft by means of a second clutch, commonly referred to as the "tail clutch," which was located right aft near the stern-glands, and the motors were then driven by the engines as generators. The main engines were started by turning them over using the main-motors. Air-start was provided but was not trusted and seldom, if ever, used. With the engines in top shape the boats could make 15 knots on the surface. When dived 10 knots was possible on the main-motors, and the batteries had a capacity of about 3,800 amp hours, sufficient for at least one hour at full speed.

Aft of the main-motors were two ballast pumps. In *C1* that to port was a twin-piston rotary pump which took its drive from the main shaft by way of a gear train and clutch, while in *C2* there were two of these pumps. In *C1* the starboard ballast pump was a centrifugal pump driven by its own electric motor. Generally the piston pumps were used for pumping when deep, while the centrifugal type were preferred when shallow. The speed, and therefore the pumping rate, of the piston pumps could be varied by adjusting the speed of the main motors, whereas the centrifugal pump had a constant speed and its pumping rate decreased considerably as they went deeper. Aft of the pumps were two identical two-stage high-pressure air compressors also driven off the main shafts. Each of these could produce about 10 cubic feet of compressed air per hour at around 2,000 psi.

The after torpedo tube rear door was situated near the top of the after internal bulkhead, while the stern cap operating gear was located directly above the door in a small raised enclosure. The main-shaft stern-glands exited the hull to left and right below the torpedo tube, and the after hydroplane and steering gearing and shafting were in the centre directly under the tube.

At the extremities of the boat were trim and ballast tanks, while additional ballast tanks were located in the spaces under the battery tanks and between the battery tanks and the ship's side. To dive the boat these tanks were flooded through the Kingston valves and to surface the water was blown out through the same valves with high-pressure compressed air. All ballast tanks were connected to the main pumping and flooding line by branch pipes and screw-down stop valves. The forward, aft and amidships trim tanks were connected to the trim pump by way of a distribution manifold to permit fine adjustments of trim. The trim line and main line could be cross-connected if necessary. All Kingston valves and main vents were operated by hand, hydraulics would not make an appearance in submarines until the British K class in 1917.

Once the boats had been dry-docked, refitted and properly ballasted, they proved to be handy little submarines but would always be plagued by mechanical problems resulting from design limitations, substandard materials and the poor workmanship of the original constructors.

First class of RNCC cadets. Rear: Hibbard, Hatheway, Jones, Murray, Tingley, Laurie, Dand. Middle: Maitland-Dougall, Worth, Palmer, Lawson, Moffatt, Cann, Silver. Front: Oland, (Eng. Lt.), (Lt. Cdr.), Reid, Grant. On deck: Gabruverau, Watson. Hatheway, Cann, Silver and Palmer were killed at Coronel. Maitland-Dougall, Watson and Lawson went into submarines. Jones and Murray both became admirals. – author's collection

3 THE CC BOATS IN ACTION

THE TRADE

They bear in place of classic names,
Letters and numbers on their skin.
They play their grisly blindfold games
In little boxes made of tin.
Sometimes they stalk the Zeppelin,
Sometimes they learn where mines are laid
Or where the Baltic ice is thin.
That is the custom of "The Trade".

Few prize courts sit upon their claims.
They seldom tow their targets in.
They follow certain secret aims
Down under, far from strife or din.
When they are ready to begin
No flag is flown, no fuss is made
No more than the shearing of a pin.
That is the custom of "The Trade".

The Scout's quadruple funnel flames
A mark from Sweden to the Swin,
The Cruiser's thundrous screw proclaims
Her comings out and goings in:
But only whiffs of parrafin
Or creamy rings that fizz and fade
Show where the one-eyed Death has been.
That is the custom of "The Trade".

Their feats, their fortunes and their fames
Are hidden from their nearest kin;
No eager public backs or blames,
No journal prints the yarns they spin
(The Censor would not let it in!)
When they return from run or raid.
Unheard they work, unseen they win.
That is the custom of "The Trade".

Sea Warfare, Rudyard Kipling 1916

Canada and Canadians were about to learn a bit about what it was like to belong to "The Trade."

Ships without men are little more than cold steel shells filled with cleverly arranged pieces of machinery having neither life nor purpose. To bring the new boats alive crews had to be found and found they were. What was wanted first, however, was a man to head the enterprise, a man with a knowledge of submarines and the gift of leadership. Fortunately for the embryonic submarine service, such a person not only existed in Canada but had already been recruited. When Sir Robert Borden had mentioned in his message to McBride that the submarines could be manned by Canadians, he had done so from personal knowledge, as Vice-Admiral Kingsmill had already interviewed a highly qualified submariner nearly a week before in Toronto. The story of how all of this came about has been handed down to us in a letter written by another Canadian submariner, Jock Edwards, which describes those turbulent days.

John Grant Edwards, as Jock was christened, was born in 1893 at Liverpool, England. His mother and father were both descended from old Scottish families and the Edwards' ancestral home, "Craigton," was at Kessock in Rosshire, deep in the Scottish Highlands. He was raised along with his two younger sisters in the comfort of a moderately prosperous middle-class family. At the age of 12 he was accepted into the Royal Navy as an officer cadet and attended the Royal Naval College, spending his first two years at Osborne, on the Isle of Wight, and finishing aboard the training hulks at Dartmouth, as was the custom before the opening of the new Naval College. In 1909, just prior to commencing the final phase of his training, Jock Edwards contracted rheumatic fever and was invalided out of the Navy.

Undismayed and having made a good recovery from his illness and from having to leave the Navy, he enrolled at Repton, a prominent public school, intending to seek a career in the Army. In March 1911 he passed the Army Board Qualifying Examinations but failed to make the entrance requirements for either Sandhurst or Woolwich. When his father fell seriously ill and died during 1912, young Jock was forced to abandon his search for a military career and look for civilian employment to help support his family. This was not easy, as he had no previous experience or training for a civilian position, nor could he find any sympathetic benefactors among his many relatives.

The only solid offer of employment came from Major Arthur Peuchen, a wealthy friend of his father's, who offered Jock a position as a clerk with a company he controlled in Toronto. Though reluctant to leave his family and England, the young man accepted and the two booked first-class passage aboard the RMS *Titanic*. Edwards fortunately developed bronchitis, a serious matter in the days before antibiotics, and remained at home to mend. Peuchen, however, embarked on that tragic maiden voyage and survived the sinking of the *Titanic* by taking charge of a lifeboat. He had apparently been president of the Toronto Yacht Club at one time and this seems to have qualified him for the job. Jock eventually came out to Canada early in 1913, settled in Toronto, where he found digs in a Spadina Avenue rooming house, and took up his job as a clerk with the Standard Chemical, Iron and Lumber Company.

During the summer of 1914 Jock spent the weekend of July 18 and 19 in the popular Georgian Islands, as did many, to escape from Toronto's unrelenting heat. While enjoying his holiday he had a chance encounter with another, somewhat older, Englishman who also had a naval background. This was Adrian Keyes, younger brother of then Captain Roger Keyes, RN, Commodore Submarines. Keyes was working in Toronto for the Temiskaming & Ontario Northern Railroad and, like Edwards, was seeking some light entertainment and relief from the heat of the city. During their conversation, which was mostly about the coming war, for there could be no doubt of it by then, Keyes discovered Edwards' naval background. After the weekend break both men returned to their jobs in

Toronto. (Shortly before that fateful weekend Jock Edwards had joined the Queen's Own Rifles, a Toronto-based Militia regiment. He was issued a uniform and rifle and was told to carry on with his job and wait for the order to mobilize.)

Adrian St. Vincent Keyes, "Tubby" to his peers, was a big, rough-hewn sort of a man in his early thirties. The younger son of General Sir Charles Keyes, he had entered the Royal Navy as a cadet around 1895, attended Osborne and Dartmouth, and first went to sea in 1898 as a midshipman aboard HMS *Talbot* on the North America and West Indies Station. He progressed to sub-lieutenant in 1901 and a year later, having made five first-class certificates (quite an achievement, especially in those days), was promoted to lieutenant. In 1903 he joined submarines, becoming a pioneer of that arm of the service. His first submarine was a Holland boat, one of the RN's original submarines, in which he served as second captain to Alexander H. Quicke. Keyes quickly rose to a command of his own, one of the A class, and in 1905 transferred to HMS *Forth* at Devonport, where he became an instructor for officers and men joining submarines. After a year he returned to General Service and 13 months later went back to *Forth*, where he was given command of the tender HMS *Onyx* and the four submarines attached to her. It was during Keyes' appointment in *Onyx* that Bertram Jones took his basic submarine training, and it is probable the two men became acquainted with one another at that time. His last submarine was the *C13*, which he commanded until leaving RN submarines for good in 1909. In June 1912 he retired voluntarily and shortly afterward came out to Canada. Like most prematurely retired officers, Keyes was on the Emergency List, making it obligatory for him to report for duty once war became imminent. He was not married.

In the middle of the last week in July, probably on Wednesday the 29th, the day after the Admiralty warning telegram had been dispatched, Edwards received a telephone call from Keyes asking him if he'd come down to the Yacht Club, where a recruiting depot had been set up by the Navy League, and help with organizing the servicemen reporting there for duty. Jock Edwards spent all day working at the Yacht Club and on returning to work the following morning found he had been sacked.

Reporting to Keyes later in the day, he was surprised to find himself being interviewed by none other than the Director of the Naval Service, Vice-Admiral C.E. Kingsmill, who was visiting Toronto and who had already interviewed Adrian Keyes. In recognition of his Royal Naval College training Edwards was granted a temporary commission as a midshipman, RCN, and told to report aboard the *Niobe* at Halifax. Edwards refrained from making any mention of his enrollment in the Queen's Own Rifles. Keyes was reactivated as a temporary lieutenant, RCN. Neither had uniforms, but they were definitely back in the Navy. Later that same day Keyes approached Edwards and asked him about his posting. Upon hearing Edwards was going to the cruiser, Keyes told him, "You are coming with me to help man two submarines expected at Esquimalt. I'll fix it with Ottawa." And so he did.

While whiling away the hours before boarding the westbound train the following evening, Edwards spent the time secluded in his room on Spadina Avenue certain that the Army was about to arrest him for desertion while Keyes was being fêted by his friends. Stashing the rifle behind his bed, he rolled his uniform into a bundle, wrapped it in brown paper and took it with him to Union Station. In due course Keyes arrived with a group of high-spirited, well-wishing friends who gave their companion a boisterous send-off. Edwards, who took no part in the revelries, slunk aboard as inconspicuously as he could and was considerably relieved when the train started to move and no one had tried to arrest him. At the first opportunity he tossed the incriminating Army uniform into a wide, fast-flowing river. His spirits improved considerably as the miles rolled away under the wheels of their speeding train.

Submarine pioneers Alexander Quicke (left) and Adrian Keyes (right). Both would have an influence on Canadian submarines.
- RN Submarine Museum

In the meantime another young officer was also making his way west to join the submarines. Midshipman William McKinstry Maitland-Dougall, who had been serving aboard the *Niobe* at Halifax, was the first serving RCN officer to respond to the request for volunteers. He was a few days ahead of the others and appears to have arrived at Victoria sometime before August 4. He was known to Vice-Admiral Kingsmill through family connections and it is quite probable he had been extended a personal invitation to join the submarines. Eighteen-year-old William was the eldest son of a former police constable, and later magistrate and B.C. provincial government agent, James "Handsome Jim" St. Leger Maitland-Dougall and his wife, Winnifred (nee McKinstry-Watson). He was born in 1895 and raised at Duncan, on Vancouver Island, where he attended Mr. Skrimshire's Quamichan Lake School, a local, privately funded preparatory school, where he was considered a bright student. His paternal grandfather was the late Admiral William Heriot Maitland-Dougall, RN, and he was directly related to the Maitlands, hereditary Earls of Lauderdale. The family estate, "Scotscraig," was at Tayport, in Fife, Scotland. The Maitlands had a long association with the Royal Navy. Not only had the Admiral seen action under sail in India and China, but his uncle was a retired commander and cousin Arnold a serving lieutenant. It was not surprising that William's father should choose a career at sea for his eldest son. William passed his entrance exams in the summer of 1910 and entered the RCN as an officer cadet in the first class to undertake its training at the newly opened Royal Naval College of Canada at Halifax. On completion of his two-year course at the college, he graduated second in the class. A year later, in January 1914, he finished his sea training aboard HMS *Berwick* at the top of his class, with three first-class certificates. Along with ten of his classmates, William was posted to the *Niobe* at Halifax.

Lt. Henry Byng Pilcher, RN, who was acting SNO Esquimalt when war began. — PABC

In the meantime, at Esquimalt, another would-be submariner had already entered naval service but at that time had no inkling of what the future held for him. A pilot for the B.C. Pilotage Service, Captain Bernard Leitch Johnson, "Barney" to almost everyone, was 36 years old and had already seen a lifetime at sea, having joined his first ship as an apprentice seaman at Liverpool, England, on his fifteenth birthday. In the hectic days immediately preceding the declaration of war, he had been asked to serve as pilot for the cruiser *Rainbow* on inshore patrol duties and had volunteered his services for the duration of his one-month's annual leave. He reported for duty at Esquimalt on August 3, only to be told that he would not be needed aboard *Rainbow*, as the cruiser was headed south, but to stand by until she returned. He busied himself about the base, observed the arrival of the submarines and, when Lieutenant Jones took over as SNO Esquimalt, agreed to act as his secretary.

After a tedious train ride across central and western Canada and a short steamer trip from Vancouver, Adrian Keyes and Jock Edwards arrived at Victoria on the 4th and entrained for Esquimalt. It was not a long ride but the two men livened things up a bit by "borrowing some of the train conductor's gold braid." This they draped around the sleeves of Keyes' blue civilian jacket to give him some semblance of a naval officer. According to Edwards' recollections of many years later, the authorities must have frowned on their behaviour, for they were met at Esquimalt by a group of officious people with large revolvers, placed under close arrest and escorted to the cells on the base. This did not seem a fitting beginning to their new naval careers. According to Barney Johnson, however, the cells were being used as overflow accommodation at the time and it's just as likely Keyes and Edwards, who were probably more than a little inebriated, were simply given cells instead of the usual cabins, all of which were occupied.

The next morning Adrian Keyes managed to arrange an audience with the near prostrate Lieutenant Pilcher, and he and Edwards were released in time to witness the arrival of the two boats they were to serve in. Shortly after his somewhat conspicuous arrival at Esquimalt, a message was received appointing Lieutenant Adrian Keyes "Officer in Command of Submarines." He immediately assumed command of *C1*, while Jones was given command of *C2*. Both Jones and Johnson, however, would be temporarily occupied in the SNO's office until the arrival of *Shearwater* a week later, when they were relieved by her captain, Commander Troubridge, and Lieutenant Chalmers, his first lieutenant.

Morale along the West Coast, already bad, was beginning to worsen as the German cruisers successfully eluded their pursuers and disappeared among the labyrinth of Pacific islands. The need to protect British merchant shipping in the Pacific had diverted fully two thirds of the forces available to hunt down the Germans, warships that now had to be parcelled out for employment on escort duties because of the presence of Von Spee's ships and the unpredictability of their movements. The Admiralty had confidently predicted that Japan would declare war on Germany on August 12, an event that would free British ships for the pursuit of Von Spee's squadron. Realizing the vulnerability of the Canadian situation, and relying on the Admiralty's prediction for the Japanese entry into the war, Vice-Admiral Jerram dispatched the modern cruiser *Newcastle* to the West Coast to reinforce *Rainbow*, but she would not arrive at Esquimalt until the last week in August.

The Japanese, however, were not in such a hurry to open hostilities. They not only deferred their declaration until the 23rd, but also made their decision dependent on the British assigning a battleship to assist in besieging the Germans at Tsingtau, much to the discomfort of the Admiralty and the British Admirals in the northwestern Pacific. Not only were they going to lose ships, but their new ally would only put two cruisers into the North Pacific, claiming that the rest of their large, relatively modern navy would be needed to support their attack on the German possessions in China.

The German Admiral, meanwhile, took full advantage of his freedom of movement and devised a plan that was to cause the maximum amount of disruption for the least expenditure in forces and precious fuel. On August 13 he detached the *Emden*, under Captain Karl von Müller, with orders to harass British shipping to the westward for as long as he could hold out. Taking a collier with him, Von Müller set out for the Indian Ocean and Bay of Bengal, there to wage a 70-day campaign that was to win the grudging admiration of even the British for its audacity and effectiveness. He was to remain undetected until August 28. Von Spee, meanwhile, was planning his own campaign and preparing his ships for the coming contest. It would be a month before he really got started, and in the meantime the Germans laid low, first at Ponape and then at Pagan, in the German Marianas, where they coaled ship. From intercepted wireless signals they knew that Admiral Jerram's force was hunting them far to the south of their lair.

SMS *Leipzig*, operating against British shipping along the American West Coast, had steamed north to take up a station off San Francisco, where she arrived on August 11. She found no targets, however, as by then all British shipping in the area had been ordered to remain in port. At the same time the British sloops *Shearwater* and *Algerine* also steamed north, making for Esquimalt. On the 4th Commander Hose headed the cruiser *Rainbow* south at 15 knots to shepherd them home from the vicinity of San Francisco, all the while expecting to encounter at least one German cruiser. Fortunately for her there was no meeting, for the *Leipzig* would have made short work of the old ship; she had no armour-piercing ammunition aboard and was manned by a very inexperienced crew. At one point there were fears for *Rainbow*'s safety when pieces of the ship were recovered on the beaches of Oregon, but these were only wooden furnishings and fittings discarded overboard when she cleared for action.

All of this activity hastened the need to get the submarines into an operational state, and Adrian Keyes lost no time in getting started. When another Emergency List officer, Lieutenant Wilfrid T. Walker, RN (Retired), turned up from the *Rainbow*, Keyes made him first lieutenant and appointed Maitland-Dougall as his third hand and navigator. Johnson was nominally first lieutenant in *C2* under Jones, with Jock Edwards as their third hand. Completely lacking in naval and submarine experience, Johnson's experiences as a ship's captain and as a pilot were utilized to navigate whichever boat was doing training exercises while he learned the ropes. The American captain, Lieutenant-Commander Smith, had been retained by McBride to act as a consultant while the Canadian officers became proficient at handling the boats. This was to cost the Naval Service $5,000.

For crew, about 50 volunteers were recruited from among the RNCVR, *Rainbow* and the remnants of *Shearwater's* ship's company. When the loosely screened volunteers had fallen in, Keyes explained the seriousness of the task ahead and told them there would be no loss of respect should anyone decline to volunteer. All hands stood fast, no one was going to back out. The orders were given for the seamen to take one pace forward, stokers one pace back, electricians one pace to the left and steamfitters one to the right. Anyone not included in those groups was dismissed. From among those remaining, two 15-man crews were selected by Keyes himself, who chose the most physically fit and technically best qualified. A chief engine room artificer and two other artificers were needed for each boat, as well as a senior artificer to act as the flotilla engineer. Chief Artificer Engineer Wood, himself a promoted ERA, scoured the base and *Rainbow* for volunteers, preferably those with experience in the rare diesel engine. It is to his credit that many of the artificers he selected remained with the boats until the end of the war.

When the selection process was completed, *C1* was manned by three regular ratings and 13 RNCVR men, while *C2* got six naval ratings and 10 RNCVRs. As Barney Johnson observed, "Several volunteers from *Shearwater's* personnel gave us about a strand of disciplined men but not a thread of submarine experience. We greenhorns were endowed with the valour of ignorance." Two men did in fact have previous submarine experience. Coxswain Jas. Addison of *C1* had served in the boats attached to HMS *Thames* in 1906 and Stoker PO Roberts of *C2* had also seen service in Royal Navy submarines.

Training then began in earnest. All leave was stopped and under the personal guidance of Keyes and Jones the men were turned-to aboard the boats, getting them ready for sea and familiarizing themselves with the strange machinery. One of the early tasks to be undertaken was the changing of hundreds of tally plates from Spanish to English. The two midshipmen, Jock Edwards and Maitland-Dougall, along with a curious Barney Johnson, literally lived in the bowels of their boats, learning the operation and layout of every system and the location and function of every valve and each piece of equipment from personal experience, an exercise that would stand all of them in good stead later on.

With the boats secured to the jetty by slack lines, the crews were exercised in diving and surfacing procedures in slow time. Each tank was carefully flooded in turn so that the boat settled on an even keel and then was pumped or blown out to surface the vessel. From here they were taken to deeper water, where, with extra positive buoyancy, the drills were repeated with the boats under way. With the excess of buoyancy they would only sink up to the conning tower, even with all the ballast tanks flooded, a necessary precaution as things didn't always go as planned. During these exercises Barney Johnson

Crew of HMCS/M CC1. A fine bunch of pirates! – Nat. Def. E48718, N. Cuthbert

manned the conning tower, where, using the compass and electric steering control, he would act as pilot. The captain in the command position below would give all depth and speed orders. In this manner they perfected diving and surfacing drills. At the same time the two submarines conducted surface torpedo firing and recovery exercises. At first using wooden dummy torpedoes and later on the real thing with practice heads fitted, they would launch their torpedoes at the Dallas Road. This was a popular thoroughfare and the locals who promenaded there would gather to watch and found this to be great sport. Within a few weeks the crews were sufficiently experienced to try diving in deeper water and the boats started to exercise in Royal Roads.

It was during these exercises that the Canadians discovered one of the peculiarities that had deterred the Chileans: the boats had a tendency to take on severe bow-down or stern-down angles without warning. Assistance was sought from the Electric Boat Company, who sent out a trials captain to help solve the problem, Lieutenant-Commander Smith having already collected his fee and returned to the States.

During one of these trial trips Adrian Keyes demonstrated the value of his seasoned experience and submarine knowledge. They had dived the boat, set a good trim and were running at slow ahead on both motors when she took a sudden bow-down angle and started to nose-dive. The American ordered, "Full ahead both electric motors and blow bow main ballast." Before anything was done Keyes countermanded the orders with, "Full astern both, blow all main ballast." Keyes' orders were obeyed without hesitation and they surfaced safely. Those who remained in boats soon learned that Keyes had made the correct and safest decision, as his actions immediately arrested their downward plunge and gave the boat full overall buoyancy, whereas the American captain's method would have taken them deeper before the boat started to rise and she would then have been light at the bows, which would only have reversed the angle, thus compounding their problem. Barney Johnson particularly was to benefit from this experience when he found himself faced with a similar, but much more dangerous, situation in the North Sea 18 months later.

While engaged in these training exercises the two boats made several courtesy and recreational visits to small isolated communities along the coast. As well as providing experience to the crews, these short cruises were instrumental in improving morale among the civil populace. At the same time Ottawa was conducting a submarine propaganda campaign, sending and receiving contrived movement signals to give the impression the boats were operational and actively employed.

About the middle of August nine torpedoes arrived from Halifax. These had to be modified to fit the submarines' torpedo tubes. One of the alterations involved heating the air vessel to remove a redundant fitting, and during this operation it was dramatically demonstrated that one "tin-fish" had reached Esquimalt with a fully charged high-pressure air reservoir. Once the steel skin had reached a good heat it swelled out like an orange, fortunately for the fitters it didn't burst, but the air vessel itself was ruined. The eight remaining warhead-fitted torpedoes were embarked, four forward and one aft in *C1*, two forward and one aft in *C2*.

On September 8 the sloop *Shearwater*, which had been taken into the RCN upon her return from Mexico when most of her crew was sent east to help man the *Niobe*, was allocated to the submarine flotilla as a depot ship. She was fitted out with a workshop and other amenities for supporting her new charges and was commissioned in the RCN on October 1. The old sloop had no heating and was overcrowded, but she provided a much-needed home for the submariners and a base for the submarines.

HMCS Shearwater *with* CC1 *and* CC2 *alongside.*
> – Maritime Command Museum

CC1 *returning to Esqui-*
malt after diving exercises,
September 1914. Midship-
man Maitland-Dougall
facing the camera.
> – Vancouver City Archives

Aboard CC1 *on a cruise to Cape Flattery. Coxswain James Addison on the right.*
– RN Submarine Museum

CC1 *and* CC2. – Maritime Museum of BC

A glimpse of life in *Shearwater* has been provided by ERA Dickie Pearson, who joined the boats early in 1915. He relates that what the men lacked in knowledge they made up for in enthusiasm and a determination to excel. A favourite pastime was for the hands to divide into two teams and try to stump one another with questions about submarine equipment, machinery and systems, and on what the correct procedures were for operating different systems and equipment under normal and in emergency circumstances. This pastime will sound all too familiar to even today's submariners.

Jock Edwards also had some observations to offer on this aspect of life in those early days. In one of his letters he mentions that, "We considered ourselves most efficient. Competition — in speed of diving, firing and surfacing to pick up our own torpedoes — the two boats endeavoured to outdo each other in everything, yet never was there anything but complete harmony with rivalry."

ERA Pearson left a description of the escape equipment and training given to the early submarine crews. The equipment was reminiscent of the Drager mine rescue gear of the period. It consisted of a helmet fitted with a front scuttle and attached to a canvas jacket. The jacket was equipped with an inflatable life jacket, a four-pound lead weight at the back to keep the wearer upright and a two-pound detachable weight at either side. Two small, manually operated air bottles were provided, one of low-pressure air for inflating the jacket, the other of high-pressure air for maintaining air in the helmet. A small container of oxylate crystals, with a pipe leading to the mouth and one to the top of the helmet, and nose-clip completed the equipment.

Escape training was done in the Victoria Public Baths. In this the man donned his equipment, entered the pool, walked from the shallow to the deep end, all the while regulating his helmet pressure manually, then dropped the two small weights and popped to the surface. Here he was supposed to inflate the life vest and then open the scuttle on the helmet. Some performed this last procedure in the wrong order, only to find themselves having to be fished out by the instructors as their helmets began to fill. Two successful trips from shallow to deep end and up to the surface qualified a man in escape procedures.

By the end of August the naval defence situation on the Canadian West Coast had improved considerably. The Japanese declared war on Germany on the 23rd and this was followed two days later by the arrival at Esquimalt of the Japanese heavy cruiser *Idzumo*, an event that was greeted with mixed reactions in the B.C. communities. On the 28th the light cruiser *Newcastle*, detached from Admiral Jerram's force over a fortnight before, also arrived at Esquimalt.

The German cruisers were still at large and their plans and exact location were unknown to the Allies. At the end of the month they were all at sea, the main body headed for Christmas Island while the *Nurnberg* steamed for Honolulu to send and receive dispatches. She would rejoin the squadron a week later, having stopped at Fanning Island to cut the Fiji-Honolulu cable. *Emden* had only just opened her campaign in the Indian Ocean. Admiral Jerram, meanwhile, was fruitlessly searching the Java Sea, frustrated by a shortage of modern warships and with having to consult Whitehall at every stage.

In mid-September, having stayed with the submarines for several weeks longer than he'd agreed to, Barney Johnson broached the subject of his return to the Pilotage Service. Both Keyes and Jones rejected the idea. He had become a capable submariner and his experience as an officer and navigator were of great value to the little flotilla. On their next refueling run to Vancouver the matter of his service was referred to the Pilotage Commissioners, Keyes and Jones strongly supporting the notion of somehow keeping Johnson with them. After some discussion the Commissioners agreed to give Johnson a leave of absence for the duration of the war. On returning to Esquimalt he was granted a temporary lieutenant's commission in the RNCVR and told to get into uniform. He also applied, through the proper channels, for a Royal Navy Reserve commission, to which he was entitled by virtue of his Master's certificate, but this was never acknowledged.

On October 1 Lieutenant Adrian St. Vincent Keyes was appointed to the position of "Lieutenant in Command (Temporary) of HMC *Shearwater I* and for command of Submarine Flotilla." NSHQ was taking its submarines seriously.

At the end of September, when *Scharnhorst* was reported heading north (at the time the entire squadron was in fact coaling and provisioning at the Marquesas Islands), the two submarines went out on patrol in the Strait of Juan de Fuca. Each boat would go out for a 24-hour patrol and return to harbour, being relieved by the other en route. In another letter written by Jock Edwards, we have been favoured with some of the details of these patrols. The boats by this time were only taking three minutes to dive, as compared to the 45 minutes taken for the first dives. They were able to remain submerged for eight hours comfortably and could stay down longer if necessary, although the atmosphere soon became fouled with battery fumes. Until the longitudinal stability problems could be properly rectified, the forward and aft fuel tanks were left empty to give some buoyancy at the extremities. Periscope depth was 20 feet on the gauge, datum at that time being at the water line, not the keel as it is now. Normally they patrolled on the surface, trimmed well down, and dived on sighting a ship. These alternating patrols were carried out for at least a fortnight without rest and required constant effort from the crews. At sea the men were always in two watches, it only took nine men to run a boat of that size. Even during the 24 hours alongside there was little time for relaxation. The batteries had to be charged (a long and tedious job), the boat stored, torpedoes pulled and checked, maintenance performed, repairs made and cleaning done. The men were given little time to rest or even to take a bath. This was their first real taste of what it meant to be submariners in wartime.

When possible the crews were given a two-day break to clean up and catch up on their rest. For *C2* this happened when they went to Vancouver to take on fuel, and Edwards recalls that they all enjoyed "such a wash." The officers were put up at the Vancouver Club, where they were given a very warm reception. How the hands fared is not recorded, but no doubt they were as well treated, for the West Coast was very proud of the achievements of "their" submarines and submariners.

The naming of the boats had taken an unusual course, in that it became common to call them CC boats instead of Canadian C, as had been intended, or submarine No. C1 or No. C2, as was sometimes noted. Somehow this was explained to Ottawa and a message dated October 6, 1914, made the CC designation official. From then on they were to be known as *CC1* and *CC2*.

By the second week in October the German squadron was reported far away in the southeastern Pacific and the crisis was apparently over, for the time being at least. It was decided to take advantage of the lull to rectify some of the accumulated defects and correct the longitudinal trim problem. *CC2* had already been put in dock for a short period during September to repair some structural damage apparently caused during her Chilean trials. At that time a number of defective valves had been discovered and repaired. At Keyes' behest it was decided to give the two boats a thorough inspection and both submarines were scheduled for docking.

With the help of some technical advice from Sir Philip Watts, who had addressed the problems as described by Captain Plaza, and through their own experiments and deductions, the submariners had defined three basic faults with the boats:

(1) With all main ballast tanks full, as they should be when dived, the boats had uncontrollable negative buoyancy. With the tanks only partially full to give neutral buoyancy, they became susceptible to nose or tail dives.

(2) The flooding and emptying of some tanks was uncertain and could be described as "temperamental."

(3) The main engine cylinder heads could not stand the heat generated at full speed; they generally cracked after about six hours of running.

The first problem was corrected by removing all excess weights in the form of spare gear, unnecessary stores and surplus fuel. These alterations prevented the boats from making long cruises in diving condition, but as they were used primarily for coastal defence, this was of little consequence. This overall lightening permitted the ballast tanks to be fully flooded, giving the boats their proper trim as the designers had intended.

In correcting the second problem, which was done over a number of dockings, the matter of the faulty workmanship and lack of quality control, as perpetrated by the Seattle Drydock and Construction Company, was exposed. Valve seats were scored, spindles bent, bonnets warped and solid debris was found trapped in valve seats and lying loose throughout the piping systems. Repairing these valves and cleaning out the piping made a tremendous difference in the ability to properly trim the boats. Some large pieces of debris were also found inside the tanks, such as a pair of coveralls, several cleaning rags and a piece of plank.

Another defect discovered concerned the sacrificial zinc anodes installed in the tanks to reduce corrosion. Nearly all of these were installed on top of the paintwork with no contact whatever with the metal they were supposed to protect. Over time all the zinc anodes were removed, cleaned and properly remounted. This job was made more difficult because of the location of the access holes to the internal tanks, most of which were on the outside of the hull, making it necessary for the boat to be in dock so as to get at the tanks.

It was also found that the hull plating in the vicinity of the waterline was suffering severe pitting and was completely bare of paint. Over a long period frequent observation of this phenomenon gave rise to a number of theories for its occurrence, one being that it was caused by electrolytic action between the steel-hulled boats and the copper sheathing on *Shearwater*'s timber-clad steel hull. Early in 1915 the copper was stripped off, but the corrosion persisted. Ultimately it was proven that the pressure-hull plating had not been properly pickled during manufacture. Only frequent inspection, thorough cleansing and preservation would keep the hulls from rusting through.

Nothing, however, would keep the rivets from rotting. Hundreds of these had to replaced at almost every docking. The engineers at Esquimalt, and later at Halifax, learned a great deal about hull preservation after dealing with the two subs for a few years, for they presented them with some very unusual problems.

The engines were a constant source of anxiety. In some cases breakdowns were caused by a lack of expertise on the part of the operators, but as a rule were mostly due to the obsolete design of the engines and the poor quality of the materials used in making them. The reversible camshafts were not a success. The timing had to be reset frequently, while continuous excessive wear of the camshaft drive gearing was another source of misery. As mentioned in the list of problems, the cylinder heads had a relatively short life and this was never satisfactorily corrected. A contributing factor to the problem was the impossibility of keeping water out of the fuel system, as a result of which it found its way into the piston heads, giving rise to unequal temperatures, which would cause the head to crack. This undesirable ingress of water was caused primarily by leaky valves.

CC1 *on the cradle at Yarrow's, Esquimalt.* HMS Newcastle *astern.* – DND E65-851

Material failures were fairly frequent. The engineers received a bit of a setback when *CC1* suffered a cracked main crankshaft in June 1916, and it was discovered the item had been manufactured by Krupp's of Germany. As it was most unlikely the manufacturer would be willing to supply a spare, a new one had to be made locally. Although the extent of the problem would not be discovered until much later, the batteries had little endurance and would not stand up to the rigours of prolonged usage.

The engine and battery problems were not unique to the ex-Chilean Canadian submarines. Similar problems were being experienced throughout the USN submarine fleet, as most of their boats had also been built to Electric Boat Company designs from parts supplied or manufactured by that company. The Americans would be forced to re-engine a large number of their submarines in 1915-16 and to replace batteries as well. Even the most advanced 1915 American-manufactured submarine batteries were not up to the standard of the contemporary British and European types, although much-improved engines were being built by that time.

All considered, however, the CC-boats were at least as successful as their American contemporaries and they did achieve the purpose for which they had been purchased. Despite breakdowns, trim problems and material failures, they remained manned, armed and on patrol throughout the crisis that existed on the West Coast from August to December 1914, after which they continued to give good service until the end of the war.

Von Spee's ships reached Easter Island on October 12. Here they remained for a week while they coaled and provisioned for the next leg of the journey, which it was intended would take them to Chile, a neutral but sympathetic refuge. During this time the squadron was reinforced by the arrival of *Leipzig*, which had made a slow passage south from San Francisco, and *Dresden*, which had rounded Cape Horn from the Atlantic a month earlier. Von Spee now had a concentration of two armoured cruisers and three light cruisers. He also had the AMC *Prinz Eitel Friedrich*, which had been forced to abandon her commerce raiding off Australia because of a lack of coal. Von Spee sent the liner on ahead to Valparaiso, as he couldn't spare any fuel from his seriously depleted stocks; these were reserved for the warships.

In the meantime the British had assembled a force in the South Atlantic to intercept Von Spee should he attempt to break through into the Atlantic. These ships were under the command of the capable and respected Rear-Admiral Sir Christopher Cradock. His force consisted of an old battleship, HMS *Canopus*, two obsolescent heavy cruisers, HMS *Good Hope* and HMS *Monmouth*, a modern light cruiser, HMS *Glasgow*, and the AMC *Otranto*. Cradock flew his flag in *Good Hope* and aboard her were four RCN midshipmen. The eager youngsters had been taken aboard when Cradock called at Halifax shortly after the beginning of the war. HMS *Defence*, a fast, modern armoured cruiser, had been delegated to relieve *Canopus*, but her orders were changed by the Admiralty, leaving Cradock insufficient strength to match the German armoured cruisers. *Canopus*, apparently suffering from boiler problems and too slow in any case, had been left behind at the Falklands when Cradock passed through the Straits of Magellan into the Pacific for the last time on October 24. Although Cradock ordered *Defence* to join him, it was too late.

Late in the afternoon of November 1, 1914, Cradock's squadron of obsolescent ships, manned largely by reservists, engaged Von Spee's Asiatic Squadron off the coast of Chile, near a place called Coronel, in a brave but futile contest. The battle was over in less than three hours. Between 7 p.m. and 9:30 p.m. the vastly superior gunnery of *Scharnhorst* and *Gneisenau* reduced *Good Hope* and *Monmouth* to flaming, shell-shattered hulks. Although no one witnessed the tragedy, *Good Hope* was the first to go sinking, at about 8 p.m., taking all hands with her. Seriously damaged and listing heavily, *Monmouth* was attempting to escape in the dark when she was spotted by the *Nurnberg*. As the British ship's ensign was still flying, the German cruiser, after playing a searchlight over the wreck and waiting a reasonable time for her opponent to surrender, opened fire at point-blank range. There was no reply. The end was inevitable, and 90 minutes after the flagship had gone, *Monmouth* joined her, taking her entire complement of 700 men with her. *Nurnberg* stood by, a helpless witness to the tragedy. The combination of a worsening gale and utter darkness made any attempt at rescue impossible, even had anyone survived to be picked up. *Glasgow* and *Otranto* made good their escape under the cover of darkness, heading for the Falklands and the dubious protection of *Canopus*'s 12-inch guns.

When the cold, dark South Pacific poured into the blazing remains of Cradock's sinking flagship, it claimed the lives of close to 900 British sailors, including the four Canadian midshipmen: William Palmer, John Hatheway, Arthur Silver and Malcolm Cann. All had been friends of William Maitland-Dougall and their deaths must have been a severe shock. He and Palmer had enjoyed a rivalry for first place in class standing throughout their three years together. Canada had suffered her first battle casualties of the Great War and the RCN its first ever. The loss of the four midshipmen served to bring the war into the homes of the many Canadians who until then had remained aloof from its reality.

The Battle of Coronel had a tremendous impact on both the British and the German peoples, obviously for opposite reasons. In Germany it was hailed as a great naval victory, which it undoubtedly was. In Britain it was mourned as a national tragedy, for not only had close to 2,000 men and their gallant Admiral perished and two ships been lost, but the Royal Navy had suffered a defeat upon the high seas. Like salt added to a wound was the fact that *Emden* was still loose in the Indian Ocean causing havoc with British shipping in that part of the world.

In British Columbia the public mood was close to panic. This despite the fact that there was a strong Allied naval force mustered for the defence of the West Coast, to which the Japanese had recently added the pre-Dreadnought battleship *Hizen*.

Retribution was swift and devastating. First to fall was the elusive *Emden*. She was destroyed on November 9 by the cruiser HMAS *Sydney* from Admiral Jerram's pursuing forces. Caught in the act of smashing the cable station on Cocos Island, she attempted to escape but was shelled into a wreck by the 6-inch-gunned Australian cruiser. Von Muller was forced to beach his ship on a reef, where he surrendered.

A few days later it was reported that *Scharnhorst* was steaming north accompanied by a collier and headed for the coal stocks at Nanaimo, and that she would shell Victoria. At the same time the Canadian authorities were warned that a group of German saboteurs was headed overland to attack the submarines in their berths alongside. British Columbia was having its share of alarms and the boats were once again sent out on patrol. Von Spee's squadron was in fact safely anchored at Mas-a-Fuera, off the coast of Chile.

In the South Atlantic, Britain assembled a truly formidable squadron of its own under Vice-Admiral Sir Doveton Sturdee. This squadron included two modern battlecruisers, HMS *Invincible*, flagship, and HMS *Inflexible*. Each was armed with eight 12-inch guns, protected by 6 inches of armour, and was capable of 25½ knots. These two battlecruisers, together with the cruisers *Carnarvon*, *Cornwall*, *Kent* and *Bristol*, converged almost leisurely on the Falkland Islands, where they joined with *Glasgow* and the old *Canopus* on December 7.

A few minutes before 8 a.m. the following day, the British, with their boilers at two hours notice for steam and in the act of coaling their ships, were surprised when columns of smoke announced the approach of a large number of vessels from the southwest. Von

Ship's company HMCS/M CC2 at Esquimalt circa April 1915. Back row, L to R: L/STKR Warner, SPO Roberts, ABST Lock, LTO Moulder, STKR Simmons, L/STKR Finmore. Middle, L to R: STKR Lee, AB Herrod, STKR Flannigan, unknown STKR, LS Foreman, STKR Sutherland. Front, L to R: ERA1 Pearson, COX'N Purves, LT Johnson, RNCVR, MID Edwards, RCN, CERA Hunting, ERA3 Conroy. – PAC 142539

AB ST Fred Crickard circa 1915. Fred served in the CC-boats from 1914 to 1917.
– Rear-Admiral F.W. Crickard

Spee had no inkling of the presence of such powerful forces and had unwittingly led his ships to their doom. The old *Canopus*, too slow to keep up with the modern ships, had moored herself inside Stanley harbour as a floating fortress, and a few rounds from her 12-inch guns convinced the Germans to try their luck elsewhere.

Sturdee wasn't the man to panic. All ships were ordered to raise steam and cast off their colliers. Three hours later his powerful command was clearing the harbour and by 1 p.m. the opposing squadrons were engaged in a number of separate ship-to-ship actions.

The Germans were outnumbered and vastly outgunned. By 7 p.m. both *Scharnhorst* and the *Gneisenau* had been sunk, to be followed within the hour by *Leipzig* and then *Nurnberg*. There were very few survivors, as many of those who lived through the battle were claimed by the icy waters. Although the seas were calm, the British had trouble finding boats without shrapnel holes in them with which to rescue the survivors.

By a miracle of good luck and Herculean efforts on the part of her stokers, *Dresden* managed to escape back into the Pacific. Nearly out of fuel and low on ammunition, she hid out for three months but was finally brought to bay on March 14 at the Mas-a-Fuera by *Kent* and *Glasgow*. After a brief engagement *Dresden* was abandoned by her crew and scuttled. Coronel had been avenged.

For the Canadian West Coast the destruction of Von Spee's squadron effectively ended the war in the Pacific. The threat of German raiders was completely removed in that one devastating action and nearly four months of tension vanished as the thoughts of the populace turned to Christmas. It was to be the last carefree Yuletide for many years to come. By that time over 30,000 Canadian troops were in France, but they had yet to take part in any actions and the tragic casualty tolls that would mar the next five Christmases were still in the future. The land war in Europe had come to a standstill while the trenches were being dug from the Channel to the Alps, but all of that was far away.

With no operational role to play the submarines were reduced to a care and maintenance routine alongside *Shearwater* while McBride urged for their retention and Ottawa debated whether or not to keep the boats at all. In the end it was decided to keep the flotilla intact. The boats were to maintain their operational capabilities so as to be available for deployment by the Admiralty. While their fate was being decided, the subs lay idle and crew morale slowly deteriorated.

Late in December Adrian Keyes requested to be allowed to resign his temporary RCN commission. There was a real naval war going on across the Atlantic and he wanted to be part of it. NSHQ reluctantly gave its approval and on January 9 he left Esquimalt for England. His leaving was a blow to many, for he was a strong leader and popular with all ranks. His leadership, forthright manner, ability as an instructor and willingness to share hardships had endeared him to his men. Adrian Keyes and Barney Johnson had got along particularly well and they formed a friendship that would last until Keyes' untimely death in 1926. Command of the flotilla passed to Bertram Jones, a duty he would continue to perform with ability and distinction until the end of the war.

Prior to Keyes' departure for England, Midshipman Maitland-Dougall was appointed to NSHQ. Reluctant as he was to leave the submarines, he had a long career ahead of him and a chance to work at Headquarters was not to be lightly dismissed. His place was taken by one of his classmates, Midshipman Robert F. Lawson. From the new year onwards the reservists who had manned the boats from the beginning started to move on to other duties and their places were taken by regular personnel. A few of the RNCVRs would remain, notable among these was Able Seaman Torpedoman Frederick W. Crickard. He would survive the war to father a son who in his turn would become an admiral in Canada's Navy of 60 years later.

At about 8:45 a.m. on October 27, 1914, the 23,000-ton battleship HMS Audacious *hit a mine while exercising off Tory Island. The White Star liner* Olympic *attempted to take the stricken warship in tow, without success.* Audacious *sank that evening after an internal explosion. This was the scene witnessed by Charles Schwabb while on his way to London for talks with the War Office.* – Author's collection

4 THE MONTREAL H-BOATS

The value of the submarine as an effective and affordable warship requiring only a small crew had not escaped the Canadian authorities at NSHQ. Experience with the CC-boats on the West Coast would soon demonstrate that even one or two submersible torpedo boats stationed off a major harbour not only provided a deterrence to would-be raiders but also inspired public confidence in the Navy out of all proportion to their expense and manpower requirements. They were cheaper to run and required far fewer men than a destroyer, yet carried a greater number of torpedoes. Possessing but indifferent seakeeping abilities in comparison to a patrol vessel and somewhat limited in submerged mobility, it was appreciated that the small submarine's potential could best be exploited by restricting its deployment to harbours and their approaches and to inshore waterways where geography would force the intruder onto the defender. As the authorities were only seeking a means for local defence, these small boats offered an economical solution to the problem.

The Canadian government had been approached as early as 1903 by a concern calling itself the British Submarine Boat Company Limited, which held the patents for a design known as the "Volta" submarine. This was a 17-ton, three-man submarine carrying two torpedoes. They were propelled by electric motors only and had no independent means of charging their batteries. Designed for portability the company literature claimed the "Volta" boats could be carried aboard larger ships, to be dropped whenever it was tactically desirable, or they could be used in swarms for protecting harbours and river estuaries. The philosophy of close-range action, as it existed before the Russo-Japanese war and the introduction of the Dreadnought type of battleship, is evident in the concept of these miniature submarines. They were designed to defend against attackers who forced their way into a nation's harbours and waterways in a time of war, implying a degree of invulnerability for the attacking ships against defending warships and shore defences that didn't exist. Their radius of action was extremely limited, and although a top speed of around 9 to 10 knots was claimed, this would have drained the battery very quickly if sustained. The government was not enthusiastic about these little submarines and the original proposal was declined. They were offered again in 1909, when it was apparent Canada would be getting its own navy, but again the offer was politely, but firmly, refused.

When the war broke out, Canadian Vickers had only recently opened their shipyard at Maisonneuve near Montreal and were relying to a large extent on government orders. In this respect the shipbuilders were disappointed by the failure of the naval building schemes as proposed by both the Laurier and Borden governments. Had either plan succeeded, large orders for naval ships would have gone to Canadian Vickers, but this had all evaporated when neither a national navy was built nor any contracts received from the Admiralty. The plant had recently been given two government contracts, one for an icebreaker and another for a large dredge, but these occupied only a fraction of the capacity available and the company was actively seeking additional work.

A short two weeks after the war had begun, Canadian Vickers made a proposal to the Deputy Minister for the Naval Service, George J. Desbarats, to build submarines for the Canadian Navy. It is well worth examining this offer, for the vessels they were going to build and the speed at which they proposed to build them were forerunners of dramatic events to come.

Canadian Vickers wanted to construct two or three of the design 20E Holland-type submarine as produced by the Electric Boat Company. These were very similar to the *CC1*, being 144 feet 1½ inches in length, 15 feet on the beam, with a displacement of 336 tons surfaced, 400 tons dived. They had four 18-inch torpedo tubes forward but none aft. Three similar but slightly larger vessels had already been supplied to the American Navy as the USS *Seawolf*, *Nautilus* and *Garfish* at a cost of $491,000 each. Ordered in 1912 the USN subs entered service in 1913. The engines used in these boats, and proposed for installation in the Canadian boats, were not altogether successful and the three USN submarines were re-engined in 1918.

The price Vickers was quoting for the submarines was $572,000 per boat, of which they estimated the government would recoup $50,000 in customs duties, as most of the machinery and raw materials would be subject to importation duties. The balance of the increase in cost over what the USN had paid was accounted for by the higher rates paid to Canadian labour and by wartime inflation. It is interesting to note that the price for these more modern Canadian-built submarines was $3,000 less than what was paid for the new, but obsolescent, CC-boats. The Vickers proposal stated that the first two vessels would be ready for trials in time for the 1915 opening of navigation on the St. Lawrence, or in about eight months from receipt of the order, provided it was placed before August 28, 1914. The third vessel would be ready a month later. By comparison it was taking Vickers' Barrow shipyard anywhere from 20 to 30 months to build the standard 800-ton British E-class submarines. This excessive building time would later be halved, but the original contracts had been let at the peacetime rate of production and couldn't be changed. In view of what was to follow, both the price and the delivery date were realistic, and Canadian Vickers appears to have offered the government a reasonable deal.

Lacking the expertise to evaluate the proposal, Ottawa sought the advice of the Admiralty, as they had done for the CC-boats only three weeks before. On August 26 NSHQ sent a message to Whitehall with the details of the proposal and requested an urgent reply. Two days later the following telegram was received:

28 August, 1914
Purchase of three submarines offered Canada Vickers Company are not recommended. Apart from objections design and other difficulties, date given for delivery is considered impossible.

On the strength of this communication and notwithstanding the earlier favourable report rendered on the very similar CC-boats, Desbarats politely declined Canadian Vickers' proposal. This decision was disappointing to Vickers, who badly needed the work, and to the Naval Service, which wanted to station the submarines at Halifax for local defence. Considering what the same Admiralty advisers were to undertake on their own behalf three months later, it is difficult to fathom the reasoning behind the position taken by the British authorities.

With the United States neutral, and there being no indications of increased domestic arms production and sales, entrepreneurial American businessmen were looking to Britain and France for orders that would get their industries working to capacity. One of these enterprising individuals was Mr. Charles M. Schwabb, President and Chairman of the Board of the Bethlehem Steel Corporation, a conglomerate based on steel-making that also included the shipbuilding firms of Union Iron Works, San Francisco, and the Fore River Shipyard, Quincy, Massachusetts. Late in October 1914 Schwabb sailed for England aboard the S.S. *Olympic* to discuss armaments orders with Lord Kitchener.

A few days later, on October 27, the handful of passengers aboard the White Star liner were witnesses to the 12-hour drama of the sinking of the new British battleship HMS *Audacious* after she hit a mine off the coast of Ireland. The mine had been laid two nights before by the converted liner *Berlin* in the first minefield to be laid outside the North Sea. Despite heroic efforts to save the great ship, she foundered in high seas after all survivors had been safely removed.

Not wanting the loss made public the Admiralty quarantined the liner in Lough Swilly, while the passengers were questioned and briefed on the role they were to play in keeping the matter quiet. Schwabb, however, grew impatient at the delay and demanded he be released to pursue his business with Lord Kitchener. His protestations were so insistent and his credentials so impressive that he was interviewed by Admiral Sir John Jellicoe, Commander in Chief of the Home Fleet.

During their conversation Jellicoe asked Schwabb if his company could build submarines, to which Schwabb replied they could and quoted a building time much shorter than anything in Britain. Jellicoe, sensing an opportunity, asked that he call on Admiral Fisher and, receiving Schwabb's assurances that he would do so, released him. Travelling under an assumed identity, the American industrialist went about his business.

Seventy-four-year-old Admiral "Jackie" Fisher was a dynamic and controversial individual who had already held the post of First Sea Lord from 1904 to 1910. He had come out of retirement at the insistence of the First Lord of the Admiralty, Winston Churchill, to resume his old position following the unexpected resignation of the incumbent, Prince Louis of Battenburg. Between them, Winston Churchill and Jackie Fisher had been putting together a crash submarine-building program but were having difficulties due to lack of capacity and slowness of construction in British yards. Fisher, father of the Dreadnought battleship and outspoken proponent of its battlecruiser sister, was also a staunch supporter of the long-range patrol submarine. He had been lobbying for a strong force of these boats for years and eventually won Churchill over to his cause. During 1912-13 an ambitious submarine-building program, including experimental as well as standard types, had been started but was proceeding at an almost leisurely production rate. This was far too slow for Fisher's strategies.

At the outbreak of war Britain possessed only 18 submarines capable of overseas operations, eight D and ten E class. Only seven additional overseas boats, six E and one experimental S class, would enter service between August and December 1914. A dozen new boats were due to reach the fleet in 1915 but none of those before May. It was into this submarine-building crisis that Charles Schwabb stepped after completing his talks with Kitchener.

On November 3 Schwabb and Fisher discussed many armament options and proposals, but it only took five minutes to strike an agreement whereby Bethlehem Steel would build 20 Holland-type submarines for the British Admiralty. Schwabb proposed a building time of less than six months per sub, with the entire 20 to be delivered inside of ten months. The price would be almost twice what it was costing the Admiralty to build a comparable submarine in a British yard, but the quantity and speed of delivery would make the deal well worth the expense. The specification selected was a modification of the latest type supplied to the USN. Though not by any means the largest design available, it was the most modern Electric Boat Company design of a suitable tonnage for which the main components were already in production. There would be no delays in making moulds or drawings or in designing new equipment. These were already in place with the manufacturers. These submarines were to be known as the H class, as that was the next vacant designation in the British scheme of class identification.

Even before leaving England for the States, Schwabb had telegraphed details of the deal to his legal team and set them to work finding ways of circumventing the question of American neutrality. By November 9 the keels were being laid, 12 at the Fore River shipyard and 8 on the Union Iron Works' slips. The submarines' hulls were to be completely erected then disassembled, crated and shipped to England, to be reassembled and finished there using complete outfits of mechanical parts as supplied from the United States. The procedure of shipping the boats in this knocked-down condition and reassembling them in the yards of their new owners had been perfected during the Russo-Japanese war, when five submarines were supplied to Japan and seven to Russia in this way. The parts for the first four British boats were to be delivered in five and a half months, the next six within eight months, and the final ten within ten months of the start of the contract. The price agreed to was $500,000 per boat with a bonus of $10,000 per boat per week for early completion or a penalty of $5,000 per week for late delivery. A contract for 40 diesel engines was given to NELSECO, the New London Ship and Engine Company, an Electric Boat Company subsidiary. The engines supplied for the H class were a big improvement over those installed in the latest USN submarines and were to prove both reliable and durable. Bethlehem Steel would produce the plating and angle bars, while Electric Boat would provide the other components through their own works or subcontractors.

Schwabb's company stood to make a handsome profit as long as the deal went through as planned, while Fisher would get 20 operational submarines at a time when British production would be at its lowest. Back in the United States, however, all was not smooth sailing. President Woodrow Wilson's Secretary of State, William Jennings Bryan, did not view the submarine-building deal favourably. The whole operation was in serious jeopardy when the matter was passed to the Joint State and Navy Neutrality Board for a ruling. In late November the U.S. government came out against the contract and proposed contesting its legality in the courts.

The administration's decision to oppose the deal was a serious blow to Schwabb's concept of the leading role Bethlehem Steel was to play in supplying armaments to the Allies. The submarine contract was to be a demonstration of his company's performance as an industrial supplier which could deliver in quantity and on time. Potentially, billions of dollars' worth of future orders were at stake. The government's position lacked popular support both inside and outside the administration and in some quarters was considered anti-Allied if not pro-German. Finding a means to get around the delays that would be caused by a battle in the courts only acted as a challenge to Schwabb's already well-proven ingenuity. He immediately began a furious round of visits to British diplomats and American politicians, including a personal appeal to his antagonist, the Secretary of State. Somehow or other, the deal had to go through.

The announcement by Secretary Bryan that the government was opposed to the Admiralty-Bethlehem Steel contract was good news to the depressed Canadian shipbuilding industry. If the Americans wouldn't do the job, they certainly could. The Prime Minister's office received offers from almost every yard of any size in the country: they all needed the work. One shipyard on the West Coast was willing to build up to four of the boats at the same speed and cost as their American competitors. They also mentioned that they had in their employ the very hull superintendent who had assembled the CC-boats. The reply received by this yard from the Minister of Naval Service, J.D. Hazen, admitted that the government knew nothing of any such opportunity being put forward by the Admiralty but that he would pass on their offer. The government would have been only too happy for the shipyards to have the contracts, but without a formal request from the Admiralty they could admit to nothing nor do anything to assist. Getting this kind of work would bring big economic benefits to the country, as well as serving to establish a Canadian naval shipbuilding industry. Borden lost no time in communicating the Canadian offers to the British government.

On the night of December 2 Charles Schwabb took the train to Montreal to visit the Canadian Vickers shipyard, where he held talks with the general manager, Mr. P.L. Miller. Two days later he returned to New York and to all appearances was prepared to submit to the government's position on neutrality. Work on the hulls, the most visible part of the operation, ceased, although production of all other assemblies continued, but under a tight security blanket.

By the 5th Schwabb was aboard the RMS *Lusitania* bound for Britain and more talks with Fisher. Ten days later the terms of a second deal had been hammered out, this time for ten of the submarines to be built in Canada. These boats were to be fully assembled, launched, fitted-out and trialed at the one location. Each would cost $600,000 and the Admiralty was to pay for leasing the Canadian Vickers yard, for all importation duties levied on materials brought into Canada and for part of the wages of the managerial staff that Schwabb would bring up from the States. The overall building time was about the same as specified for 20 boats in the original contract, but the actual completion time was considerably shortened. The first two boats were to be afloat and ready for trials in 4½ months rather than ready for shipment in crates in 5½ months. The first pair of submarines were to be launched by the end of April, with two boats to follow at the end of each of the next four months.

In the end all of the boats were launched early, while the final pair was handed over almost ten weeks ahead of the contract schedule, netting Schwabb and Bethlehem Steel a considerable profit in completion bonuses even though these had been cut in half by the new terms. The remaining ten submarines would be built, fitted out and trialed at the Fore River shipyard at normal building speed for delivery after the war or at such a time as suitable diplomatic arrangements could be made with the American government. The possibility of America entering the war was not discussed openly. On returning to the United States, Charles Schwabb publicly declared that he had been to Britain to cancel the contracts for the submarines to be built in American shipyards.

The building of the submarines at Montreal was to be a well-kept secret, not even the Canadian government being consulted or even informed. The Canadian Vickers yard had been leased to the Admiralty by the parent company, Vickers Limited of the UK, for the exclusive use of the Bethlehem Steel Corporation. As of January 1, 1915, the entire resources of the yard were to be devoted to the building of the submarines, all other work was to cease, the official reason being given as "the lack of parts." The vice-president of the Union Iron Works arrived from San Francisco on January 4 to head a team of managers and specialists brought in from the Electric Boat Company and the Fore River shipyard. The existing Vickers' work force was retained and extra labour was hired locally. The entire yard was fenced in and guarded by the Militia around the clock. All personnel were issued with passes and nobody was allowed in without one. Almost immediately material started arriving by rail and soon reached a volume of about 50 tons a week. The first keel was laid on the slips inside the big building sheds on January 11, six were down by the 14th, and all ten by February 9.

The first word that anyone of authority in Canada received about the building of the boats in Montreal came in the form of a cable dated January 6, 1915, from Sir Cecil Spring Rice, the British Ambassador at Washington, addressed to the Governor General, HRH the Duke of Connaught. In his telegram Spring Rice mentioned (erroneously) the construction of five submarines in the United States and 15 in Canada, and that Bethlehem Steel had been warned to avoid any kind of publicity regarding the construction of subs in Canada. Informing the Governor General, however, was not necessarily informing the government of Canada. This telegram was forwarded to NSHQ, where it was received on the 13th and duly noted for the information of the Minister.

The next official communication came from Sir George Perley, the Canadian High Commissioner in London, it was dated January 16. In this communication to the Prime Minister, Sir George mentions the construction of ten submarines with the possibility of more later and dwells on the matter of the importation of American workmen into Canada, citing the need to satisfy Admiralty requirements in fulfilling the contract. This was followed on the same date by another telegram to the Governor General, this time from Lewis Harcourt, the Colonial Secretary in London. In this he informed the Governor General that "the Admiralty has found it necessary to undertake the construction of submarines for H.M. Government in the Canadian Vickers yard at Montreal and that it is feared this will interfere with the construction of the icebreaker." This was received in External Affairs on February 8, when it was passed to the Prime Minister.

The Prime Minister, however, was not entirely ignorant of what was taking place at Montreal. He had been privately informed about the submarine contract by the President of Canadian Vickers, Fredrick Orr Lewis, but not until mid-January, by which time work was well under way. There was little Borden could do about an Imperial fait accompli except fume inwardly. What did immediately concern him was the fact that American workers may well have been imported illegally. If the allegation was substantiated it would create serious problems between Canada and the USA and with the vociferous Canadian labour movement.

Indignant though he may have been over the high-handed and insensitive manner in which the matter had been handled by London, Borden had been urged to secrecy and had little choice but to accept that this was necessary from the viewpoints of international relations and military security. After all, the nation had decided against equipping a proper navy of its own and the maritime defence of Canada had been entrusted to the Admiralty. For that privilege there was a price to be paid. Upset though he undoubtedly was to see the contract in place without any consideration whatever for Canadian interests, and with all of the profits going to the USA and Britain, there was little Borden could do about it publicly. Privately he vowed never to allow such an act of Imperial arrogance to happen again.

It was not until February 8 that the Secretary of State for the Colonies, Lewis Harcourt, sent a telegram to the Governor General in which some regret was expressed at the secretive way in which the matter had been handled by the Admiralty. The right of the Admiralty to act in such an arbitrary manner, however, was never questioned. Their Lordships only promised to try to keep the Colonial Secretary informed should such an action again become necessary. Imperial arrogance died hard.

H-boats under construction at Montreal. – PAC 32270

H-boats nearing completion in the sheds at Canadian Vickers. – author's collection

Launching an H-boat. – RN Submarine Museum

Borden, through his High Commissioner, continued to press Whitehall for more building contracts. If not submarines or other naval ships, then merchant ships to replace those already commandeered. With the completion of the Canadian Vickers contract almost 2,000 men would be thrown out of work. With the loss of work, the skilled workers would soon disappear and the industry would once again be in a slump. A proposal to build subs for the Imperial Russian government at a yard near Vancouver was also put forward and passed for consideration. Churchill, who had been a strong supporter of the Naval Aid Bill and had even considered building battlecruisers in Canada before the war, turned down all the offers. In a direct contradiction of his 1911 assessment of Canadian shipbuilding potential, Churchill now declared that Canadian yards were only suitable for the assembly of parts manufactured in the United States or elsewhere. The best that could be arranged was the refit of a cruiser at Vickers after the spring break-up.

The building of the submarines — for building it was, despite the First Lord's pronouncements — was proceeding at a furious pace. By March there were over 2,000 men employed in two 12-hour shifts working around the clock. There were a few labour difficulties, particularly when it became common knowledge that a large number of aliens were in the work force. The unions also objected to the 12-hour shifts, particularly as an 8-hour shift was the Canadian norm and acceptance of their grievance would get another 1,000-man shift to work. The Montreal Trades and Labour Council made representation to Canadian Vickers and were told that only 150 American specialists were being employed out of the entire work force and that the 12-hour shift was not negotiable. The Council was not satisfied but, lacking the power to buck Vickers *and* Bethlehem Steel, was unwilling to take any further action against the plant.

The type of work and the manner in which it was being conducted was a matter of concern to the government. Considering the size of the contract and the international implications inherent in its fulfillment, the Minister for the Naval Service ordered an inquiry into the work being carried out at the Vickers plant. The Germans too would have liked it thought that Vickers was merely assembling finished parts supplied from the United States. If the charges were to be proven, these details could be used very effectively in a propaganda campaign directed against the Americans. The Minister for the Naval Service was himself uncertain as to exactly how the building of the boats was being accomplished and, anticipating some awkward questions in the House, sent his deputy to Montreal to make a detailed investigation.

J.G. Desbarats arrived at Canadian Vickers on April 29, 1915. He immediately began a round of discussions with the Vickers, Bethlehem Steel, and Electric Boat Company managers involved in the project. At the time of his arrival three boats had already been launched, while two more were nearly ready to take the water. The remaining five were in various stages of completion. By the information he was given, it was disclosed that the work force had peaked at 2,800 men, but by the time of his visit was down to 2,400. He was shown how the steel plate and angle bar for the hull plates and ribs was received uncut and unshaped and that all laying out, cutting, shaping, rolling and punching was done in the yard itself. The special steel castings of patent design arrived from the States in an unfinished state, while several subcontracts were let locally for large quantities of small steel castings and shafting. Orders for common bronze-bodied valves were also placed with a Canadian manufacturer. All of the cast-bronze items, such as the conning tower sections, periscope shears and large valve bodies, came from Electric Boat and their subcontractors in New England, as did the engines, storage batteries and the electrical equipment. These major items were accepted as being of a common commercial type such as would normally be procured from an outside source. It was also pointed out that Canadian industry had neither the facilities nor the expertise to produce many of the specialty components. Desbarats was satisfied that, as much as any ship was ever actually manufactured in a particular Canadian yard, these could be considered as having been built in Canada.

Desbarats went to some pains to secure proof that none of the material previously prepared for the West Coast and New England yards had made its way into Canada for use in the Vickers-built boats. To all appearances this material had been stockpiled at the Fore River yard for incorporation into the ten boats being built there. Because of American concerns that they might be accused of helping the Allied war effort too vigorously, USN officers had been stationed at the Fore River yard to monitor the construction of the boats and ensure that none of the prepared materials found their way into Canada. How rigidly this security was enforced is a matter for conjecture. There was considerable sympathy for the Allied cause in the USN, and Bethlehem Steel and Electric Boat seem to have had a pretty free hand in the conduct of their affairs.

The Canadian authorities had, even if somewhat belatedly, made the correct political moves and were now beyond reproach in the matter. In naval parlance Hazen and Borden had effectively "covered their yardarms." It is to their credit that they did so, for although the Canadian government had no connection whatever with the Canadian Vickers-Bethlehem Steel arrangements, the Admiralty would make demands on the government in the future as if they had engineered the whole deal.

Lt. Wilfred B. Pirie, RN, senior officer of the first group of H-boats and CO of HMS/M H1.
– author's collection

5 FOUR PLUS SIX

While Montreal bustled with the building of the H-boats and Ottawa became entangled in the diplomatic problems arising from their existence, the Drafting Office of HMS *Dolphin* at Fort Blockhouse near Gosport, the British submariners' "Alma Mater," was busy rounding up the officers and men needed to man the new boats. To the distress of those whose job it was to find and allocate suitable personnel, it soon became apparent that the submarines were not only going to be ready much earlier than was forecast, but they would have to be manned in batches, beginning with the first four, and not in well-spaced pairs as originally anticipated. These developments would cause the authorities some severe headaches. It was one thing to find and dispatch two crews at a time at well-spaced intervals, but to have to provide four all at once was going to be hard enough, after which they would be faced with the need for six more, and that was going to prove almost impossible in the time available.

For the passage to their operational bases each boat was to be provided with a nucleus crew consisting of a captain, a navigator and a complement of 15 men. The remaining officer and anywhere from six to ten men required to complete the crew in each submarine would join later, when the boats reached their operational depots. To meet these sudden manning demands Britain's fleets and naval establishments were scoured for suitable personnel, several experienced men serving in the Royal Fleet Reserve and even a few boy signalmen being accepted.

By the beginning of April the crews for *H1* through *H4* had been assembled at Fort Blockhouse under the overall command of the senior commanding officer and captain of *H1*, Lieutenant Wilfrid B. Pirie. Early on the morning of April 9 the party of 68 officers and men entrained for Liverpool and on arrival trooped aboard the S.S. *Missanabie*, a nearly new G.P. Allan tourist-class liner, to begin the seven-day Atlantic crossing to Canada. As the St. Lawrence was still choked with ice, they would have to land at Halifax and travel to Montreal by rail. Aboard ship the sailors were well received by their fellow passengers and the liner's crew, most of whom were well aware of their reason for going to Canada. The thought of challenging the mighty Atlantic in a tiny submarine displacing a mere 355 tons was a daunting prospect that could well be appreciated by mariner and landsman alike from the comfort and relative safety of a large ocean liner of 14,000 tons. During the voyage the submariners, with the help of a few other passengers, gave a benefit concert in the saloon for the Mercantile Marine Orphanage, which proved to be a great social and financial success.

After a safe and speedy trip the *Missanabie* made landfall off Nova Scotia on schedule, where she went alongside one of the big ocean-liner docks at Halifax. The 8 officers, 8 chief petty officers and 52 ratings were hustled straight aboard a waiting train to begin the 24-hour journey to Montreal. The party arrived at its destination on the evening of Sunday the 18th and were met by members of the Admiralty Overseer's party who had been in Montreal working with Canadian Vickers since January. Their hosts explained that the submariners had arrived only a few hours too late to have witnessed the launching of the first boat, *H1*, which had slid down the ways stern first that very afternoon.

The British sailors were uncertain as to what sort of a reception to expect in Canada. In Britain the one-time colony was commonly regarded as being pro-USA and at best lukewarm to the Allied cause in Europe. It was the impression among the British at the time that Canadians, like the Yankees to the south, were prepared to help the "Old Country" only so long as it was profitable and they didn't have to take any risks.

The fact that by that time over 30,000 Canadians were serving on the Western Front, where they had already distinguished themselves in the bloody fighting at Ypres and Festubert, had gone almost unremarked in the British and Canadian press of the day. Like the newspapers in England, the Canadian press failed to single out Canadian Corps successes from those of the British Army as a whole and frequently reprinted the British press releases verbatim.

Doubts were soon dispelled, however, for the sailors were warmly welcomed by Canadians throughout their journey to Montreal. On arrival the men were put on "lodging and compensation allowance," while the officers took rooms at the Ritz Carlton Hotel. It wasn't long before the British matelots found lodgings with the local English-speaking populace, many of whom hadn't been out from the British Isles very long themselves and held it as their duty to look after the "boys in blue." Later, the sailors were befriended by the men of the Royal Highlanders of Canada, who were in garrison at Montreal. During the next few months many an enjoyable evening was spent in the Royal 42nd Regiment's messes.

The submariners were surprised to be refused entry into the Vickers works that first morning. Despite their uniforms and the protestations of their officers, all had to wait until each was issued with his pass before they could enter the shipyard. The British tars had never expected to encounter such strict security this far from the war. They would soon learn that the works were guarded 24 hours a day and that the passes were their only sure means of gaining entry.

As had been the case on the West Coast there was concern about German agents and sympathizers coming up from the United States to conduct sabotage operations against military targets in Canada. Although the fear of actual sabotage may have been unfounded, the German Diplomatic Mission to the USA certainly availed themselves of every opportunity to foment criticism of American military assistance to the Allies and to spread anti-British sentiment.

For the submariners, familiarization with their new vessels began at once. Officers and men alike had a great deal to learn in the four weeks it would take before *H1* was fitted out and began her acceptance trials. Although descended from the old Holland boats with which the USN and the RN had both started their submarine forces, development had taken different courses in the two navies and the layout of the H-boats was foreign to the British submariners. This was a real opportunity, especially for the officers and engine room artificers, for seeing just how the submarines were put together, a knowledge that would be invaluable later on. With ten hulls in various stages of construction, they were able to observe the work in nearly every phase of completion from a near-empty shell to a fully equipped boat in the water. It was observed by many that, although the workmanship was good, the speed of construction was being deliberately pushed by the American supervisors so as to win the substantial early completion bonuses provided for in the Schwabb-Churchill contract.

On May 5, *H4*, the last of the first group of boats, was launched by Mrs. W.B. Pirie, the wife of *H1*'s captain, who had followed her husband across the Atlantic. On the 9th *H1* left Montreal on the 325-mile trip downriver to Murray Bay, where the boat would spend the next nine days completing acceptance trials. Although Pirie and his crew were aboard for the passage to Quebec City, the vessel was manned by a civilian crew under the command of an American trials captain provided by the Electric Boat Company and assisted by a St. Lawrence River pilot. While trials were in progress the British crew went aboard their boat as observers and for training only. Not until the tests were finished and the boat accepted by the Admiralty Overseer would they take over from the civilians.

During this period, probably on May 12, the cruiser HMS *Carnarvon*, a veteran of the Battle of the Falkland Islands, made her way upriver to Canadian Vickers for repairs to a damaged bottom received when she had grounded some time previously — Churchill's promised work for Canada's near-idle shipbuilding industry.

On the 18th *H1*, having finished most of her trials, started upriver for Quebec to take on stores before completing the schedule of tests. The day was overcast with intermittent rain squalls and visibility was generally poor. While passing Point St. Jean the submarine accidentally collided with and sank the small steamer *Christine* with the unfortunate loss of six of her crew in the frigid, choppy waters. The steamer sank quickly, her screw still revolving as she disappeared beneath the surface. There had been no time to get any boats away.

Lieutenant Pirie immediately relieved both the trials captain and the pilot and personally took charge of the rescue of the survivors from the steamer's crew, all of whom were floundering in the cold, fast-flowing river. Able Seaman Moyse distinguished himself in helping to rescue the steamer's signalman and injured captain. On his own initiative Moyse fastened a line around his waist, dived into the icy river, swam out to the half-drowned survivors, and secured his line about them. They were all hauled to safety aboard *H1* by the sailors on deck. Moyse was later decorated by the Humane Society for his bravery, while the *Christine*'s grateful master presented him with a fine silver wristwatch. The brave and resourceful submariner was later lost aboard an E-class boat. The damaged submarine put in at Quebec to report the incident, exchange pilots and to land the American captain. The next day, under the sole command of Lieutenant Pirie and with a new pilot embarked, *H1* returned to Montreal, where she was quickly repaired, much to Pirie's surprise and delight.

Four days later *H1* returned to Murray Bay to successfully complete a 200-foot test dive, after which the boat was accepted by the Admiralty representatives. That afternoon she steamed upriver and secured alongside the Customs pier at Quebec City. The following day, May 26, the little submarine, her two officers and 15-man ship's company were inspected by His Royal Highness the Duke of Connaught, Governor General of Canada, accompanied by Her Royal Highness the Princess Patricia. Following the inspection *H1* was formally commissioned into the Royal Navy. The vice-regal party was impressed with the submarine and expressed their belief that the crew should have no problem in getting across the Atlantic in their fine new boat.

In the meantime the other three submarines had been making steady progress toward commencing their trials. On May 19 the British collier *Glenalmond*, chartered by the Admiralty to carry the spare gear, towing equipment, stores and torpedoes for the boats, left Montreal for Quebec with the crews for *H2*, *H3* and *H4* aboard. The subs

The H5-H10 group fitting out. The cruiser Carnarvon *is in the* Duke of Connaught *floating dock undergoing repairs.* – RN Submarine Museum

H1 *arrives at Vickers for repairs after colliding with the steamer* Christine. *The collier* Glenalmond *is alongside taking on cargo for the Atlantic crossing.* – RN Submarine Museum

followed in the charge of civilian trials crews. *H3* left Montreal on the 25th, *H4* on the 28th and *H2* on the 29th of May.

While awaiting their boats, and when not actually working on board or standing guard duty on the pier, the sailors were billeted at the Citadel, guests of the Militia. Any time not spent on trials was devoted to cleaning and painting the boats and in embarking stores, water, fuel and torpedoes in preparation for the long voyage ahead. Other than *H2* suffering a badly damaged engine and falling ten days behind, the submarines got through their trials without accident or exceptional difficulty.

On June 7 Lieutenant Pirie was officially informed that his destination was to be the Mediterranean, not England, as most had expected. This was stimulating news for the submariners, for at that time going to the Med meant the exciting possibility of getting a crack at traversing the infamous Dardenelles. The exploits of the English submariners in the Sea of Marmara had recently been making world headlines and it was expected that the British would keep up the pressure on the Turks. On the 10th the submarines were ready to depart, an incredibly short five months after the first keel had been laid. At 5 a.m. the little convoy set out downriver bound for St. John's, Newfoundland. The four submarines were accompanied by the *Glenalmond* and escorted by the ex-fisheries protection gunboat HMCS *Canada*.

H1's run of bad luck played its last card when she fouled a pontoon and badly damaged her port propeller on leaving the berth at Quebec. Keeping *Glenalmond* to assist and to supply a spare propeller, Pirie sent the other ships on ahead. *H1* was then secured alongside the steamer and, by flooding tanks forward and emptying those aft, the sub was trimmed down by the bows to expose the injured screw. Within a few hours the boat's own ERAs had replaced it with a new one. That evening *H1* and *Glenalmond* set out to catch up with the others, their rate of advance restricted to the collier's best speed of about 10 knots.

As the second group of boats, originally thought to be just *H5* through *H7* but soon expanded to include all six, started to take shape, the second contingent of officers and crew began arriving at Montreal. The senior officer for this group was Commander Alexander H. Quicke, one of the very early British submariners and Adrian Keyes' first submarine CO. Upon arrival he assumed the position of Senior Officer, Submarines, and took command of *H10* for the passage to England. Quicke, who had brought the officers and crew for *H5* with him, arrived around May 5 and booked into the Hotel Place Viger. He speedily took over the reins of command from Pirie, who by then was fully occupied with mastering his own boat and in supervising the completion and trials of *H1* through *H4*. Two weeks later the crews for *H6* and *H7* arrived at Montreal, having made the crossing aboard the RMS *Scandinavian*.

On leaving Quebec City the Mediterranean-bound boats journeyed down the picturesque St. Lawrence River valley and into the gulf in fine early summer weather. By noon of the 12th, however, this tranquil scene had changed completely. As they were entering the Cabot Strait the convoy found themselves in the thick of a worsening gale with high winds and rough seas from the northwest.

That first stormy night was one of great apprehension for the submariners. They were in unfamiliar waters, aboard untried vessels, had no logs, gyros or wireless sets and, to complete their discomfiture, their compasses had not been corrected and could not be relied on. The submarines had been instructed to keep station on their escort, but in the gale and darkness this proved to be impossible.

Sometime during the night of the 12th-13th, *H4* Lieutenant Henry E. Smyth, CO, and Sub-Lieutenant Anthony G. Cunard (a grandson of Sir Samuel Cunard), first lieutenant and navigator, got separated from the group and disappeared, having been last seen about ten miles west of the island of Miquelon. During the forenoon of the 13th *Canada* reported to Halifax that she only had *H2* in sight and requested assistance to help locate the others. A few hours later she reported finding *H3* but confirmed the disappearance of *H4*. *Canada* then led her remaining charges into a sheltered anchorage at Bay Virgin, in the lee of Miquelon, where they waited for the weather to improve. Around seven the next morning they were joined by *H1* and *Glenalmond*, who had heard of the *H4* episode the previous day from the Armed Merchant Cruiser HMS *Calgarian*, one of the ships on charter to the government that had been ordered to search for the missing submarine. *Canada*, leaving her convoy at anchor, set out to join in the search for the missing boat.

By midnight of the 13th no fewer than five steamers, including two large troop transports, had been diverted from government business to search for *H4*, while all shipping in the area between Cape Ray and Cape Race was warned by wireless to keep a lookout for the lone submarine. This was not as effective a precaution as it would be today, for in 1915 fewer than a quarter of the ships at sea were fitted with wireless and many of those that were did not man their sets continuously. It was necessary for ships which had received the message to relay it by flag signals or word of mouth to any other vessels they encountered. Added to the concerns for the possibility of *H4* having foundered in the gale was that of the submarine being discovered on the surface, mistaken for a German U-boat and attacked by the large, fast, steel-hulled steamers, many of which were armed. Her unescorted presence might also precipitate a panic among the local fishermen if she were spotted in an area frequented by the large fleets of inshore fishing craft that plied those waters.

H4, however, was oblivious to all of this and was in fact quite safe and set upon following the instructions she had been issued when the trip started. These required any boat that got separated to put into the nearest port with a telegraph office and report their position and circumstances. At the height of the gale *H4* had put about and for nearly two days steamed with her head to the weather, during which the boat covered almost a hundred miles in the direction from which it had come. When the weather eased early on the 15th Lieutenant Smyth found his bearings and put into Rose Blanche Bay, near Port Aux Basques, where he was able to telegraph their position and intentions to NSHQ, Ottawa. For some unexplained reason it took nearly 24 hours for Ottawa to get word back to Halifax and from thence to the searching ships. By the evening of the 15th *H4* was reported passing Lamelines Light at the tip of the Burin Peninsula, about 24 hours behind the main group and well on her way to St. John's.

Glenalmond and the other three boats had weighed anchor at noon on the 14th and set course for St. John's, to be joined by the *Canada* shortly afterwards. Upon rounding Cape Race the following morning, they encountered massive icebergs and banks of cold, thick fog, all of which heightened their anxiety for the missing *H4*.

Shortly after noon that same day the three storm-battered submarines went alongside in the historic seaport. Hundreds of spectators had gathered on the quayside to see the first submarines ever to visit the old colony. But it was as if there was an invisible barrier between them and the submarines, for the crowd would not approach closer than about a hundred feet. It was several hours before the crewmen could entice the cautious locals to come closer for a good look. The submarines must have seemed alien craft indeed to those accustomed to simple sail-driven fishing vessels and the occasional steamer. Once they had overcome their shyness, however, the Newfoundlanders' tradition of generous hospitality prevailed and the British sailors were made heartily welcome. The next day the submariners' minds were put at rest when news of *H4*'s good fortune and progress reached

H2 and H3 *arriving at St. John's.* – RN Submarine Museum

A storm-weary H4 *safely alongside* H2 *at St. John's.* – F. Gordon Bradley collection

them from the telegraph office ashore. That night the British tars really had something to celebrate.

Early on the morning of the 17th the tardy *H4* put into St. John's, salt-stained and rust-streaked but none the worse for her adventures. The H-boats, it had been discovered, were very good seaboats, riding the long Atlantic rollers with buoyant ease, quite unlike their consorts, which had plunged through the high seas, their upper decks awash. With *H4*'s safe arrival HMCS *Canada* took her departure and returned to Quebec, leaving the convoy in the care of their escort for the transatlantic voyage to Gibraltar, the 21,000 ton AMC *Calgarian*. Once the largest liner in the G.P. Allan Line's fleet, she was on a trooping run from Halifax to Liverpool by way of St. John's and Gibraltar. While at St. John's Boy Signalman William Wilkes of *H2*, who had been too sick to be useful, was traded for a seaworthy signalman from *Calgarian*, RNVR Signalman Junniper from Eastborne.

After an abortive start on the 19th, called off because of dense fog outside the harbour, the convoy finally got under way at 10 a.m. on Sunday, June 20. Aboard the *Calgarian* the 242 blue-putteed soldiers belonging to F Company, Royal Newfoundland Regiment, and 85 Naval Reservists, also from Newfoundland, gave the submarines a wild, song-filled send-off as they filed past the liner while leaving harbour.

The first few days of the passage were plagued by heavy fog which reduced the convoy to a crawl. Once into the open Atlantic this gave way to brilliant sunshine and aboard *H1* the crew celebrated by rigging a large canvas bath on the forward casing, in which four men at a time could get a saltwater scrub down. Photographs of this event were eventually published in the British newspapers.

H3 developed a variety of mechanical problems during the trip and spent much of the time under tow, which reduced the convoy's speed to about 10 knots. *Calgarian* made a diversion to the Azores, where she anchored off a lee shore, took *H3* alongside to effect repairs, and offered the other boats an opportunity to come alongside and replenish their supplies of fresh water and food. Despite the best efforts of her ship's company, both of *H3*'s engines quit shortly after leaving the Azores and towing was resumed. Sometime later *H3* finally got her ailing engines going and the ships were able to make better progress. Shortly afterward *H1* brought the convoy to a halt when both her engines quit at the same time. A frantic investigation revealed that the fuel tank selected for use was full of water instead of oil. The "Yankee" suppliers were roundly cursed (perhaps without cause, as it was normal to fill empty fuel tanks with water for trimming purposes). Tanks were switched over, fuel lines and cylinders purged, engines restarted, and the ships got under way once again. Three days out from Gibraltar the convoy ran into a howling gale and the submarines were forced to find what little shelter they could in the lee of the high-sided liner. During the gale *H1*'s starboard engine finally stopped, having given trouble for several days, but Pirie refused the offer of a tow. They'd made it this far unaided and he fully intended that his boat would arrive under its own power. By the time the "Rock" was sighted, at 8 a.m. on July 2, the weather had calmed considerably. Two-and-a-half hours later the submarines secured alongside the mole at Gibraltar, 13 days and 25 minutes after slipping from the jetty in St. John's.

At Gibraltar the four boats were dry-docked for inspection and repairs while the crewmen enjoyed some recreation ashore. On July 12 they sailed for Malta in company with the monitor *M-15*, which was enroute to the island to be fitted with her main armament. The trip was broken by a stopover at Algiers to report meeting a strange, fast warship which refused to identify itself. There was some speculation that she might have been the *Goeben* or *Breslau* making a break for home or on a raid, but this was not the case, as the ship turned out to be an Allied vessel.

Calgarian and the subs leave St. John's, June 20, 1915. – PAC CN 6405

In the bath on H1. – author's collection

The crew of H5, *a typical ship's company. Officers (L to R): Lt. W.L. Thompson, the first RNVR officer in submarines; Lt. Cromwell H. Varley, captain; Lt. Frank Busbridge, first lieutenant. Sixteen-year-old Boy Signalman Mills is seated in front of Lt. Thompson.* – RN Submarine Museum

"Young Billy," Sub-Lieutenant William McKinstry Maitland-Dougall, RCN.
– Maitland-Dougall family collection

On the 19th the four submarines and their escort reached Malta, where they were berthed alongside the famous *E11*, which, having already made two trips up the Dardenelles, was in Malta to have a deck gun installed. The next day work was begun in fitting the H-boats with wireless equipment, special jumping wires and six-pounder deck guns. Gyros were not available. Less than a month later Pirie and his *H1* would be in the Sea of Marmara harrying the Turks ashore and afloat and making submarine history.

Back at Montreal the building of the second group of boats was rapidly nearing completion. *H5* and *H6* had already been accepted and *H7* finished her trials on the day the first group left St. John's. By the time Pirie reached Gibraltar the entire group of six was ready to depart Quebec City, so quick was the progress.

Because of the unexpected speed with which the boats were completed, a manning crisis was coming to a head. When Quicke had arrived in May he had only brought one crew with him and was followed shortly after by two more in anticipation of the boats sailing in two groups of three boats each, one in July and the other in October, but now he was going to have to man all six at once.

As far back as late April Vice-Admiral Kingsmill, appreciating the manning difficulties being experienced by the Royal Navy, offered to man one or two of the submarines with Canadian submariners to help get the boats to England. The crews would be drawn from the CC-boats and all personnel would return once the boats concerned had reached the UK. When the call went out for volunteers, all of the submarine-trained officers and men attached to *Shearwater* and the CC-boats offered to go, except for one petty officer and one able seaman. Ultimately it was found that only 18 men could be spared. Because of the disparity in pay between the RN and the RCN, Quicke proposed keeping these together as a crew for one boat. At first this was to have been *H8* with a Canadian captain, but later he changed it to *H10* with himself in command. When the Admiralty moved to retain the crew indefinitely the Prime Minister insisted that the Director of the Naval Service withdraw his offer. Kingsmill was reluctant to comply with his superior's instruction, reasoning that the government had, after all, placed the resources of the RCN at the Admiralty's disposal for the duration of the hostilities. The Admiral also pointed out that all but four of the men serving in the CC-boats originated with the Royal Navy in the first place and that should they desire, their Lordships could order them all back to England or to any other duties they chose. He was overruled, however, for the Prime Minister was in no mood to give in to Admiralty demands, especially with regard to submarines.

All of these negotiations took time, and during the first week of June Quicke suddenly found himself deprived of the Canadian crew he had been counting on and in need of three complete crews instead of only two. Some relief was available locally, as four candidates for engine room artificer had reported off the street at Montreal, while one Canadian, Lieutenant B.L. Johnson, RNCVR, had been appointed by the Admiralty to command *H8* (presumably with some urging and advice from Adrian Keyes), and a pair of midshipmen, John Grant Edwards and William McKinstry Maitland-Dougall, had volunteered to make the passage. When some doubts were expressed concerning Maitland-Dougall's qualifications, his application was fully endorsed by Vice-Admiral Kingsmill, who professed he considered him to be "as competent as the ordinary sub-lieutenant." To these could be added three submarine-trained ERAs from the Admiralty Overseer's party, who could return home in the boats. In the end the four volunteer ERAs were recruited while Johnson arrived in Montreal around May 14, and a month later Maitland-Dougall appeared and was taken aboard *H10* as spare officer. In the meantime Blockhouse had scraped up the other three crews and sent them over aboard the S.S.

Corsican. They arrived at Montreal around June 14, which allowed the men very little time to get acquainted with their boats before taking them to sea.

Barney Johnson had been both pleased and relieved to be given command of one of the new submarines. Not only was the appointment an acknowledgement of his professional standing, but it also served as a much-needed boost to his drooping morale. He knew it meant leaving his wife and son and going overseas, but that was all a part of the war, and by then he was determined to get into action. With Adrian Keyes' departure from Victoria earlier in the year and the laying up of the CC-boats for the winter, life at Esquimalt had become somewhat pointless and depressing. With no new challenges to demand the level of activity he had become accustomed to in those early, frantic days, Johnson's spirits slumped into a condition he described as "mouldy." The nature of the flotilla had changed too. The innovative sparkle that had characterized those first six almost desperate months had disappeared as professional naval routine took over. Most of the early volunteers had left the boats then, many being taken into the RCN proper, only to be drafted elsewhere. Their places were taken by regular naval personnel, most of whom were RN men on loan or ex-RN sailors who had enlisted in the RCN for the duration. They were capable enough, but of a very different brotherhood.

It was May before the CC-boats tried to dive again, and the first exercise, a submerged attack on the *Shearwater* carried out off Ladysmith, almost ended in tragedy. Bertram Jones by that time was the only qualified submarine captain left. He was in command of the entire flotilla, which put heavy demands on his time and energies, as well as which he was captain of the *Shearwater.* During the attack the combination of a defective depth gauge and the lack of alertness on the part of the captain and his crew, resulting from their long period of idleness, caused *CC2* to go much deeper than she'd been before, or since. In all likelihood it appears that the submarine was only saved by the operation of the safety blowing valve, which automatically blew the ballast tanks, causing the boat to surface before she could exceed her designed depth.

Johnson wanted out, gracefully if it could be managed. He no longer felt he belonged. He had joined to fight against the Germans and they had long ago disappeared from the coast of British Columbia. He was committed to seeing the war through but couldn't visualize himself engaged in an endless round of exercises while waiting for the call to action that now seemed far from ever coming. When the request for volunteers to man the H-boats had come near the end of April, Barney had volunteered along with the rest. It was shortly after this that they sailed from the exercise off Ladysmith.

After the flotilla returned to Esquimalt from its near tragedy in the Strait of Georgia, Johnson was handed a telegram appointing him to HMS *Dolphin* for command of *H8* and transferring him to the Royal Naval Volunteer Reserve. Barney Johnson was both elated at having been selected and relieved at not having to take some sort of drastic action to free himself. After a hurried round of farewells he boarded the train at noon on May 9 to start his journey to Montreal.

The telegram he received at Esquimalt instructed him to report to Commander Quicke at the Place Viger Hotel, so it was quite natural that Johnson should book accommodations there upon arrival. He had no way of knowing that the other officers were staying at the Ritz Carlton. His reception by the British officers, most of whom were Royal Naval College graduates, was not encouraging. The only exception was another RNVR officer, Lieutenant William Lowell Thompson, who sympathized with Barney's predicament.

Johnson had several counts against his being readily accepted, the first being that he was a Volunteer Reserve. Even had he been a member of the Royal Naval Reserve, his appointment would have been more acceptable, but his application of the previous September had never been answered. The appointment of a "colonial civilian officer" to the command of a submarine was unanimously considered an unprecedented step for the Admiralty to have taken, even if it was only to get the boat to England. Other things that set him apart were his age and sea-going experience. At 37 he was older than all of his new brother officers, with the possible exception of Alexander Quicke, and if truth be told, Johnson had seen more time at sea and in command than any of them.

His familiarity with the American submarines also told against him, at least at first, for Johnson soon became known as a proponent of the H-boats and their "Yankee gadgets," while most of the British officers had not had the time nor the experience to appreciate the finer points of the new submarines. The only immediate factors in Barney Johnson's favour were his friendship with Adrian Keyes, who was well known and respected in the Submarine Service, his natural good nature, and his long experience in handling men. While at Montreal he would be accorded an attitude of aloof acceptance by the younger British officers, and it was probably fortuitous that he was living apart from them, at least for the time being. In any case, *H8* was about to be launched and everyone was much too busy to be overly concerned with social niceties.

When the British crew for *H8* was formed, Johnson was assigned an acting mate for his first officer. As Johnson was probably the most experienced navigator in the group and his first hand the least experienced, there was perhaps a purpose behind his appointment to *H8*. Unfortunately for the mate, Mr. Alfred Brewster, he and his new captain did not hit it off very well and Brewster's lack of navigation skills caught Barney by surprise and probably left him feeling a bit browned off. As Brewster and the bulk of the crew did not arrive from England until the boat had completed its trials, Johnson had no opportunity to even recognize the problem let alone have anything done about it. In the meantime, getting the boat ready was his only goal as he began the arduous five weeks of fitting out and trials with a borrowed crew. From the very start of his new venture it appeared the Fates had given Barney Johnson a difficult role to play.

On the other hand, when Midshipman William McKinstry Maitland-Dougall arrived later that same month, he was immediately accepted as one of the family. For despite being of colonial origins, he was at least a "properly" trained naval officer and belonged to a privileged family whose name had long been featured in the Navy Lists. Although one could hardly have compared the facilities at the Naval College in Halifax with those of Osborne and Dartmouth, the training was comparable and his British compatriots would not have been aware of the differences, that would come later. Commander Quicke, in requesting his services, described him as "a good sort and very keen on going."

Maitland-Dougall's six months experience in submarines would stand him in good stead with his new messmates. Adrian Keyes' insistence on his junior officers gaining an intimate mechanical knowledge of whatever boat they were aboard provided him with a worthwhile set of objectives to apply to the H-boats. His time spent crawling around in the bowels of *CC1* and *CC2* with Jock Edwards was going to pay off.

The young midshipman had arrived in Montreal by a somewhat circuitous route. After leaving Esquimalt in January Maitland-Dougall had served for 3½ months at Headquarters in Ottawa then joined the cruiser *Niobe*, which was engaged in making patrols along the East Coast. This he had done at his own request in order to complete his lieutenant's qualifications. It was during the process of trying to alleviate the manning difficulties that Vice-Admiral Kingsmill put his name forward as a suitable candidate for navigating one of the submarines to England. At about the same time a request had been received by Quicke from a member of the staff of Commodore (S) in London, asking that Midshipman John Grant Edwards be considered. A decision was made based on the two candidates' abilities in navigation and, as he had more experience in this department, Maitland-Dougall was selected as the most suitable.

In expectation of his being accepted, Maitland-Dougall was transferred to HMCS *Canada* at Montreal on May 25. It was during this period that he first made the acquaintance of Alexander Quicke. He was aboard *Canada* for the adventurous trip to St. John's when the gunboat escorted the Mediterranean-bound H-boats. In the interim the Admiralty appointed Lieutenant Noel Dixon to *H10* as first lieutenant. On June 24 Maitland-Dougall went aboard as third hand. It was a wise decision, for Dixon did not arrive in time to make the next part of the journey.

During the five-week fitting out and trials period Barney Johnson encountered an old acquaintance from his early CC-boat days in the person of Captain Smith, the former USN submariner who was employed by Electric Boat as their senior trials captain. Johnson was able to bring him up to date on the progress of the CC-boats and Smith was very surprised to find the Canadians had made such a success of them. By way of explanation he told Johnson of the results of the Chilean trials, something Barney had not known about. The two men got along well together and the American was instrumental in helping Johnson to acquire an intimate knowledge of the new boats.

The remaining six submarines came down the ways in rapid succession and by the end of May they were all in the water fitting out. An account of the preparations for launching one has survived in the notes of ERA1 Richard Pearson, who along with Chief ERA J.T. Jones was loaned to the H-boats from Esquimalt. According to Pearson, who was assigned to *H10*, in order to ensure the watertightness of the all-riveted hull prior to launch, the boat was shut off internally and the outside of the hull was lathered in soft soap. A pressure of a few pounds per square inch was built up inside the hull and any air leaking out caused the soft soap to bubble, indicating the exact location of the leak, which was then attended to. This sufficed for launching. There would be further tests for diving, the first of which were completed in the fitting-out basin where shallow, static dives were conducted while moored fore and aft.

Deep dives, down to 200 feet, were carried out at Murray Bay in the St. Lawrence River. In this final series of tests *H10* had to make eight descents before all of the leaks were corrected. On the last dive the boat had reached 180 feet when it started to drop like a stone, reaching 240 feet before the frantically blown ballast tanks took effect and she surged to the surface. "The dive had revealed no new leaks so the boat was accepted," recalled Pearson.

The sudden plunge was explained by the presence of a deep layer of water of a lesser density than that above. The St. Lawrence, which is mostly salt water at this point, has several cold, freshwater streams emptying into it, which causes considerable density stratification. The extent of this phenomenon was not appreciated at the time, but it would play an important role in submarine operations in the same part of the river during another war 26 years later.

The last three crews were slow in coming from England, and Johnson had to begin *H8*'s acceptance trials with just his own ERAs (whom he'd had all along), the assistance of the civilian trials crew, and the loan of half of the men from *H7*. In this fashion he completed the trials program. His own crew joined at Murray Bay on June 15, and the next day they commissioned the boat and sailed for Quebec. When going alongside, *H8* struck *H7* and damaged her own starboard screw. This was replaced by the crew a few days later. As soon as he could Johnson began training his men in the way he had learned from Adrian Keyes.

Trials party taking a break at Murray Bay on the St. Lawrence.
– C.H. Varley collection

H8 and H7 with H10 and H6 astern at the Customs Pier, Quebec City. – RN Submarine Museum

In the Gut of Canso en route to Halifax. – C.H. Varley collection

It had originally been intended to sail the boats to Halifax in two groups of three. This was later changed to one convoy of four and a second of two. From Halifax they were to sail to England in one six-boat convoy. Because of delays in completing the trials of *H5*, *H6* and *H7*, all six submarines commissioned in the two-week period between July 10 and 28. Because of the constraints of time and the shortage of escorts, it was no longer practical to divide them into two convoys, and all six boats were rescheduled to sail together with HMCS *Canada* as escort. If needed, an additional steamer or sea-going tug would be hired to accompany the convoy, but this did not prove necessary. At Halifax the submarines were to conduct a final series of tests in the safety of Bedford Basin and wait for their transatlantic escort and assisting ships, the cruiser *Carnarvon*, which was still in dock at Vickers, and two colliers hired by the Admiralty.

Accordingly, the convoy of six H-boats and their escort left Quebec on the morning of Saturday, July 3, 1915. This time care had been taken to ensure that all compasses were properly adjusted prior to leaving the St. Lawrence, and an elaborate plan had been worked out in the event any boat got separated from the group. Four days later the convoy arrived safely at Halifax. The only incidents of note during the trip were the prevalence of fog in Chedabucto Bay, which caused the convoy to go to anchor off Arichat, and the lack of illumination for the compasses (someone had forgotten to install or even to supply the necessary electric bulbs).

At Halifax they were met by the Canadian authorities and *H10*'s first lieutenant, whose steamer arrived at Quebec after the convoy had sailed. He caught a train and reached Halifax a few days before the submarines.

The officers were billeted in the cadets' dormitory at the Naval College in the dockyard; it was summer leave period for the cadets, so there was more than enough room

Three of the H5-H10 group at Halifax. – RN Submarine Museum

for the submarine officers. The men were accommodated in the barracks. This was the first opportunity that Johnson and the other officers had been given to assess one another at close quarters. By this time the British officers were becoming accustomed to their new boats and their feelings toward the Canadian VR captain were becoming more positive. The evenings were spent in long, sometimes heated, discussions concerning the attributes of the H-boats, comparing them to other classes of submarine and deciding how they could be improved to meet operational needs, a matter of some concern to the British captains, some of whom had already experienced considerable wartime service.

The officers were generally satisfied with the new vessels, particularly with their submerged handling characteristics, diving capabilities and the performance of the engines. As completed the boats lacked many of the refinements they were accustomed to in British-built submarines, such as gyros, echo sounders and wireless sets. Even at that early date some improvements had already been made to their H-boats. This included the fitting of British depth gauges after the Electric Boat-supplied gauges proved too sluggish for accurate depth-keeping. Many other alterations were noted down to be carried out once they reached England. Even at this early date defect reports were beginning to arrive from the Mediterranean H-boats, and correction of some of these was made in the second group before they left Canadian waters.

While at Halifax the submarines spent much of their time conducting trials. This included testing and perfecting communications between each other while submerged by means of the underwater signalling apparatus known as Fessenden gear, after its Canadian-born American inventor. The primary feature of this equipment consisted of two large oscillators located inside number-one main ballast tank, arranged facing outboard, one each to port and starboard. In practice this equipment proved satisfyingly effective, with ranges of several miles being achieved. The underwater signalling was conducted by sending messages in Morse code and was particularly useful when working in close company with other submarines.

By the time the H-boats were ready to leave Halifax the crews had become fairly proficient at handling the new submarines. Each boat had received two of the new Mark VIII, 18-inch torpedoes with which to make the passage, and all fuel tanks had been filled to capacity with diesel oil from the tanks at Bedford Basin. By July 21 the two steamers, S.S. *Midlands* and S.S. *Prophet*, and the convoy leader, HMS *Carnarvon*, had made port and were ready to depart. The two colliers were ballasted to obtain seaworthiness and permit maximum speed for the crossing. All three ships had been provided with towing cables and the submarines themselves carried as much spare gear as they could manage — after the experiences of the first group, some breakdowns were expected. Prior to their departure Chief ERA Jones and ERA1 Pearson were landed, with some reluctance, to begin their journey back to Esquimalt. Able Seaman Galaway remained aboard *H5* for the voyage and would return to Canada during August. Johnson and Maitland-Dougall had plans of their own.

At 5 a.m. on the morning of Thursday, July 22, the submarines, the cruiser and the colliers sailed out of Halifax harbour without fanfare. A few miles out to sea they formed convoy with the boats and colliers in three columns astern of *Carnarvon*. The voyage was relatively uneventful and, although the expected breakdowns did occur, the ships' companies managed to cope. During the passage each submarine was towed for 24 hours, both to conserve fuel and to allow time for repairs and adjustments to be made to the engines. The weather remained seasonally co-operative and a good minimum speed was maintained. By August 4 all of the submarines were safely alongside HMS *Onyx*, the submarine depot ship in Devonport dockyard, after a passage of 13 days.

At the beginning of May 1915, the Canadian Naval authorities made another effort to acquire a pair of submarines for the defence of Halifax. Feeling somewhat cheated out of the submarines that Canadian Vickers had proposed building in September 1914, it was reasoned that the Admiralty might be persuaded to let the Canadian Navy have two of the ten H-boats being built at that same yard, to station at Halifax, while two replacements were built at Ottawa's expense. These two boats were to be manned by two of the three crews available from Esquimalt, leaving one complete crew on the West Coast, sufficient to exercise one boat at a time, while more men were trained to fill out the numbers for two full crews on each coast. This proposal would also have served to alleviate Vickers' problems when the British contract ended. A letter for the Admiralty was duly prepared and forwarded from the Prime Minister's office to the Colonial Office by way of the Governor General. The Admiralty's (Churchill's) response was short and revealing for its lack of foresight. As there was no perceived threat to Canada's East Coast, there was no need to protect the approaches to Halifax. The ten submarines were badly needed overseas and would sail for their bases as planned. It was also suggested that Canada might like to buy two of the boats being built at Fore River — after the war.

In June 1915, toward the end of the British H-boat building program, Canadian Vickers made one more offer to the Naval Service of Canada. They proposed building two H-class submarines for the RCN, identical to those being produced for the Admiralty, at the going price of $600,000 apiece. So that they would be finished before the freeze-up, they were to be built on a 24-hour, seven-days-a-week schedule.

The Naval Service was agreeable and passed the proposal on to the Prime Minister. Borden appears to have been startled by the cost, despite his previous experience with the CC-boats, the Canadian Vickers offer of August, and a patient, detailed and thoroughly realistic defence of the pricing of the boats by Canadian Vickers. He would not be moved. The offer was declined. It seems the Admiralty had finally convinced the Prime Minister that Halifax was not, and never would be, threatened by units of Germany's navy.

The Admiralty, however, had one more assault to make on Borden's credulity. In November 1915 a letter from Downing Street suggested that the Canadian government might want to refund the import duties levied on the materials brought into the country to build the British H-boats. As the sum involved amounted to just under $600,000, it would nearly equal the cost of one submarine and give Canada the opportunity to contribute a boat to the Admiralty. The request was passed to the Customs Department and nothing further is recorded of the matter.

H5 *picking up a tow from* Carnarvon *during the Atlantic crossing.*
    – C.H. Varley collection

The depot ship Onyx. – RN Submarine Museum

6 THE NEW FLOTILLA

Farewell and adieu to you Greenwich ladies,
Farewell and adieu to you, ladies ashore!
For we've received orders to work to the eastward
Where we hope in a short time to straffe 'em some more.

We'll duck and we'll dive like little tin turtles,
We'll duck and we'll dive underneath the North Seas,
Until we strike something that doesn't expect us,
From here to Cuxhaven it's go as you please.

The first thing we did was to dock in a minefield,
Which isn't a place where repairs should be done;
And there we lay doggo in twelve fathom water
With tri-nitro-toluol hogging our run.

The next thing we did, we rose under a Zeppelin,
With his shiny big belly half blocking the sky.
But what in the heavens can you do with six-pounders?
So we fired what we had and bade him goodbye.

Untitled poem by Rudyard Kipling from *Sea Warfare*, 1916

When the six brine-encrusted submarines had been secured alongside the ark-like HMS *Onyx* their crews trooped inboard for baths, tots and a hot meal. Having refreshed themselves the eight officers assembled in the wardroom to be officially welcomed by Commander Charles J.C. Little, personal assistant to Commodore (S), who had been sent to meet the flotilla upon its historic arrival. Once the formalities were concluded and matters concerning the care of the submarines attended to, Johnson was asked to meet privately with the Commander.

When they were alone Little came straight to the point and stated that he was surprised, even shocked, to find that Johnson was a Volunteer Reserve officer and not RNR as he had assumed. He professed he could not understand the actions of the Admiralty in making such an unprecedented appointment, as at the time only Royal Navy officers commanded submarines. He informed Barney that, so far as he was concerned, if he wished to remain in submarines he would be obliged to revert to the command of a non-operational A-class boat after delivering *H8* to Portsmouth. As the commander saw it, Johnson, assuming he was even allowed to remain in submarines, should be required to work his way up the command ladder in the approved fashion in order to qualify for an operational command.

Charles Little was a big, aggressive man, certainly not the sort to be challenged without good reason. Although Johnson was somewhat taken aback by his belligerence, he was neither surprised by his comments nor was he unprepared. At Halifax Barney had been warned by Thompson and the other British submariners of the likelihood of a hostile reception because of his Volunteer Reserve status, and he was firmly resolved to stand his ground.

In reply he informed the Commander that he was not prepared to voluntarily relinquish command of *H8* and that if ordered to do so he would request a transfer to General Service and ask for an appointment to a Fleet Reserve ship. He stated that, "After being in command of my own ships for 12 years in the Merchant Navy and serving for a year as handyman in the RCN, I have no desire or heart to commence another apprenticeship." Appointments being beyond his authority, there was nothing Little could do at the time except pass Johnson's remarks on to Commodore Hall, which he did upon his return to Whitehall the next day.

The submarines slipped from *Onyx* early the following morning and shaped a course for Portsmouth harbour and Fort Blockhouse. Within a few days of their arrival they crossed the harbour to the dockyard, where all six were taken in hand to be outfitted for operations.

On August 9 William Maitland-Dougall joined HMS *Dolphin* and was posted to a Submarine Officers' Training Course to undertake the Royal Navy's basic submarine training. This was of six weeks' duration and candidates had to achieve a minimum mark of 70 percent in all subjects in order to pass. Failure meant returning to General Service.

A handful of midshipmen made an appearance in the Submarine Service during late 1915 and early 1916, particularly in the Mediterranean Theatre. Maitland-Dougall, however, was the only "snottie" serving in submarines at that time and may well have been the first ever to do so.

To establish his eligibility for the course the young Canadian needed permission to remain overseas, the recommendation of his commanding officer, to be physically fit, and to have achieved a first-class pass in torpedo work or to have had equivalent experience. Vice-Admiral Kingsmill had given him permission to serve with the RN before leaving Canada, and Alexander Quicke recommended him without hesitation, for he already thought well of the young officer's abilities. He was certainly physically fit, and having already served seven months in submarines under a recognized expert, he encountered little difficulty in establishing his qualifications or in achieving a first-class pass. After finishing his course, and taking leave to visit some of his relatives, he rejoined *H10* in Portsmouth dockyard toward the end of September.

When he started his career in Royal Navy submarines William McKinstry Maitland-Dougall, "Billy" to family and friends, was 20½ years old. Standing one inch over six feet tall, he had a lean, straight-backed, well-proportioned body and almost girlish good looks, so much so that he was given the nickname "Mary Jane' while at college. He had sandy-brown hair, a pronounced widow's peak, and large, well-spaced blue eyes enhanced by dark bushy eyebrows, a straight nose, generous mouth, and a firm, slightly dimpled, rounded jaw. His prominent ears were made all the more noticeable by the very short service-style haircut then in vogue. The young Canadian was genuinely likable, naturally modest, possessed pleasant manners and was enthusiastic without being effusive.

Even as a midshipman William exhibited a natural command of men and a healthy respect for his seniors, with whom he associated easily. His marks throughout his career show him to have been a bright student, while his record of achievements indicate an unusual dedication to his profession, even among submariners, who were well noted for their zeal. Later in the war he confessed in a letter to his mother that he did not enjoy reading for recreation and that perhaps he spent too much time and money in the mess. As was usual for young officers of the period, he was fond of sports, having a reputation as a centre forward on the soccer team and being noted for a good reach in tennis. While in the United Kingdom he took up fly-fishing and golf. He was also an avid amateur photographer and had his own developing equipment, not an unusual possession in those days. He smoked cigarettes and drank his fair share of spirits, as did most of his contemporaries, and liked a lively evening in the mess or in town at the popular music halls and clubs. Women found him attractive and he enjoyed their company. The young Canadian officer wouldn't have been in England very long before becoming almost indistinguishable from his Royal Navy contemporaries.

Maitland-Dougall was almost as much at home in Britain as he would have been on Vancouver Island, despite never having been abroad before. He is known to have made at least one visit to Scotscraig during the autumn of 1915, where he met his uncle William, aunt Charlotte (affectionately known as "Sissy") and cousins Claire and Arnold. William, "Handsome Jim's" elder brother, then in his early sixties, had retired from the Royal Navy with the rank of commander. He was a justice of the peace and the owner of Scotscraig. The old gentleman had spent much of his early career at sea on the North America and West Indies Station and had been in action on a number of occasions during the Turko-Servian and Russo-Turkish wars. Cousin Arnold, eight years older than Billy, was a lieutenant in the Royal Navy and serving as Torpedo Officer in the battleship HMS *Hercules*. William had relatives on both sides of his family in many parts of the country and was particularly close to his paternal aunt, Mary Catherine, who was living at Scotscraig.

Young Billy with his Aunt Mary at Scotscraig winter, 1916.
– Maitland-Dougall family collection

H8's officers (left to right): John Mansfield, Cap' Johnson, "Whiskers" Thompson. – C.H. Varley collection

Cap' Johnson, RNR.
– C.H. Varley collection

H10's officers (left to right): Maitland-Dougall, Byron Carey, Noel Dixon. – C.H. Varley collection

While in the south of England the handsome young Canadian was a welcome visitor at "Fryern," the King family residence at Storrington, near Worthing in Sussex, less than an hour's journey by rail from Portsmouth. This was the home of his aunt Charlotte's family. Well known for the beauty and artistic abilities of their women, the Kings were related to the Maitland-Dougalls by more than one marriage. In the diaries of old Mrs. King, the family matriarch and herself a Maitland-Herriot, his visits are fondly recalled and he was recorded as "Billie from Canada."

In Johnson's case Commodore Hall's ruling was swift in coming and precedent-setting in its implications. Commander Little, much to his own chagrin, was personally charged with conveying to Lieutenant Johnson, RNVR, the Commodore's wishes. He was to be allowed to retain command of *H8* without having to undergo any further formal training or examination provided he transfer to either the RN itself or to the RNR. As Barney remembered it, Little would have preferred he enter the Royal Navy proper. In this way the precedent would have been invisible. As an RN lieutenant Johnson would have been indistinguishable from any other submarine CO. Barney, however, felt that after all his years in the Merchant Navy he had no right to wear the straight stripes and elected to enter the Royal Naval Reserve and ship the intertwined stripes of a lieutenant, RNR. As Johnson recalled many years later, "He [Little] cursed me for my obstinacy but I think he approved." That night Barney Johnson was well and truly féted by his fellow H-boat officers.

With this decision his seniority was post-dated to the date of his original Admiralty appointment and the fact that he was the first RNVR to captain a British submarine became obscured in the official records. No other Volunteer Reserve officer would command an RN boat until 1943, when another Canadian would uphold the precedent. Johnson, however, undeniably holds the distinction of having been the sole RNVR and the first of only five RNRs to command British submarines during the Great War.

Barney, however, was not the first RNVR to enter the RN Submarine Service, that distinction belongs to Lieutenant William Lowell Thompson, who the Canadians had already met in Montreal. There is some evidence to indicate that Thompson may have been a Canadian, but this has not been substantiated. He was brought into the Service in April 1915, apparently by Commodore Hall himself, who sent him directly to Montreal to stand-by the H-boats. Thompson did not have sufficient sea-going experience to become a first lieutenant but made the transatlantic crossing nevertheless as third officer in Lieutenant Cromwell H. Varley's *H5*. Upon returning to Great Britain he remained connected with the H-boats for the rest of the war.

That he had been retained to command an operational submarine at all, and without being required to undergo additional training, speaks volumes for the Commodore's assessment of Barney Johnson's abilities as a captain and as a submariner. Barney was being inducted into one of the most exclusive bodies of professionals in the Royal Navy entirely on his own merits, an extraordinary accomplishment indeed, particularly in those days of strict social and Service delineations. Already a well-respected mercantile seaman when he entered the Service, Johnson quite openly credited Adrian Keyes with his acquired ability as a submariner. Whether or not Adrian Keyes had any influence in Hall's decision to retain Johnson is not known, but the possibility certainly exists.

There can be little doubt that Barney did all he could to foster his cause while his status was under review in Whitehall. When *H8* was inspected by the authorities from HMS *Dolphin*, they were impressed both by the boat's spotless condition and the proficiency of her scratch crew.

Once Commodore Hall's decision was made public, Johnson was whole-heartedly accepted into that very elite family of seafarers known somewhat derisively throughout the Service as "The Trade." He was extended every courtesy and assistance and it was to his credit that he never attempted to disguise his shortcomings, particularly in the area of naval operations.

Despite his own preference for being called "Barney," the British submariners dubbed him "Cap'" Johnson, the sobriquet by which he is still remembered in Dolphin. A man with his kind of experience was something of a novelty in the Submarine Service. There was no denying that he was a four-ringed Master Mariner in his own right, and despite having been reduced to the rank of a naval reserve lieutenant, he would always be a fully fledged captain in their eyes, so "Cap'" it was to be.

One of the first improvements to be made to Cap' Johnson's lot was to provide *H8* with a replacement first lieutenant to take over from Mr. Brewster. A promising young officer, Sub-Lieutenant John M. Mansfield, was sent down from Sheerness, where he had been first lieutenant aboard the *C2*. He joined *H8* on August 18. According to Johnson, his new first lieutenant "set a pattern of behaviour and efficiency that was reflected throughout the ship from the youngest Stoker to the Captain!" Alfred Brewster was posted to the 4th Flotilla at Ardrossan, where he took over as first lieutenant aboard the *C35*. Despite his awkward time with Johnson, Brewster would go on to command his own submarine before war's end.

There is no written record of who *H8*'s third officer was during this period, but photographic evidence shows that RNVR Lieutenant William L. Thompson filled the position for at least some of the time. Cap' Johnson's command was shaping into a happy, efficient, well-run operational submarine.

At Portsmouth dockyard the H-boats were provided with the latest electronic marvels of the day, beginning a seemingly never-ending process of improvement. The most important items to be fitted were the Sperry gyro-compass and a wireless transmitting and receiving set. The gyro equipment was mounted in the starboard forward corner of the after battery compartment, where there was plenty of space for the bulky gyroscope and its associated electrical cabinets and components. At the time only two gyro-compass repeaters were provided, one each in the conning tower and at the lower steering position, but additional repeaters would be installed on the bridge and in the wardroom at a later date.

To accommodate the wireless set a small, soundproofed office, measuring four feet square and extending to the deckhead, was erected over the battery boards in the forward compartment close to the control room bulkhead next to the head. This was designed to be portable and could be disassembled in order to gain access to the battery tank underneath. To carry the aerial aloft a light telescopic pole was fitted to the back of the fin and the aerial wire was strung from the bows to the top of the pole then aft to the salvage U-shackle at the end of the casing. The aerial was raised and lowered by means of a hand-crank mounted on top of the housing. The signalling mast was removed from the front of the fin, which was then modified to accept the watertight, insulated pigtail conductor that connected the aerial to the wireless set in the compartment below.

To deflect submarine nets, explosives-laden sweep wires and mine-mooring cables away from upper deck obstructions, a jumping wire was rigged from the bows to the top of the periscope fairwater and down to the salvage shackle at the end of the casing, which it shared with the aerial wire. At the fairwater the jumping wire divided into two parts and was led around the tops of the periscopes on a light steel frame so as to allow the periscopes to raise and lower without fouling the wire.

In order to improve navigation a Forbes log was fitted in the hull under the control room, while its speed and distance-run indicator was mounted by the helmsman's position. An echo sounder was also provided. While the installation of the new equipment was in progress a considerable amount of finishing work was carried out, particularly on hatch seatings and valves, many of which, despite the best efforts of the Admiralty Overseers at Montreal, exhibited symptoms of their hurried and not always careful assembly. These modifications were common to all six United Kingdom-based H-boats.

The most serious defect to be encountered with the new submarines had already made itself apparent when the original batteries began to show signs of deterioration during the first months of operational use, and it was decided to replace them with an improved type manufactured by the Exide Company. *H10* was one of the first to receive a new outfit, and her batteries were removed and replaced by the crew during the last week in August.

On the night of September 27-28 the new battery was put on charge at a rate of 600 amperes. Part way through, serious overheating of the cells developed and the charge was stopped. So intense was the heat that both battery tanks had to be half filled with water in order to cool the cells. Three days later the entire outfit was landed for examination and correction of the problem. A fortnight later the errant *box*, as the battery was called, was back aboard, secured and taking a charge at 600 amperes without any problems. *H5* is also known to have received a new battery at this time and the rest of the class was outfitted either as the problem became acute or as the operations schedule permitted.

While the new submarines were being equipped efforts were under way to assimilate them into the operational scheme of things. To the delight of the ships' companies the H-boats were rated as "suitable for overseas patrols" — a classification that Pirie in *H1* was in the act of establishing in the Sea of Marmora, where he remained continuously in action for 28 days despite a contaminated fresh water supply. To the men this meant that their boats, which they had dubbed "Ford submersibles" because of their North American origins, mass construction and reliable engines, would be assigned to operations off the German coast in common with the much larger and very successful E-class submarines. By this time the British submariners had become fully acquainted with the new craft and held their "Ford submersibles" to be the equal of any submarine afloat, except in very rough seas, when their small size would tell to their disadvantage.

Commander Quicke left *H10* shortly after arriving at Fort Blockhouse. His place was taken by Lieutenant the Hon. Byron Cary and *H10* retained her position as senior H-boat. Quicke, meantime, was appointed to the command of HMS *Alecto*. His new command would be stationed at Great Yarmouth on the Norfolk coast. There she would act as parent ship for a small group of submarines, including the six H class.

Alecto, like her sister ship HMS *Adamant*, was a small submarine depot ship of only 935 tons. With her elegantly raked masts and funnel and graceful clipper bow complete with bowsprit, she resembled a yacht more than a naval support ship. Perhaps in keeping with her appearance her facilities are reputed to have been totally inadequate for her purpose.

At Great Yarmouth, or simply Yarmouth but not to be confused with the town of that name on the Isle of Wight, *Alecto* was berthed a few miles upstream from the mouth of the narrow River Yare, on a stretch of waterfront known as Bryants Wharf. Within a short time of her arrival a line of wooden sheds was erected between the quay wall and the edge of Southgates Road, in which were accommodated a baggage store, workshops and the piles of spare gear and other equipment that soon exceeded the limited capacity of the

HMS Alecto, *Alexander Quicke's new command.* – RN Submarine Museum

Alecto's *depot and the subs, Bryant's Wharf, Yarmouth.* – C.H. Varley collection

ship's own storerooms. The little flotilla base was close to the centre of town, the railway station and the main roads. This location also placed her within a few minutes' walk of the sandy pleasure beaches and their amenities, as well as within easy range of a variety of public houses so necessary to the well-being of the submariners.

Once assembled *Alecto*'s brood would form a part of the 8th Flotilla with headquarters aboard HMS *Maidstone* at Harwich. To the 8th fell the task of maintaining the watch on the principal German anchorages in the Wesser and Ems estuaries and of conducting reconnaissance patrols along the routes commonly used by the ships of the enemy fleet. The area assigned to the Harwich and Yarmouth boats extended from Hiorns Reef, off the Danish coast at Jutland, to Terschelling Island, off the coast of neutral Holland. This area encompassed the notorious Heligoland Bight and included the whole length of the Frisian Island chain. This was a huge area, and a dangerous one. Continuously mined by both sides, it fell within range of all kinds of hostile naval support and was increasingly patrolled by Zeppelins and aircraft. From a network of patrol billets the British submarines acted as advance scouts for the Grand Fleet and as the eyes of the Whitehall planners.

These operations made heavy demands on the submariners, particularly on the eager young captains. Unlike the early months of the war, when submarines had been few and captains had been given large areas in which to conduct what amounted to independent hunting cruises, the submarines of late 1915 were becoming game pieces on a vast strategic mozaic. Under these conditions they were required to remain within the confines of relatively small billets, frequently with orders to watch and report, leaving them little independence and few opportunities to seek out and engage the enemy. The Admiralty wanted the High Seas Fleet at sea, intact, confident and unmolested, so as to give the Grand Fleet the opportunity of destroying it in one great Trafalgar-style naval action. Targets for the boats on station were few and far between, while the dangers that had to be endured almost daily were many and varied. Success, it seemed to some, was going to be measured by the number of enemy sighting reports transmitted to Headquarters rather than the number of attacks delivered against German ships.

Although the submariners would never be told of it, the allocation and positioning of their submarines was to some extent determined by the Admiralty's ability to predict German warship movements based on intercepted German wireless signals. In the closing months of 1914 the Naval Intelligence Division acquired copies of the German naval wireless codes and set up a secret section, the now famous "Room 40," to exploit them. Within a short time the cryptographers had cracked the German naval cyphers and, by means of a series of wireless direction-finding stations set up along the southeast coast, were able to intercept German wireless signals and even pinpoint the location of individual ships. The interception and interpretation of enemy wireless traffic soon began to play a prominent part in the war against Kaiser Bill's *Kriegs*marine.

Once the modifications to the H-boats were completed, captains and crews were encouraged to test the new gear and practise their drills by carrying out dives, exercise firings, emergency procedures and manoeuvres in the safely enclosed waters of the Solent. The opportunity was also taken to give the officers and men some leave and to send them on courses to improve their technical qualifications. During this period personnel undergoing basic submarine training at *Dolphin* were given short trips aboard the H-boats as a part of their course; something of a departure from going out in the old B- and C-class submarines that usually provided these services.

By the beginning of September the easy times were coming to an end. On the 4th *H5*, *H6* and *H7* left their berth in Haslar Creek and set a course for Yarmouth via Dover and

Harwich. Three days later found the three boats secured alongside: Varley's *H5* at Harwich, from where she would operate until the following summer, and the other two on *Alecto* at Yarmouth. The remaining three H-boats all joined *Alecto* before the month was out.

At their new bases the crews soon found themselves hard at work striving to attain the high standard of operational efficiency demanded of the submarines of the 8th Flotilla. It would be another month before any of them were ready to undertake real "Ops."

In between frequent visits to the exercise grounds, the inevitable customizing of the boats continued as each commanding officer vied with his flotilla mates to make his submarine the most up-to-date and efficient of them all. The unauthorized installation of individual modifications would not be tolerated in today's navies, but it was accepted practice then. Internally each boat began to take on a distinct individuality, while externally they all remained much alike. The hull areas were painted black and the fin and casing a medium shade of grey. Some originality was achieved when the latest scheme of camouflage was applied and the fin and casing were enlivened with large patches, or "splodges," as one CO described them, of olive green, light blue and dark brown, in an effort to break up the boat's silhouette and make identification and range-finding difficult for the enemy. The periscope fairwater was given a coat of very light grey to make it less conspicuous should it inadvertently break surface while on patrol. The top few feet of the main periscope were painted with black and white tiger stripes or leopard's spots, so that it blended with the sea's surface. Each boat's number, prefixed with the letter H, was prominently displayed on either side of the fin in large black block capitals.

By early November *Alecto*'s "Yankee boats" were ready for action, warpaint and all.

The first of the "Ford submersibles" to make a war patrol was *H5* under Lieutenant Cromwell H. Varley. Following reports of German destroyers and possibly even a cruiser leaving the Baltic for operations in the Kattegat, it was decided to send three submarines into the area to intercept the enemy warships and keep watch on the Sound, that narrow waterway between Sweden and Denmark that joins the Kattegat and the Baltic Sea. Leaving Harwich on November 15 Varley headed for his billet in the southern half of the Kattegat. The other two boats, *D3* and *D4*, were assigned patrol areas closer to home and left the following day.

While patrolling in the Sound, Varley encountered sea-water conditions of such high density that it became very difficult to keep the boat submerged even with every trim, compensating and ballast tank full. As a last resort he flooded the entire compartment under the control room and only through this extraordinary expedient did he manage to stay under. Once back in the Kattegat the compartment was pumped out and dried with rags. This patrol lasted 18 days and *H5* returned to Harwich on December 3 without having seen anything significant.

On Friday, December 17, 1915, a little over ten months after her keel had been laid, *H10*, with her Canadian third officer, who only a fortnight before had been promoted to acting sub-lieutenant, set off on her first overseas war patrol. *H10*'s billet was typical of those assigned to submarines on reconnaissance patrols, being about ten nautical miles square, covering the channel between the islands of Terschelling and Ameland, known as the Akkepolle Gat, in a stretch of water that was to become very familiar to the Yarmouth H-boats. Here she was to keep watch for any German attempts at sweeping the British minefields.

These two islands form part of the Frisian Island chain which lies about 10 to 20 miles off the European coastline and extends for 150 miles from the estuary of the River Wesser to Den Helder on mainland Holland. In the days before the invention of radar, warships making raids in the North Sea could steam close to the seaward side of these

Alongside Maidstone *at Harwich, September 1915. The subs are, left to right:* E4 *(Cdr. E.W. Leir);* H5 *(Lt. C.H. Varley);* H6 *(Lt. R. Stopford);* H7 *(Lt. E.G. Ebblewhite);* F1 *(Lt-Cdr. D.I. McGillewie);* D7 *(Lt. Charles de Burgh).* – RN Submarine Museum

H5 *embarking torpedoes at Yarmouth.* – C.H. Varley collection

islands, remaining almost invisible against the camouflage backdrop to ships patrolling offshore. In most places the water between the islands and the mainland was too shallow for major warships, but there were channels which could be used by smaller vessels, and for these the Frisians provided a protected waterway all along the coast, from which they could debouch into the North Sea almost undetected. The Akkepolle Gat was one of the primary accesses to this protected coastal waterway and the approaches to the channel had been mined by both sides, making patrols in the area ever hazardous for surface ships and submarines alike.

H10's first patrol lasted six days. She sighted and correctly identified a British force but otherwise nothing of interest was observed. *H10* returned to Yarmouth on December 23, just in time for the festive season.

Christmas came and went amidst the preparations for a busy new year. The year 1916 was to bring with it the introduction of a novel type of operation, or "stunt," for the submariners serving with the Harwich forces. This was the carrier-launched air attack.

The aeroplane, in the form of the float-fitted seaplane, had been appreciated by the Admiralty as a means of taking the war deep into enemy territory from the sea since 1913, when aircraft launching and recovery trials had first been carried out from an old cruiser. During 1914 a handful of seaplane carriers converted from freighters and passenger ships had been used with qualified success, most notably in a raid on the Zeppelin base at Cuxhaven, as well as for gunnery spotting and reconnaissance over the Dardenelles and the English Channel. Experimentation had proceeded space and by late 1915 two seaplane carriers with flying-off decks over their forecastles had entered service. One of these, HMS *Vindex*, was assigned to Harwich for operations in the Bight.

The plan for the first operation of 1916, code-named "ARH," was fairly straightforward. *Vindex*'s seven seaplanes were to attack the Hage Zeppelin sheds near Norddeich on the Norderney coast. The British aircraft were only light, two-seater, single-engine biplanes, each with a very limited bomb load, but given an opportunity, they were capable of inflicting considerable damage. The strategic objective of the exercise was to provoke the Germans into pursuing the British with their own fighter aircraft and supporting them with warships from the fleet anchorages. These, it was anticipated, would attempt to intercept *Vindex* and her light escort. On leaving their bases, however, the German ships would be running an unseen gauntlet of six British submarines positioned in an arc across the mouth of the Ems. The ultimate success would have been the escalation of the raid into a series of counter-strokes, leading to a major confrontation between battle fleets. According to Johnson's recollections, this was known as "Operation Dog-Fight" and the air raid was but its prelude.

The four submarines — *H8*, *H10*, *D3* and *E23* — were allocated billets covering the channels between the East Frisian Islands shielding the mouth of the Ems, while *H6* and *H7* were positioned to seaward of the Eastern and Western Ems access channels respectively. As well as patrolling, passing along intelligence and awaiting opportunities to torpedo German ships, the submarines had an interesting secondary role to play in acting as air-sea rescue ships.

The boats had all been instructed to surface at a predetermined time coincident with the return of the aircraft from the raid. In the event that a plane had to crash-land because of injury to the pilot, damage to the aircraft or shortage of fuel, the pilot could make for one of the boats. Should an aircraft land in their vicinity, the submariners were instructed to rescue the aircrew, remove the plane's gyro and any other confidential material, and then destroy the aircraft. It was dangerous to remain on the surface for any length of time in daylight so close to the German bases, and the submarine captains were relieved when the waiting period was over and they could get dived once again.

The date for the raid was set for January 18. Two additional days were allowed on station should the weather be unsuitable for flying operations. Although the seaplanes could be launched from the carrier's foredeck in choppy weather, flat, or nearly flat, calm conditions were necessary for them to land on the sea, from where they would be recovered by the ship's cranes.

Some of the submarines sailed on the 16th, the remainder left on the morning of the 17th accompanied by Captain Waistell in HMS *Firedrake* with four Harwich destroyers. Commodore Tyrwhitt and the rest of the covering force sailed that afternoon. In 1916 scientific weather prediction was in its infancy, and the force, which sailed in a lull between an almost continuous succession of gales, left port more in the hope of finding good conditions than with any certain knowledge of what to expect. On approaching the enemy coast on the morning of the 18th the British ships found themselves in a fog and with the wind rising from the southwest. By noon the operation had been called off and *Vindex* was ordered back to Harwich. The submarines, however, were not recalled and for the most part remained on station until the expiration of the three-day period.

Cap' Johnson's H8 *leaving Yarmouth on her first patrol.* – C.H. Varley collection

In accordance with normal patrol practices the boats remained submerged as much as possible during daylight. Under the circumstances, however, running dived soon became almost as rough as remaining on the surface. The strong rise and fall of the swell subjected the small boats to a constant, and almost uncontrollable, up-and-down pumping action. This could be overcome in three ways, either separately or in combination, all of which were either dangerous or wasteful of a submarine's resources. That most commonly employed was the use of radical hydroplane angles, but unless done with great skill there was always the possibility of losing control altogether, either sending the boat crashing to the bottom or through the surface. Applying bursts of speed to overcome the grip of the swells was another method, but this caused rapid depletion of the battery. As a last resort, ballast and compensating tanks could be successively blown and flooded, but this entailed the expenditure of large quantities of high-pressure air which could only be replenished on the surface. Any way they looked at it, the submariners were in for a hard time.

Ordinarily the submarines would have withdrawn to seaward and surfaced, but as this was a combined exercise there was no choice but to stay put and suffer it out. During daylight they remained dived, surfacing only when required to do so by the pre-arranged, and unknown to the captains, futile air-sea rescue schedule and at night to charge their batteries. They were happy to remain submerged, both to escape the worst effects of the weather and the attentions of the German patrols.

In keeping dived while remaining on station, the H-boats had the advantage over their home-built counterparts in that they were provided with a submerged one-ton mushroom anchor in a housing under the bows. The anchor could be operated from within the boat. This "weight," as it was called, allowed them to come to anchor while remaining submerged. To do this the captain would select his spot, drop the weight, then haul in on the mooring wire, all the while adjusting his trim to maintain a near neutral buoyancy until the submarine was at a comfortable depth, clear of the bottom yet well below surface turbulence. The weight was one of the more useful "Yankee gadgets" to be found in the "Ford submersibles."

The weather, however, was taking its toll. Lieutenant Robert N. Stopford's *H6*, while heading for her assigned area off the Eastern Ems, had strayed far from her course. Around 4 a.m. on the 18th she went aground on the sands to seaward of the island of Schiermonikoog, in the Friesche Zeegat, about 15 miles to the southwest of where she should have been. *H6* grounded 2½ miles inside neutral Dutch territory and opposite, but inshore of, *H8*'s position. Try what he would, there was no help for the unfortunate Stopford; the currents had put his boat hard and fast onto the sands and the receding tide soon left her high and dry, well clear of the battering seas. Down below, a worried telegrapher tapped out a coded distress message to the British task force, which was received by Commodore Tyrwhitt's flagship, HMS *Arethusa*. Captain Waistell was ordered to set off with his ships, find the errant submarine and render what assistance he could.

Stopford's dilemma was made all the more acute by the knowledge that another Harwich submarine had suffered a similar mishap only 12 days before. On that occasion the *E17* had gone aground in bad weather during darkness in the same general area and was severely battered by the seas. At daylight she broke free on the rising tide only to find herself in the midst of a group of warships. To avoid discovery she dived, but was in such a leaky state that her captain was forced to surface and abandon ship. The crew was rescued by the warships, which turned out to be Dutch, not German as they had supposed, and the British submariners were interned in Holland.

The stranded *H6* was first spotted near dawn by a pair of patrolling Dutch cruisers, who immediately called for assistance, shortly after which a lifeboat and a tug arrived. While the cruisers and lifeboat stood by, the tug attempted to get a line aboard but was prevented from doing so by her own deep draught.

Firedrake reached the scene early in the forenoon. At great risk to the tiny vessel she slipped her steam launch and sent it shoreward to pick up the higher-trained crewmen and confidential documents from the stranded submarine. Because of the dangerous conditions the boat was only able to make one trip, on which she retrieved the first lieutenant, ten men, including the boy signalman, and the ship's papers. Stopford, his navigator and remaining nine men were taken off by the Dutch after the next high tide, when it became obvious there was no hope of freeing the submarine. They went ashore to join the crew of *E17* in the internment camp, where they remained for the duration of the war. A month later the Dutch pulled *H6* off the sands and, after negotiating her purchase from the British, commissioned her into their own Navy as the *O-8*.

Not too distant from the scene of *H6*'s disaster, Cap' Johnson's command was having difficulties of her own. Strained by the conditions arising from the foul weather, the battery had begun to break down. By the end of the second day on station, so many damaged cells had been disconnected that Johnson calculated he could not have remained dived for much more than an hour and from that time onward remained on the surface, hoarding a rapidly deteriorating battery against the appearance of the enemy.

Inside the submarine the upheaval caused by having to attend to the defective battery at the height of the gale must have made life very uncomfortable for the crew. Every time a cell needed to be disconnected, the appropriate battery tank had to be opened up, which entailed clearing away the area of deck above the cell and taking up the 17-foot-long planks of the deck to get at it. Even if Johnson dived to carry out the work, this would only have dampened the effect of the seas somewhat, for there was no escaping the swell in those waters. It was especially hazardous work for the electrical ratings, for whom one careless slip meant painful, if not fatal, electric shock and the possibility of sulphuric acid burns from electrolyte spilling out of the wildly heaving cells.

Thanks to the ingenuity of the personnel aboard *H8*, they were at least able to maintain an efficient watch while on the surface yet remain snug and dry down below despite the gale. By opening the conning tower ventilator, the H-boats could continue to run their engines with the upper conning tower hatch shut to prevent the high seas from pouring down the tower. The biggest problem with running in this condition was the need to leave the officer of the watch and a lookout isolated on a very wet bridge where they were in danger of being carried away. Bringing them below and using the conning tower ports and the periscopes was not good enough in wartime, so another solution had to be found.

Before leaving Portsmouth, Johnson's crew had managed to wangle a steel tractor seat from somewhere, which they bolted to the back of the periscope fairwater about five feet above the bridge deck. Seated on this perch and hanging onto the jumping wire for support, the officer on watch could command a superb view and still communicate with the conning tower by shouting down the ventilator, the open top of which was only inches away from his face. The upper lid still had to be opened to change the watch, but this was of little consequence compared with running opened up. According to Johnson, while seated in the tractor seat, "It was a sight for the Gods to watch a sea roll over the conning tower and to see the little ship emerge like a porpoise and almost smile." Even during good weather the tractor seat made a fine vantage point from which the lookouts could keep their watches.

During the forenoon of the third day Cap' Johnson set a course for Yarmouth but encountered such heavy seas that he decided to wait out the storm in the vicinity of his original station where the waves were not so high. He sent off a wireless message advising Flotilla of his intentions but received no acknowledgement. A full day later *H8* began the 12-hour journey back to Yarmouth, where she arrived on the evening of the 21st only to find she'd been posted as missing.

Glad as everyone was to see *H8* safely alongside, the abandonment of the operation, the stranding of *H6* and the internment of half her crew made for a discouraging beginning to the new year. *H10*, with Maitland-Dougall aboard, had experienced a rough but otherwise uneventful patrol and arrived alongside *Alecto* on schedule.

H8 and *H10* were both taken in hand for repairs and improvements. *H8*'s battery had to be replaced before she would be fit to go on patrol again. Johnson was told to take his boat to Portsmouth where a new box would be installed.

H10 went to Reavells at Ipswich where a long list of repairs and modifications was undertaken. Although the submarine was brand-new, she was the senior boat and as such seems to have pioneered a semi-official class improvement program. When she finally emerged from Reavells in mid-March, *H10* would represent the ultimate in H-class efficiency and comfort. She would have power-assisted foreplanes, built-in berths and a wash hand stand for the officers, pipe-frame and canvas bunks for the crewmen, separate messes for the petty officers, seamen and stokers, as well as a long list of other improvements, including a seat on the back of the periscope fairwater just like *H8*'s.

In faraway Esquimalt the CC-boats were operating on a peacetime routine but managing to maintain a good standard of efficiency. The boats were now manned almost entirely by regular service men although a handful of the original POs and RNCVR volunteers remained. Bertram Jones had been promoted to lieutenant-commander the previous autumn and Jock Edwards had been advanced to acting sub-lieutenant in January 1916. Lieutenant Francis B. Hanson, RN, was proving to be a capable CO, while two RNCVR officers, Lieutenants Arthur Pitts and Godfrey Lake, were settling into their positions as first lieutenants.

Although Ottawa would not release either Jones or Hanson for service overseas and the RN would not accept the RNCVRs, the midshipmen were allowed to go and by the middle of 1916 two more Canadians had joined the RN Submarine Service. Fredrick Lawson, who had originally relieved Maitland-Dougall in *CC1* and nine months later went aboard the patrol vessel HMCS *Hochelaga* for watchkeeping experience, set off on a six-week journey aboard the cruiser *Leviathan* at the end of January. He would join his Submarine OTC at *Dolphin* in the middle of March.

When he left *CC1* for *Hochelaga*, Lawson exchanged positions with another member of the first class of RNCC cadets, Midshipman Robert Cameron Watson. Watson joined the Esquimalt boats in mid-September 1915. He too was eager for an overseas appointment and after nine months' experience would be sent to England aboard HMS *Casandra* to begin his training at *Dolphin* commencing in June 1916.

7 FOR A FEW BOB A DAY

The British sailor of 1915, though not particularly well paid for his services to the Crown, was liberally rewarded for being in submarines. In 1915 a Continuous Service able seaman with six years seniority received one shilling ("bob" in popular parlance) and 11 pence per day (about 48 cents total) in basic wages, while his submarine allowance of two bob (50 cents) a day more than doubled his basic income. Senior ratings, whose basic take-home pay varied between three shillings a day for a newly made petty officer and seven shillings and six pence for a senior chief ERA, received two shillings and six pence in submarine allowance, proportionately less than the junior men when considered as a percentage of income but substantial nonetheless.

Officers were well rewarded too. A lieutenant whose basic daily rate was around 12 shillings *per diem* ($3) received an additional six shillings a day in submarine allowance — a fairly respectable sum when considered as a percentage of earnings. For all ranks the improvement in income to be gained from serving in submarines was an obvious inducement.

To these figures could be added a truly impressive range of special payments and allowances. These included additional pay for a man's standing in his non-substantive rating, or "trade," and allowances for additional duties, such as an extra tuppence a day paid to a sailor for doing the job of "lamptrimmer," seven pence per day for a chief or PO performing coxswain's duties, and a captain's command pay of about four shillings a day.

Prior to and throughout World War I the British submariner was a volunteer. In 1915 the submarine was considered to be on the leading edge of military technology, much the same as nuclear-powered submarines are today. As a consequence they attracted men seeking something technically challenging, different, or simply more adventurous, as well as those who were prepared to put up with the danger and discomfort strictly for monetary gain. There was no lack of volunteers until the overall manning shortages began to make themselves felt toward the end of the war, when manpower resources generally were severely depressed.

Provided he was physically fit, had good assessments and a clean record, the volunteer's name was passed to the Submarine Depot at Fort Blockhouse where it was entered on the waiting list. In due course the candidate would be drafted to Fort Blockhouse for training. In peacetime this could happen more or less quickly, depending upon how valuable the man was to the ship in which he was serving or how long it took to get a relief for him. In wartime such requests were supposed to be handled with dispatch.

The historical records are unclear as to the actual length of the course, but it is thought to have been between six and eight weeks long in peacetime and shortened to four weeks during the war, although as little as six days formal instruction has been noted in the case of one man. During their training the men were observed for signs of personality disorders, whilst the standards demanded in the curriculum soon determined the extent of their technical knowledge and abilities. Anyone who proved unsuitable for whatever reason was returned to General Service without further ado. Those who passed were sent to the various flotilla depots, from where they were drafted to their first boats to begin a probationary period of practical training. Once over this hurdle the man normally remained in submarines for five years, unless he elected to return to General Service (as many did to advance in their non-substantive field), was invalided out, discharged, retired or, on rare occasions, was sent back as a punishment. The five-year term appears to have been renewable, depending on a man's non-substantive rating and was waived altogether in wartime.

Officers followed a similar route to the men and their course content was almost the same except they went into it in more detail and were expected to pass with higher marks. Upon attaining his lieutenancy an officer was returned to General Service for a period of service in surface ships, after which he was free to return to submarines should he wish to do so.

When war was declared, the Submarine Service had a sufficiency of personnel already serving in the flotillas. A reserve of trained submariners was available in the fleet, which included those who had returned to General Service as well as ex-submariners who were serving under the provisions of the Non-Continuous system. Under this scheme a man served for five years in the Regular force, followed by seven years in the Royal Fleet Reserve, instead of the more usual 12 years Continuous Service. A building program was under way that would see new submarines commissioned at a predictable rate and recruitment levels had undoubtedly been adjusted to accommodate this planned expansion.

The completely unexpected H-class building program, however, stretched manning resources severely. The sheer size of the contract and speed of construction was unheard of in that day and age. The entire program only lasted six months. All of the boats were commissioned within a two-month period and the sudden demand for 20 trained officers and 150 qualified men must have sent shock waves rippling through Fort Blockhouse. It is a tribute to the resourcefulness of the personnel of the submarine-manning organization that the Montreal-built boats were successfully crewed on time.

An examination of the H-boat ships' company photographs taken at Montreal and Quebec reveals cap tallies from almost all of the submarine depots as well as a sprinkling from the Royal Fleet Reserve and some very youthful boy signalmen. A few of the RFRs sported mustaches, a facial adornment they were allowed to keep under the terms of their call-up for duty but otherwise forbidden in the Navy except in the Royal Marines. Regular men were either clean shaven or ceased shaving altogether. Some styling of beards was permitted and that affected by King George V was often copied.

By modern standards there would appear to be a shortage of chief petty officers, and in most cases the only personnel dressed in the double-breasted, brass-buttoned jacket and trousers of the Class I uniform are the two engine room artificers assigned to each submarine. This situation was not unusual in the Submarine Service of the times, where younger personnel predominated and promotion was slow. The apparent shortage of senior ratings was offset to some degree by the fact that many of the petty officers were very senior.

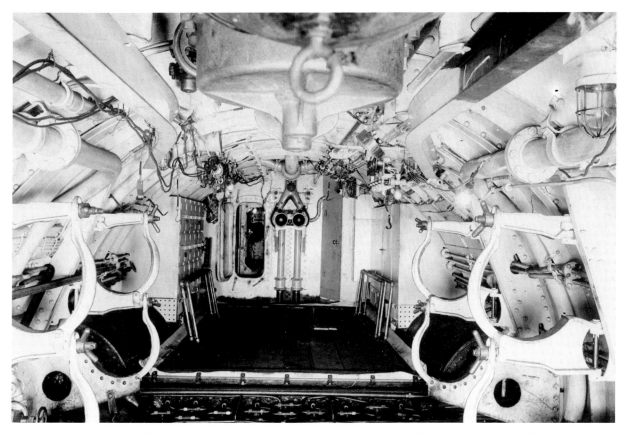

Above: Typical H-boat forward compartment. Most of the crew lived here between the reload torpedoes. – author's collection *Below: Forward compartment, looking aft, with wardroom area to the right, C and PO's mess to the left, torpedoes and sailors forward.* – PAC C-32280

H-boat control room. – Fred Wall collection

Most of the 20 H-boat officers came from the coastal flotillas, where seven of the ten captains were "getting their feet wet" in their first commands, old A-class boats. Both of the senior captains, Alexander Quicke and Wilfrid Pirie, had left the Navy before the war and were re-engaged for the duration of hostilities under the provisions of the Emergency List regulations. The tenth captain was Barney Johnson.

A captain held a god-like position aboard his boat. He was the authority in all things, be they operational, technical or administrative. Whether good, bad or indifferent, his word was inviolate and his position incontestable. As might be expected, the temperaments of the captains varied considerably, and although most were steady, middle-ground career officers, some bordered on the despotic, while others were criticized for being overly democratic. The whole tone of a submarine was often set by the personality of her commanding officer.

During peacetime it would have taken five to six years' experience in submarines for an officer to attain his first command. During the war this process was accelerated considerably, but even so, by the time he was given an operational boat the new captain was more often than not a confident, technically competent officer at the most important point in his career, that of his first real command.

The first lieutenant was known variously as the "first hand," "No. 1," "Jimmy," or even "Jimmy the One." In addition to being the ship's executive officer he also performed the duties of electrical, torpedo, and training officer. As such he was responsible for the carrying out of all drills and for ensuring that the men handled the submarine according to the requirements of the captain. On paper he was also the engineer, but during the war these duties were delegated entirely to the chief ERAs, while many of the larger boats carried warrant officer engineers.

Successful "Number Ones" quickly established a good rapport with their senior rates, delegated responsibility to them and relied on their expertise. The first lieutenant acted as divisional officer for the entire crew and, through the captain, recommended men for promotions, courses and awards, controlled leave and dealt with all but the most serious misdemeanours. Because of the control he exercised over their lives, the sailors always accorded him a subtle extra measure of deference, which in most cases was well deserved. A good first lieutenant usually meant an efficient and happy lower deck, a strong augury for success.

Normally the navigator, or "Third Hand" (a holdover from the old days when there was a first captain, second captain and third officer), was a junior regular officer and sometimes a warrant officer or a passed mate, an officer commissioned from the ranks through the Mates system. During the war, however, there was a shortage of suitable officers and those of the Royal Naval Reserve were often substituted in their stead. These Merchant Navy officers held at least foreign-going first mates' papers and some had passed the qualifications for Master Mariner and they were well suited for the position of navigator.

TYPICAL H-BOAT SHIP'S COMPANY

Captain

First Lieutenant

Chief ERA		Navigator	Coxswain
ERA			TGM
ERA	Signalman		POLTO
ERA	Telegraphist		2nd Cox'n
Stoker PO	Boy Tel.		Ldg. Sea LTO
Ldg. Stkr			Ldg. Sea. 2nd Cox'n
Ldg. Stkr			Ldg. Sea. ST (or GL)
Stoker			Able Sea. ST
Stoker			Able Sea. ST (or SG)
Stoker			Able Sea. ST

Ordinarily the navigator would have been under training for eventual promotion to first lieutenant and assessed to determine his suitability as a future commanding officer. Ambitious RNR officers were encouraged to work their way upward, as also were the warrant officers and mates serving in third-hand positions. Candidates from all these sources attained commands before the war was over, Barney Johnson (RNR) and Alfred Brewster (mate) being good examples.

As a rule Royal Naval Volunteer Reserve personnel were not accepted into the Submarine Service. William Lowell Thompson and Barney Johnson seem to have been early exceptions, and although four RNVR officers were accepted for training during 1917, none lasted more than seven or eight months. Other than Johnson, who transferred to the RNR, Thompson was the only RNVR submariner to remain in submarines until the end of the war, and he continued to serve in this capacity until his release sometime after the armistice.

As well as her three officers, a typical H-boat operating in home waters carried between 23 and 25 crewmen. Of these, eight or nine were senior ratings, while the remainder were seamen and stokers. The coxswain and chief ERA were the most senior crewmen aboard and they occupied positions of considerable importance in the ship's company. Both reported directly to the first lieutenant.

Coxswains, who were always accorded the status of the senior non-commissioned officer aboard, came from the Torpedo Branch and qualified for their positions in one of two ways. The most common method was to qualify as a "submarine coxswain," (SC). This could be attained by relatively junior petty officers and it was common for them to qualify at the first opportunity in the hopes of filling a vacancy when one occurred. There was also the formal non-substantive Branch qualification of Torpedo Coxswain, which was a more formal qualification with fleet-wide acceptability. Submarine coxswains generally started out as petty officer SCs and acquired higher qualifications and promotions later in their careers.

The coxswain was the first lieutenant's non-technical right-hand man and as such was responsible for discipline, messing, the administration of leave, and to a large extent the physical welfare of the men. His duties also included the ordering, stowing and issuing of provisions, tobacco, rum, beer, and "war comforts." It was the coxswain, with the first lieutenant's approval, who made up the "Watch and Quarters Bill" which detailed which positions the men manned when on watch and at diving or action stations. It was he who ensured the men were properly dressed whatever the occasion and that each had provided himself with the special clothing appropriate to his position in the crew. While entering and leaving harbour the coxswain traditionally closed up on the helm, and when dived on patrol he manned the after hydroplanes. When on watch on the surface he supervised the seamen on watch and assisted the officer of the watch.

The chief ERA was the mechanical expert in the submarine's crew, and he possessed an intimate knowledge of his boat and its systems. The diesels, pumps, compressors and all mechanical equipment were in his charge. Under him he had two or three ERAs, whose primary duties were the running and care of the engines, and at least one stoker PO who was generally responsible for the operation and maintenance of the auxiliary machinery and miscellaneous mechanical gear. A couple of leading stokers and three or four stokers usually completed the engineering complement of a typical H-boat.

The Torpedo Branch at that time encompassed not only torpedoes, their tubes and handling gear, but also everything electrical and seamanship generally. In addition to the coxswain, three men from the Torpedo Branch held key positions in the ship's company. They were usually petty officers, although it was not unusual that some were leading seamen, particularly in the H-boats.

Senior among these was the petty officer performing the duties of torpedo gunner's mate, or TGM. In the H-boats he was often a less-qualified petty officer, as experienced TGMs were in short supply and most were required on the larger, more complex submarines. His range of responsibilities included supervision of both the electrical and torpedo departments. The main motors, main batteries, switchboards, Sperry gyro and all other electrical equipment came under his care. A TGM usually had at least one leading seaman holding an "LTO" non-substantive rate to assist him and to stand the opposite watch. On watch he took charge of the main motor and auxiliary switchboards.

Above: Galley stove and sink on the left, door to control room in the centre, gyro and low-power switchboard on the right. – PAC C-32292 *Below: After battery compartment, looking aft. Starboard main-motor switchboard, door to engine room and a mess table.* – Fred Wall collection

The third, usually a leading seaman in the H-boats but often a petty officer in operational submarines in general, was the second coxswain. He was primarily concerned with the use and maintenance of the upper-deck equipment, including all canvas, the anchors, berthing lines and torpedo-embarking gear. On the surface he stood his watch on the bridge and when dived manned the forward hydroplanes.

Other seamen with important duties in the crew included the signalman and wireless telegraphists. The signalman, in addition to his usual duties, acted as the captain's clerk and stood lookout upon surfacing and whenever the captain stood a watch on the bridge. Signalmen were proficient in all forms of visual signalling, including signal flags, semaphore and flashing light. As only one signalman was carried, it was his unhappy lot to be constantly on call to perform his duties on the bridge.

As the war lengthened and wireless sets improved, their proper use became an important aspect of submarine operations. To keep watch on the sets, two wireless telegraphists were carried, one of whom was sometimes a boy. Ten boy telegraphists were lost in submarines during the war. When dived the telegraphists manned the underwater listening hydrophones, having been given the job purely on the basis that they were experienced in distinguishing a variety of sounds over their earphones. When first fitted in submarines, the hydrophone listening station was in the wireless office or "silent cabinet." These cubicles were soundproofed, making it easier to detect and interpret the sounds coming over the earphones, whether they were wireless transmissions in the atmosphere, sea sounds, or noise emissions from ships.

A couple of leading seamen and four or five able seamen made up the balance of the crew. These seaman torpedomen were allocated duties in the electrical and torpedo departments. When on watch they stood lookout, manned the helm and forward hydroplanes, while two shared watches in the forward compartment when dived. When a gun was fitted (only the four Mediterranean-based H-boats had guns) a gun layer and a seaman gunner would have been carried in lieu of two of the torpedomen.

Cooks and stewards were almost never carried aboard British submarines during the Great War, the only known exceptions being where stewards were carried on a few of the large steam-turbine-powered K-class boats. Canada's *CC1* and *CC2*, however, are known to have carried cooks whose primary duties were the preparation and serving of food. In RN boats these tasks were undertaken by the seamen, those of cook being taken in rotation by the sailors, while the job of steward was performed by a volunteer who received a small stipend from the officers. These domestic tasks were carried out in addition to normal watchkeeping duties.

A submarine of the Great War was no place for the fastidious. In the narrow confines of the interior of a boat packed with machinery and electrical equipment almost any movement resulted in contact with something greasy, oily, dirty, wet or all of the foregoing, and it was physically impossible to keep one's person or clothing clean, despite a very high standard of shipboard cleanliness. Although there was ample opportunity for the men to wash their clothes when at sea, there was no fresh water to spare and no clean place in which to hang washing out to dry. The same lack of fresh water reduced personal washing to an absolute minimum and engendered the acceptance of a constant state of personal grubbiness, the very antithesis of General Service, which quickly became a matter of perverse pride for the new submariner. At sea particularly, submariners were unavoidably scruffy, of necessity unshaven and, in those days, long before the invention of personal deodorants, undeniably malodorous.

Every submariner was issued a white, woollen, round-necked sweater, and for those who kept upper-deck watches, a pair of high leather seaboots that reached almost to the knees and long woollen stockings to go with them. Another item of seasonal issue was the woollen duffel coat, or "lammy," as the men dubbed it because of its golden metallic colour. "Lammy" trousers were also available for winter wear. To ward off rain and spray while keeping watch on the open bridge, oilskins and sou'westers were a necessity. When not needed on the bridge oilskins served as waterproof covers for protecting sleeping sailors from the effects of weeping seams and the ever-present condensation. A small canvas bag in which to carry this special clothing was issued.

In harbour normal working dress was the rule. For those wearing the traditional sailor's rig, known officially as Class II uniform dress, which included all seaman petty officers and seamen, this meant a white duck jumper on which blue badges were worn and bell-bottom trousers of the same material, regardless of the season. This rig was known as "Number Fives." The white duck work dress was very similar to the sailor's tropical uniform except that the jumper sleeves lacked cuffs and there was no blue piping around the cuffs and jumper bottom. In summer a flannel, short-sleeved singlet with a square neck piped in blue, the "white front" or "gun shirt" of later days, was worn under the jumper, while a blue woollen jersey was worn the rest of the time. The black, folded "neck handkerchief" or "silk," as it came to be known, was always worn, but the blue-jean, white-striped collar was only donned on rare occasions. White caps were always worn with the white working dress, regardless of the season.

When in working rig all seamen were expected to carry the issue clasp-knife. This was secured to the end of a white lanyard, which was worn under the collar around the neck with the knife tucked into a pocket in the front of the jumper, leaving a "bight," or loop, hanging below the ties that secured the silk in place. Although the regulation was complied with ashore, it was not very practical aboard a submarine, where the loose lanyard would have proved a hazard to its wearer. The knife, however, was a practical tool, and as photographs show, it was not discarded but usually ended up in a convenient trouser pocket with the lanyard around the man's waist.

When particularly dirty work was in hand, men of the seamen branches could wear a blue coverall, or "combination suit," which was part of their normal kit, donned over the appropriate singlet or jersey. Stokers and stoker petty officers, whose traditional working rig consisted of a canvas jacket and trousers, were also allowed to wear the blue coverall as a concession to the conditions found in submarines, but had to provide them at their own expense. The blue coverall was popular and appears to have been the most common dress worn aboard submarines.

For all other duties in harbour the sailors wore their traditional navy blue uniforms complete with bell-bottomed trousers, pullover jumper and including the blue-jean collar edged with three white stripes, along with the silk and, for best, a clean lanyard. Each man was issued three jumpers. One, having button-up cuffs and gold badges, was reserved for occasions when No. 1 Dress was called for, which included inspections and for wearing ashore on Sundays. Another, commonly referred to as their "Number Twos," was without cuffs, had red badges and was kept for ordinary wear ashore, while a third, not surprisingly referred to as "Number Threes," was worn when carrying out everyday shipboard tasks. At night, aboard the depot ship or in barracks, the blue collar was removed; this hybrid rig was known as "night clothing." The blue jersey and blue cap were worn with these rigs for most of the year, the white flannel gun-shirt and white cap during summer months.

For everyday wear chief petty officers, who were issued the Class I kit, wore a coarse, blue serge uniform consisting of straight trousers and a single-breasted jacket having gilt buttons and with red trade badges displayed on the points of the collars. Under the jacket a white, long-sleeved shirt with an attached fall-down collar was worn, complemented by a straight black tie. At that time most chiefs did not wear any mark of rank. The only exceptions were the chief ERAs and chief electrical artificers, who wore the three large gilt buttons spaced apart in a horizontal line a few inches above the cuff on the face of the jacket sleeve. These were to become the rank marking for all chiefs seven years after the war.

The CPO's headgear was the familiar blue peaked cap with a crown and anchor badge (such as is now worn by RN POs and Canadian sailors). For seamen CPOs the anchor was silver and the crown in gold, all on a black velvet ground. The cap was worn with a white cover in summer. Engine room artificers, who were also issued the Class I kit, wore no trade or rank badges whatever except for the CPO's anchor and crown cap badge, which in their case was all in gold on a purple ground. These senior rates were issued the blue coverall for dirty work.

When going to sea on patrol the crewmen took only the personal gear they would need for the trip. As well as a minimum of clothing, this usually consisted of books, magazines and perhaps a tin of boiled sweets or some biscuits and tobacco. Cigarettes were popular among the younger men, others preferred a pipe, corn-cob or briar, while the real old-timers still clung to their clay pipes. Most took along letter-writing materials and perhaps a few small mementos and, just in case, a towel, a bar of soap and shaving gear. For those who were proficient in their use, a small musical instrument was allowed: harmonicas, fiddles, banjos, mandolins and concertinas being the most popular. The men packed the rest of their kit away in their duffel bags and these were stowed along with their hammocks in the racks on the depot ship mess decks or in a lock-up ashore.

Stowing personal gear aboard the submarines was always a problem. Lockers were small and limited in numbers, secure dry corners in which to stuff one's belongings were hard to find. From a safety point of view it was undesirable to leave personal gear unsecured or "sculling" about. A piece of clothing hanging on, or even near, a valve handwheel would make finding and operating the valve more difficult than it already was, especially in darkness. Loose items of kit were liable to find their way into the bilges, where they clogged bilge-traps and strainers, effectively plugging vital piping. At all times thoughtlessness of this kind was severely dealt with, as it was a threat to the very survival of the submarine.

In the Electric Boat Company-designed H-boats a built-in kit locker was provided for every man. These were just big enough to hold a submariner's simple needs for a two-week trip. It was also common to provide stowages and lockers for specialized items such as the ship's charts, confidential papers and code books, the signalman's flags and lamps, wireless operators' handbooks and spare electronic gear, and the electricians' special tools, spare fuses and meters. In the torpedo compartment and engine room, all special tools, lubricating oils and greases, cleaning rags (or cotton waste) and spare gear had built-in stowages provided.

At sea in wet weather the space around the engines sometimes resembled a Chinese laundry, with wet clothing draped over every exposed piece of piping. This may have been the bane of the engineering staff but was an absolute necessity for the officers and seamen keeping their watches on the exposed bridge. Working together the men had clothes-drying down to a science. Nothing remained hanging any longer than necessary. Each man made sure his kit was retrieved and stowed away before the coxswain decided it had hung around too long and stuffed it into the "scran bag" from where items could only be redeemed on payment of a small fine or token. Such was the co-operation among the submariners that seldom did anything go missing. They were all in the same boat

Engine room, looking forward. Main motors in foreground, engine controls and door to after battery. – PAC C-32022

Machinery space, after part of the engine room. Ballast pumps to port and starboard, with compressors beyond. – PAC C-32012

together and very much dependent on one another for their communal comfort and survival.

As the crews of the H-boats were learning, once at sea their environment remained essentially the same whatever the assignment. After reaching its allotted billet — and it was usually timed so that she did so during darkness — a boat invariably dived before first light and patrolled throughout the daylight hours, alternately keeping watch with the periscope near the surface and going deeper to listen for ships' noises on the hydrophones. They would surface after nightfall to charge the battery, crank the wireless mast aloft by hand and listen for routine messages, "ditch gash" (throw the day's accumulation of garbage over the side), pump out the bilges, dispose of the contents of the sewage tank, if fitted with one, and do their cooking. Cooking was normally done while on the surface rather than when dived to prevent an additional drain on the battery and to keep the interior of the boat free of cooking odours.

Unlike General Service, where the practice was closely regulated, smoking was universally tolerated in the submarines. The men could smoke at will when on the surface, except inside the boat when the battery was exposed. While the boat was dived smoking was strictly regulated by the captain. When bottomed for the night some captains allowed the hands to "carry on smoking" for a period of time before turning in. Smoking was commonly allowed on the bridge, although doing so at night was gradually phased out as the war progressed.

Weather permitting, once the batteries were fully charged, or "bumped up," it was common for submarines on patrol in the North Sea to rest on the bottom so that everyone could get a good night's rest. In rough weather the effects of deep-running swells and unpredictable currents made bottoming difficult and unwise. During bad weather the captain had the option of running dived for the night to escape the high seas, although he would be forced to surface for a charge sooner or later, or of remaining on the surface, where he could charge and wait out the weather.

Discipline aboard these submarines was described by one captain as "a democracy of real things." With everyone's life quite literally in the hands of every other man aboard, it was of prime importance that each member of the crew do his appointed tasks correctly, consistently and reliably. There was no place for discipline of the parade ground variety aboard a submarine, yet personal discipline, dedication and the cohesion of the ship's company as a whole had to be of the highest order. When an order was given, whatever the complexity of following it through, the right action, or sequence of actions, had to be taken automatically without supervision or prompting. Complacency too had to be guarded against, for any sort of a delay or mistake in the drill could have disastrous results. Living as they did in very cramped quarters and constantly under the strain of boredom, relieved only occasionally by the actions of the sea or the enemy, it was equally important that all hands got along with one another. A well-led, experienced submarine crew was a very closely knit group of men with a strong sense of community, men who were justly proud of their technical knowledge and efficiency, and mentally well-equipped to face the dangers they would meet almost daily.

Aboard the H-boats most of the crew were normally divided into two watches, watch on and watch off, four hours about. There were exceptions. The first lieutenant's and navigator's watch-about routine was broken by the captain, who traditionally stood the morning watch and a dog watch, while the three ERAs took a watch apiece. During exceptionally cold or foul weather the bridge watches were often changed at two-hour intervals, increasing the strain yet reducing exposure time. Whenever the boat dived, surfaced, was in some kind of dangerous situation, or an opportunity to attack presented itself, all hands would be closed up sometimes for hours. This was not a hardship for the watch whose turn it was to be "on" but it was sheer bad luck for the other watch, who might find themselves spending the best part of their off-time closed up. A similar situation could be caused by a breakdown, when those responsible for the defective equipment would work until the problem was either corrected or found to be irreparable, after which the men involved could resume watchkeeping.

There were few amusements to break the monotonous daily routine while at sea. Reading and playing cards were two of the most favoured pastimes. During the war it was not uncommon for magazines, cards and games to be supplied to the boats by philanthropic societies or individuals. After the charge was finished and the boat was settled on the bottom for the night, impromptu concerts were often held. The ship's "orchestra" provided the music while the hands sang their favourite ditties, often with their own irreverent version of the words. Singing and playing musical instruments were popular pastimes then and many of the crew were likely to have been accomplished vocalists and musicians. Wind-up gramophones made an appearance in several boats, but the survival rate of these and their delicate discs was unpredictable.

The occupants of the wardrooms were well known for their snobbery and exaggerated personal mannerisms, a manifestation of the social, educational and training system in which most officers spent their formative years. These affectations of attitude, manner and language, which set the officer class so far apart from the middle- and working-class men, could have been a serious source of lower-deck alienation. The sailors, however, generally regarded their officers' behaviour as being typical of the class rather than an expression of an individual's personal attributes, unless of course such proved to be the case. Complete acceptance of the rigid class system was still a reality at the beginning of the war, although "Jack's" patience with upper-class arrogance was wearing thin by the time the war ended.

Regardless of the restrictions imposed by the social order, the personnel aboard submarines frequently lived together for long periods without class-related friction and with a mutual lowering of the social barriers that allowed for very close working relationships and the development of a strong sense of comradeship among officers and men alike. An attitude of mutual tolerance, complemented by a strong, caring attitude appears to have existed between wardroom and lower deck, all of which helped carry the submariners through some really harrowing experiences. In a book written toward the end of the Great War, a submarine captain-turned-author remarked, "I tell you, the submarine sailor, once he's past his probation time and been tested on patrol, is a hand worth writing home about!" From the other side of the wardroom curtain a one-time coxswain writing his memoirs said, "The Captain: The crew were fond of him. He was a happy-go-lucky sort, calm in all he undertook to do, no panic at any time, but at times a little too venturesome, but most of this was to relieve the crew of boredom."

Sleeping arrangements in British submarines were absolutely Spartan, and except for a bunk or two in the wardroom the crew was left to sleep on the deck and, space permitting, in a few hammocks. Aboard the older boats this was inevitable, as any other arrangement would have impaired the boat's fighting ability, but in the larger boats better arrangements could have been devised, and indeed some improvements were made as the war progressed. For those dossing down on the steel decks and battery boards, communal mattresses were provided in the form of large canvas bags called "haversacks." There were probably no more than two or three of these per boat and they accommodated anywhere from four to six "bodies." It is uncertain whether the men slept inside in sleeping-bag fashion or merely used them as mattresses. One instance is on record where a haversack was rigged as a bathing pool on the upper deck of a boat at sea. Where there was enough space for a few hammocks to be slung from the deckhead, these would have been occupied by the more senior men.

The designs for the Montreal-built H-class boats allowed for enough canvas-bottomed pipe-framed bunks to be fitted in the forward battery and torpedo compartment to accommodate most of the crew, with the rest slinging hammocks and dossing down on the tables in the after battery compartment. It is evident that these luxurious fixtures were not installed when the boats were built, except for one tier of three bunks in the wardroom and possibly another for the senior rates.

When the H-boats were refitted and customized, however, the bunks were fitted in at least some of them, and in *H10* in particular. As these boats had four bow torpedo tubes, the need to reload quickly was not considered important, and the fact that some of the bunks blocked access to the reload torpedoes was acceptable. To get to the spare "fish" the bunks could be disassembled quickly and easily.

The officers' accommodations were also considerably remodelled with space-saving cupboard-bunks being built against the ship's side in lieu of the protruding pipe-framed type. Little luxuries, such as a wash basin, compass repeater, a voice-pipe to the control room and a clinometer, were also installed in the tiny wardrooms.

The messing arrangements provided in the H-boats were unique in the RN, in that there was a combined galley and communal eating area in the after battery compartment. The galley, with its electric range, water heater, sink and storage cupboards, was very well liked but the cafeteria-style messing, where all ranks ate together, was not universally popular. Within a year of commissioning, many, but by no means all (*H5* is known to have retained the cafeteria arrangement), of the boats had reverted to the RN system of individual messes, each with its own boundaries and integral sleeping and eating facilities.

The rationing system in operation during the Great War was quite different from the universal messing that now exists. At that time the victualling stores provided only the basic staples. The men were given an allowance, not in cash but in a collective credit account for each mess, with which to purchase the balance of their requirements from the depot-ship canteen store, according to their tastes and culinary ambitions. By the dietary standards of the day, which encouraged the intake of large quantities of fats and starches in various forms and very little in the way of fresh fruits and vegetables, the submariners were reasonably well supplied both in quantity and quality.

Refrigerated storage was entirely impractical aboard the tiny submarines and most rations were supplied in a preserved condition. Meat, including sausages, bacon, boiled beef and corned beef, was provided in tins, as also were the ubiquitous baked beans. Vegetables and fruits often came in the form of bottled preserves, while "hardtack" biscuits were supplied in bulk in sealed rectangular tin boxes.

Choosing what to issue for meals was not particularly scientific, being based mostly on the coxswain's knowledge of what he had in the store allied to a formula of "so many men per tin per day." This usually sufficed for the basics and the selection was augmented by whatever else the individual messes wanted from their own supplies. When choosing staples for a trip the inboard storesman and the coxswain decided on the selection based on what was available in the storeroom and what the coxswain knew to be popular among the lads. Some bulky, long-lasting items such as potatoes, turnips and carrots may have been carried, but these would have been limited by space and the fact that they needed fresh water for their preparation.

As there was only one stove in an H-boat, all cooking was done simultaneously in the one location. Besides the standard "meat and veg" this would also have included whatever had been chosen by the individual messes. Conditions being what they were, however, all of this seemingly complex procedure would have been simplified as much as possible. Preparation depended entirely on the abilities and tastes of the man whose turn it was to cook that particular day, and it was fortunate, perhaps, that most of the food only required heating. As fresh water was almost always rationed, there was little scope for even the simplest of culinary innovations.

Wardroom officers, who received a much more generous victualling allowance than did the men, were in the habit of procuring alternative and better-quality rations for their own consumption. Ashore or aboard a large ship this would not have been particularly noticeable, but in a tiny submarine, where it was prepared in the presence of the sailors, it was painfully obvious. These specialty rations were beyond the reach of the men, wherein lay the basis for some bitter criticism.

Letters home from the men on the lower deck frequently included requests for quality long-lasting, preserved foodstuffs (fruitcake was a favourite) with which to vary the unimaginative service diet. Considering the nature of the diet and the way in which victuals were prepared, it's little wonder that one of the most prevalent medical complaints among submariners was that of constipation.

The supply of fresh water was a constant headache in all submarines of the day, and the H-boats, which were designed for short coastal patrols, were no better off. The fresh water tank itself held about 250 gallons (1,136 litres), which on a ten-day patrol allowed for one gallon (4.45 litres) per man for each day at sea, for both drinking and cooking, and perhaps an occasional trickle for washing one's hands and face. As there was only one point for drawing fresh water from the tank, a hand-pump in the galley, the use of this precious commodity was easily controlled. Other tanks could be utilized if necessary, and on long trips one of the auxiliary ballast tanks, which would normally be full of water anyway, was cleaned out and filled with fresh water. This was not always successful, as Pirie in *H1* found out part way through his 28-day sortie into the Sea of Marmora, when one of the valves associated with the tank's normal function admitted sea water and he was forced to "borrow" half a ton of fresh water from another British submarine.

Rum was consumed at sea in the submarines of World War I, in the traditional manner. Every man over the age of 20 was entitled to his "tot" of one-half gill (2¼ ounces) of the potent West Indies spirit each day. If he did not want to take his tot, a man could elect to be noted as being "Temperance" and accredited its value on his pay. The storage and discipline problems associated with the tot do not seem to have presented any unusual problems, although the need to mix it with fresh water would have meant an additional demand on the very limited supply. Doubtless the amount of water put in the men's rum while at sea was somewhat less than that prescribed in the manual. Bottled beer is known to have been carried by many boats, probably on the unassailable pretext of having to augment the meagre supply of fresh water.

Sanitary facilities were of a primitive nature. For the old coastal boats with a very limited radius of action, the Royal Navy had used open buckets half filled with fuel oil as toilets until the advent of the D class in 1911, after which each submarine was equipped with one toilet, or "head," usually out in the open somewhere aft of the control room. The Montreal-built boats, despite having been designed to American standards, which required one for the officers and one for the men, were provided with only a single head, this for the use of all hands. As was normal in USN practice, it was completely enclosed in a little cubicle and was even provided with a vent pipe tied into the battery ventilation system. In the original H-boats the head was located in the port after corner of the forward compartment. In many of the later British-built members of the class the appliance used by the men was located in the open right aft in the engine room between the thrust blocks, while that provided for the officers was located in a cubicle in the control room.

The appliance was originally of the type fitted in yachts, from which waste was pumped overboard by hand through a hull valve after each use. As these could not be operated when below periscope depth, they were later improved by the addition of a waste tank, which allowed the head to be used whenever necessary and the accumulated waste to be discharged overboard on surfacing for the charge.

The only sink in an H-boat was that in the galley, the drainpipe of which led into a bucket on the deck. The slops were either dumped overboard or into the bilges, depending on circumstances. Buckets were commonly used for personal washing purposes.

There were few medical facilities and little in the way of medical skills available aboard a submarine at sea, beyond the contents of a very basic medical chest and whatever collective knowledge and ability the officers and crewmen might provide amongst themselves. First aid courses were widely available for all hands and were well-attended, but even short-term care of the sick or injured was left almost entirely to nature and common sense.

When on patrol the sailors' world was confined to the inside of their submarine and whatever else could be seen by those who kept lookout, which was usually little other than empty sea and sky. Only the three officers had any real idea of what was going on "up top" and even they were often relying on a minimum of military intelligence and a maximum of personal deduction. The men, although deeply concerned about the war as a whole, had little interest in what was happening in the immediate strategic sense, although any kind of action was attended with keen interest and considerable speculation on "Jack's" part.

After all was said and done, wartime life in a submarine was a dangerous, demanding, physically exhausting, mind-numbing experience consisting of long periods of discomfort and boredom interspersed with bursts of intense, sometimes danger-fraught, activity. "Was it all worth it for just a few bob a day extra?" one might well ask. "You bet it was, mate. And it just wasn't the extra money either. There was a hell of a lot more to it than that."

Officers taking tea in the cafeteria aboard H5 *at sea. Lt. C.H. Varley, the captain, is facing the camera.*
- C.H. Varley collection

Engine room, looking aft. – PAC C-32161

8 H8 IN THE GAT

The ships destroy us above
And ensnare us beneath.
We arise, we lie down, and we move
In the Belly of Death.

Untitled poem by Rudyard Kipling
from *Sea Warfare*, 1916

H8 was the fourth UK-based H-boat to be provided with a new battery and the exchange was made at Portsmouth dockyard. During this operation other small jobs and improvements were undertaken, including the installation of a pressure-proof voice-pipe which was run from the vicinity of the tractor seat, through the bridge ventilator pipe and into the control room. This would facilitate the passing of orders directly to the control room with the tower shut down. It was provided with shut-off cocks at top and bottom. For the most part all of the on-board work was performed by the ship's company.

The British had been operating submarines in the Baltic since the end of 1914, but the dangerous nature of the passage through the shallow, narrow, and well-guarded waters between Sweden and Denmark, where one submarine had already been lost, deterred the sending of reinforcements by that route. Other captains, ever mindful of the opportunities to be pursued in the northern sea, did whatever they could to promote their chances of being allowed to go north, and Barney Johnson was no exception.

Through most of the Sound there was just sufficient water to allow an H-boat to remain dived, and Johnson and Mansfield worked out a plan for making the journey using the equipment they'd had installed during the battery change. Having gathered an audience of senior submariners on the Solent, *H8* set about demonstrating her answer to the dangerous passage. Trimmed down so that only the top of the periscope fairwater, voice-pipe, and the daring conning officer, in this case John Mansfield, astride his tractor seat, remained above the surface, *H8* went up and down the Solent on her main motors in the hopes of gaining official approval, for the method if not for *H8* herself. It was to no avail, however, the senior submariners were not convinced.

It must be admitted that the officer assigned to that lonely perch on top of the periscope standard would have been in a very perilous position throughout such a passage and was in distinct danger of perishing through exposure, as the attempt would have been made during the long nights of the winter months. As well as being drenched and frozen he would have been subjected to the more routine hazards of drowning and the actions of the enemy. None of the boats that had made the passage had avoided submerging fully in order to escape detection and they had not been given the chance to do anything but get down as quickly as possible. Unfortunately no one thought to open up the bridge ventilator and proceed on the engines while in the trimmed-down condition, thus preempting the invention of snorkelling by 20 years.

H8 rounded off her stay at *Dolphin* by once again giving rides to the training classes for a couple of weeks, and then it was back to Harwich and the Heligoland Bight patrols.

In mid-March *H8* and *E26*, Lieutenant Commander Dobson, RN, left Harwich to set up a joint patrol off the islands of Ameland and Terschelling, where the Admiralty indicated they might intercept some German troop ships ferrying men to the Western Front. Their task was to locate the ships and report their movements to *Maidstone*. The two submarines took up their positions near the Akkepolle Gat in clear weather; *H8* on a patrol line roughly 12 miles to seaward of the 10-fathom line, *E26* on a parallel line about 6 miles closer to shore. No sooner had the two boats settled down to their work when a dense fog blanketed the area. The fog persisted for five days. On the 19th *E26*, while surfacing at dusk, found herself less than a hundred yards away from a surfaced German U-boat. Both submarines dived hurriedly and did not re-establish contact. On March 21 the fog lifted sufficiently to expose a surfaced *H8* to three minesweeping trawlers accompanied by a destroyer. The British submarine was easily spotted in the calm seas and gunfire from the German ships forced Johnson to dive and go deep to avoid further harassment; trawlers and destroyers were hardly worth a torpedo under those circumstances. That night *E26* returned to Harwich.

March 22 was the last day on station and *H8* started her daily activities early, having spent a comfortable night on the bottom after completing a routine battery charge the previous evening. The weather had cleared; the wind was from the east-northeast at force five, the seas were choppy. As they were scheduled to head for home that night Johnson ordered a careful eye kept on the weather and emphasized that detailed notations were to be made in the log. At dawn, with the crew keeping diving watches, an observation routine was set, ten minutes at four knots at periscope depth, keeping a continuous all-around watch alternating with 20 minutes listening-out on the hydrophones at 60 feet doing two knots. A track had been plotted roughly following the ten-fathom line, and as the echo sounder was not working, their position was checked by occasionally nudging the bottom with the keel and noting the depth gauge reading. At 8 a.m. Johnson ordered a course directly to windward, north, 63 degrees east by gyro. This course was held until approximately 10:50 a.m., at which time, while at 60 feet, a scraping noise was heard coming from forward and the bows were inexplicably forced downwards. Before any action could be taken the submarine was shaken by a violent explosion, plunging the boat into total darkness and sending her stem foremost toward the seabed into which she slammed with a dull thud, leaving the boat inclined bows down at an angle of 25 degrees.

Johnson immediately sent his crew to diving stations and ordered all bulkhead doors shut. Stunned and terrified as they must have been, the men obeyed, quietly and quickly. In the inky blackness they struggled against the steep angle and the loose gear tumbling about them to get to their appointed places. Some, particularly those whose stations were forward where the blast had hit the hardest and water could be heard and felt pouring in, undoubtedly thought they were locking themselves into their own coffins.

Emergency hand-held lamps were located and switched on, providing some sense of security, and with the restoration of normal lighting less than a minute later they began to take stock of their plight. In the control room damage appeared slight; the forward hydroplanes were inoperative, the shallow depth gauge was smashed, the periscope in the tower was damaged and some light bulbs broken. A depth of 85 feet was showing on the deep gauge, which meant the bows were resting in almost a hundred feet of water.

Reports soon reached the control room over the bulkhead voice-pipes. There was no significant damage in the two after compartments. In the large forward compartment, however, the situation was bad. A broken pipe was gushing water, more water was pouring in through all four torpedo tube rear doors, the forward bulkhead was badly buckled and leaking at the seams while a fist-sized dent in the deckhead between two frames had split open and was adding its share of sea water. A check of the vents disclosed that the forward trim tank was fully flooded and open to the sea, accounting at least in part for the loss of buoyancy forward. Miraculously the hull itself and the amidships internal ballast tanks appeared to be intact. All other hull fittings were tight, the battery tanks dry, and none of the crew were injured.

Knowing full well that the only chance for survival lay in their own hands, the crew set to work making repairs. Bulkhead doors were opened up, tools located, and the pumps set to work on the flooding in the forward compartment. The broken pipe was isolated and the rear doors hammered up tight to minimize the ingress of water, while the smashed diving gauge was replaced with a spare. Johnson considered jettisoning fuel from the tanks under the forward compartment but decided not to risk the resultant oil slick; it would be a dead giveaway to an alert enemy. All of this frantic but organized activity took place in a matter of minutes.

By that point *H8*'s captain was convinced they had been bombed by a Zeppelin or seaplane, as he had not seen any ships nor heard propeller noises since the previous day. *H8* had been in the same area for almost a week and he knew there were no mines to be concerned about, and in any case, had it been a mine it would have blown them to pieces. All was quiet above the stricken boat and there were no signs of any further attacks: no eerie scraping of explosives-laden sweep wires, no churning of destroyer's screws nor the blast of depth bombs. To remain on the bottom any longer was to invite disaster and Barney Johnson decided to surface. In doing so he was reminded of the time 18 months earlier when Adrian Keyes had been faced with a sudden bow down dive in the *CC1*, and he vividly recalled the lessons they'd learned on that occasion. Now he was faced with a similar situation and he knew just what to expect and how to handle it.

Sending the crew back to their diving stations he ordered blowing started on numbers one, two and three main ballast tanks. Blowing on number one had to be stopped when shouts from forward told him it was open to sea, the high-pressure air could be plainly heard roaring out of the tank. Even so, a few seconds later the boat gave a little heave and the depth gauge needle flicked toward the shallow side of 83 feet. "Grouper switch up, full astern both motors, full dive on the after hydroplanes." Seizing the moment, Johnson gave the orders to start them toward the surface.

In the after battery compartment the big knife-switches crashed home on the switchboards as high-pressure air hissed into the tanks. Just as the boat began to lift itself from the grip of the bottom, there was a sharp bang accompanied by a blue-green flash from the starboard switchboard. The sudden surge of electric current had blown the main fuses and, for the time being at least, they lost all power to the main motors. Blowing was stopped to save the precious compressed air, and as the screws audibly swished to a halt in the near silence that followed, the battered submarine once more settled nose-first into the sandy clutches of that ancient, wreck-strewn seabed.

Minutes dragged by like hours as the two LTOs worked to by-pass the fuses with emergency links. While waiting the crew checked some of the less vital areas and discovered the gyro was out of action and unlikely to function again without workshop attention. The wireless office was in a shambles and some of the delicate equipment had been smashed.

Soon they were ready to make another try for the surface. This time when Johnson called for full power the circuits held. *H8* rose stern first, broken glass tinkling across the deck to be crushed to powder under heavily booted feet as the men shifted their balance against the thrust of her ascent. The whole boat shook and fittings rattled as the thrashing screws dragged her bodily upwards. As she came up, the coxswain swung off on the big after hydroplanes handwheel to try and bring his battered charge level. This was not easy to do while proceeding backwards with no fore-planes and very little buoyancy forward. Blowing was stopped when the depth gauges began a steady swing toward the zero mark and the expanding air could be heard rumbling out through the Kingston valves beneath their feet. When he was sure that the boat was under control and had gained positive buoyancy, Johnson handed the trim over to Sub-Lieutenant Mansfield and headed for the tower, the signalman at his heels.

As the wallowing submarine neared the surface Johnson strained to get a glimpse of the outside world through the conning tower ports and, seeing nothing of any significance, grabbed the upper lid handle with one hand and its securing lug with the other. As they broached he tapped back the securing lug, cracking the hatch just enough to allow the build-up of compressed air inside the boat to whistle past his tightly wedged body. Down below, the sudden lessening of pressure caused an eerie, sour-smelling mist to rise out of the bilges.

Once the pressure was off, Barney flung the hatch open and heaved himself up and over the rim of the tower onto the bridge deck. Before allowing his mind to think of anything else, he pulled the big pair of binoculars out of the safety of his jacket and made a fast but careful examination of the horizon and the sky above. Nothing. A few seagulls, their bodies white against the backdrop of grey overcast, were gliding on the stiff breeze and making lazy swoops at the choppy surface, but there were no ships or aircraft of any description to be seen. *H8* was gratefully alone in her distress.

Safe for the moment, Barney Johnson examined what could be seen of the injuries his boat had suffered. The most obvious indication of the extent of the damage was a great gap in the fore-casing, where a section extending from just aft of the stem-post to the deck-anchor stowage had been blasted away. The forward hydroplanes and their operating gear were located in this area, but all that was left of these was the bed they had been bolted to and a length of useless control rodding that now jutted off to one side like a piece of discarded scrap metal. Dramatic as it may have appeared, this sort of damage was superficial. From the conditions they'd encountered inside the boat Johnson knew there must be much worse and decided to take a closer look.

Swinging himself over the bridge rail, he tested the slack jumping wire with his full weight, found it was still secure and proceeded hand-over-hand down the swaying wire until his feet found the deck. Moving gingerly through the wreckage of the casing, he selected a point from where he could make his inspection. At times submerged to his waist in the cold swells that periodically swamped the sluggish bows, he inspected the blitzed area beneath the missing casing. The most startling evidence of the force of the blast was the complete absence of the huge hemispherical bowcap — over a ton of metal blown completely away. This he considered to be their salvation, as the loss of the weight of the bowcap had compensated for much of the buoyancy they had lost when the forward tanks were torn open. Beneath his feet he could see that the top and side of the forward trim tank had been smashed in against the starboard torpedo tubes, which themselves had been completely flattened. Large pieces of hull plating had been ripped off while the circumference of the bulkhead between the trim tank and the forward ballast tank was marked by a ridge of crumpled scrap. All that remained between the sea and the interior of the boat was that one last buckled bulkhead at the torpedo tube rear ends. Whenever the swell heaved the shattered bows upward, Barney could clearly discern the open muzzles of the torpedo tubes and the gleaming noses of the four warheads, each containing 200 pounds of explosives and an impact fuse. With the loss of the protective bowcap the sensitive arming pistols in each of the warheads was exposed to the full force of the seas. It took only a moment to determine there wasn't a hope of removing the deadly devices: they had no choice but to rely on the efficacy of the built-in safety mechanisms.

Having seen all he needed, Cap' Johnson regained the bridge and passed the order to "carry on cooking." He ordered up the signalman to keep lookout and instructed the second coxswain to rig the bridge screen. Greeting his two officers as they emerged to view the damage, he quickly outlined the situation and cast about for a dry cigarette and a match. As he saw it, the boat was still seaworthy and it was his intention to make a run for England during darkness. This was a danger-fraught proposition. The area he intended to pass through was known to be patrolled by the Germans and *H8* was poorly equipped to fight on the surface, lacking even a small deck gun. There would be little hope for them if caught by the patrols or if the weather turned nasty. How long the damaged forward bulkhead would last in a pounding sea was anyone's guess and he didn't even want to think about the exposed torpedo warhead pistols.

Navigation would be a problem. The gyro was permanently out of action and after such a shock the magnetic compass was probably deranged and shouldn't be trusted. Their first priority was to ensure the boat was functioning well enough to attempt the passage and make a landfall before dark, so as to get an accurate fix on the chart before heading into the North Sea. He made no mention of the naked warheads; there was no point in doing so.

In order to determine the magnitude of the magnetic compass error, Johnson proposed swinging ship where they were in order to make a new deviation table. By this means they could compensate for the compass error and steer a reasonably accurate course. Using the direction of the wave crests as noted before the blast for a datum, the evolution was begun. The boat was pivoted from north to south through west. Readings were taken every two points and a new correction table was soon worked out. While the swing was in progress four spherical moored mines bearing British camouflage markings were spotted floating on the surface. These were carefully avoided and their position plotted for future reference. As soon as the swing was completed a course was set to clear the area.

Once free of the mines Johnson had the navigator plot a course that would take them within sight of the Terschelling Bank lightship, from where they could get a fix before attempting the 160-mile overnight crossing of the North Sea. Shouting down the conning tower, the Captain ordered, "Stop main motors, engage engine clutches, away gas engines." The welcome commands spurred the engine room to action and soon the pair of faithful New England-built diesels were thundering away at full cruising revolutions, giving *H8* a speed of about 11 knots. Down below, the men began carrying out the familiar surface running routine. The hands off watch straightened away the forward compartment as best they could, while the sailor whose turn it was to cook busied himself preparing a hot meal and the coxswain gathered up his copper pots and measures in preparation for "up spirits." As yet unsure as to their destination, the crew were content to be more or less safely on the surface and under way once again, confident old Cap' Johnson would see they were all right.

It wasn't long before a new problem manifested itself in the engine room, when it was discovered that both stern bearings were running hot. Reasoning that the entire hull had been whipped in the blast, leaving the shafts and their bearings misaligned, the Captain ordered revolutions reduced to ease the friction, while the ERAs slacked-off on the hull glands, allowing a stream of cooling seawater to course over the bearings at a rate that could be handled by the pumps. Their speed was now down to about 6½ knots, which Johnson reckoned was pretty good considering the state his boat was in.

After an hour and half's running the rust-streaked hulk of the lightship hove into view and the navigator was able to get an accurate fix on his chart. Once this was done a southwesterly course was set, pointing *H8*'s battered bows toward Yarmouth. Johnson then instructed Mansfield to have the contents of number-one fuel tank pumped overboard once it was dark, to provide additional buoyancy at the bows. Satisfied with the preparations for the overnight passage, he handed the watch over to the first lieutenant and prepared to head below, having been on the bridge since surfacing. Before descending into the brightly lit interior of the boat Barney discovered that the navigator, Sub-Lieutenant Alfred Meadows, RNR, could not bring himself to go below. It was Meadow's first trip in a submarine and, although showing no signs of distress during the incident itself, he had been completely unnerved by his experiences that day. Leaving the jittery third hand to keep the first lieutenant company, the Captain went below to talk to his crew, get a change of clothes, an illicit tot, and a bite to eat.

Reaching the control room, he instructed the coxswain to muster the hands off watch. When these had gathered he explained that they would attempt to cross the North Sea during the night, first making for Yarmouth and then Harwich, where he hoped to go alongside *Maidstone* the following afternoon. Johnson told them that with the torpedo tubes wrecked they would be unable to fight if challenged by the German patrols and added that with the stern bearings already in a bad state they would not be able to run very far or fast either. Despite the risks the crew was more than willing to "have a go," for they had no desire to spend the rest of the war in a German prison camp or a Dutch internment camp, like the men from *E17* or *H6*.

Johnson's talk to the crew was followed by a more serious discussion with the chief ERA and coxswain about what could be done in the event they encountered a German patrol during the night, something he'd already discussed with the first lieutenant. Between them they worked out a plan for diving the boat, should this be necessary, and a trim was put on in preparation. Barney then inspected the remains of the wireless set, and he and the telegraphist set to work to see if they couldn't get it working again and make contact with British forces in the area. The receiver was beyond any hope of repair, but they eventually managed to get some life into the transmitter. The operator tapped out a message giving their position, a description of the damage and the position of the mystery minefield. This was repeated only once, after which they maintained radio silence. There was no way of knowing whether or not their message had got through.

H8 crossed the North Sea without incident and, considering that they were steering by a home-made compass correction table, made a remarkably accurate landfall off Yarmouth Roads during the morning watch. Even German propaganda later admitted that they were both very brave and very fortunate to have attempted, and successfully pulled off, such a fine feat of seamanship. Fortunately the weather had not worsened and the sky continued overcast. By early morning *H8* had rounded Cross Sands buoy and was safely inside the War Channel headed for Harwich. Off Lowestoft *H8* encountered a British patrol vessel and requested that she contact *Maidstone* and pass on their amended time of arrival. In any event neither this message nor theirs of the previous night ever reached 8th Flotilla headquarters.

It was a battered and weary, but much relieved, *H8* that arrived off Harwich

H8's above-water damage, dramatic but superficial. Worse damage would come to light later. –
RN Submarine Museum

A grateful H8 *heading for a safe berth alongside HMS* Maidstone *at Harwich.* – RN Submarine
Museum

The full extent of the damage is revealed in the floating dock. H8 *was very lucky to have survived the ordeal.* – author's collection

around tea time that March afternoon, only a few hours adrift of her original operational schedule. Her lack of wireless communication had caused some concern, but not until they saw that great gap in the fore-casing did anyone on Captain SM's staff realize that something dramatic had happened. Johnson soon had his half-wrecked command safely alongside the depot ship and, although the customary three days patrol leave for half the crew was suspended until after the completion of any forthcoming investigation, the men could at least go inboard to clean up and relax.

In Captain Arthur Waistell's office, however, things were far from relaxed. The first impression among the staff was that the Canadian RNR captain, or his RNR navigator, had somehow caused the boat to stray out of her assigned area and blunder into one of the many known minefields, despite Johnson's report to the contrary and his theory about being bombed. The captain and officers of *H8* were informed that a Court of Inquiry would be convened as soon as possible under the chairmanship of Commodore Tyrwhitt. This was a routine procedure, but after hearing some of the reports coming from Waistell's office Barney felt less than confident about the outcome.

The following day *H8* was ordered to proceed to the floating dock to be raised for an examination of the damage and removal of the pistols from the warheads of the torpedoes jammed in their flattened tubes. Prior to leaving *Maidstone* the flotilla navigator was embarked and he had them swing ship on their way to the dock so that he could evaluate the compass correction tables made by Johnson and his navigator.

When the dock lifted the submarine out of the water the full extent of the damage was revealed for all to see. The starboard forward part of the boat was a wreck. The space where the big bowcap had been blown away left a great gap between the heavy stem-post and the muzzles of the torpedo tubes, and it could be seen for the first time that the gash in the starboard side extended from the missing upper deck section all the way to the keel. Only then did it dawn on some of the men just how close to death they had been in the first instance and how risky was their venture of crossing the North Sea and in being prepared to dive in that condition. Only Johnson had been fully cognizant of the facts and he had told as few people as possible: Why worry the crew when there was absolutely nothing they could have done about it? Throughout their ordeal only one battered bulkhead, made of 7/16 of an inch of mild steel plate, and their own professional conduct as a ship's company had stood between them and a watery grave. Later that day fragments of an *Elia* mine were retrieved from the superstructure, firmly establishing that it was indeed a mine, and a British one at that, which had caused the damage.

At the inquiry Johnson was absolved of any blame in the incident. When called for his presentation the flotilla navigator testified to the effectiveness of the extempore compass tables and to Johnson's excellent seamanship. From the material presented in support of his claims, it was proven that Johnson's command was on station at the time of the incident and that he had not run foul of a known minefield, as had first been postulated by Captain SM's staff. In his report on the incident Captain Waistell himself commented:

Having investigated what happened after the explosion, I can with great pleasure bring to your notice the splendid conduct of the captain, officers and crew of *H8*. Lieutenant Bernard L. Johnson, Royal Naval Reserve, her commanding officer, by his coolness and prompt action probably saved the boat; any delay in getting her to the surface would have been fatal. He reports that Sub-Lieutenant John M. Mansfield, Royal Navy, and Sub-Lieutenant Alfred E. Meadows, Royal Naval Reserve, and the entire crew, although it appeared obvious to all that the boat was lost, proceeded at once to their stations without any signs of excitement, and all orders were carried out promptly and correctly.

I would submit that such conduct, in the face of apparent certain death, is an example of courage of which the whole service may be proud.

The truth of where the mine, or mines, had come from, however, was a matter for serious concern at the Admiralty and in the Harwich Command. What had actually transpired was not brought forward at the inquiry and it is conceivable that Commodore Tyrwhitt and Captain Waistell were not in full possession of the facts at the time, although they certainly were a short while later.

The mine that had damaged *H8* and those that Johnson and his officers had spotted while swinging ship off the Akkepolle Gat were irrefutably British. They had originated in a field of nearly 200 mines laid by HMS *Biarritz* nine days earlier in an area of the North Sea to the northwest of the island of Borkum. In one short week many of the mines had been carried as much as 30 miles west-southwest of their original position by a continuous succession of easterly gales. The whole area north of Terschelling and Ameland had to be declared unsafe because of the drifting mines. This effectively denied the western entrance to the Bight to the British. As a precaution British submarines were routed into the Bight by way of the Amrum Bank until the area had been proven clear.

This the enemy obligingly set about doing in very short order. The Germans had lost one ship when it blundered into the scattered field during a fog, but they were soon able to determine its extent by the many mines floating on the surface. This haphazard but visible minefield was quickly swept up in a two-day, non-stop effort to clear the German's western exit from the Bight.

In his memoirs Johnson mentioned that during the course of the inquiry an explosives expert was called. The expert testified that the mine had detonated with only a tenth of its explosive potential, resulting in limited damage to the boat rather than its complete destruction. The disclosure of the true circumstances many years later were to disprove this testimony, or Johnson's recollection of it.

It was the fact that the mine mooring cables were slack that had saved *H8* from being blown to bits. Whether the slackness of the cables resulted from the mines drifting into shallower water than where they had been laid or because the wire had paid out from the mooring reel during its rough ride along the bottom was not revealed. When the boat snagged the slack mooring wire with the starboard foreplane, her forward movement imparted a sudden tension to the wire that jerked the mine with sufficient force to cause it to detonate while still some distance from the hull. These mines did not have the now familiar horns that have to be struck to make it detonate but were armed with a sensitive inertia-activated detonator that went off when the mine was violently bumped or, in this case, jerked. *H8* and her company were incredibly lucky, but it would take almost 50 years before the facts were released and few, if any, of the crew would ever learn the truth.

A few days later *H8* was ordered to Chatham, where she could be docked, given a thorough inspection and a decision rendered as to what was to happen to the boat. She made the trip on her own engines but was provided with an escort for the short voyage. Once docked down the whole affair would take only a day or two. Meantime the ship's officers and crew had little to occupy their time and half the men were sent off on their well-earned three-day patrol leave, while the remainder stood by to assist the dockyard.

While the survey was in progress Johnson received a telephone call from Commodore Hall telling him to meet a Miss Jane Anderson and informing him that she was permitted to see his boat in dock and had permission to interview him. Johnson was to obtain the formal approval of the Admiral Superintendent to bring the lady journalist into the dockyard, meet the mid-morning train from London, make sure the good lady had lunch and send her back to London on the late afternoon train.

Barney arranged for a luncheon to be served at the barracks, persuaded some fellow officers to attend, and then obtained the Rear Admiral Arthur Ricardo's reluctant co-operation with the proviso that Johnson's guest be brought directly to him immediately upon arrival. His arrangements made, Johnson set off for the railway station.

The train, headed by a scruffy apple-green locomotive and trailed by half a dozen grimy, crimson lake coaches, pulled up to the platform with a squeal of brakes and deposited a crowd of Chatham-bound passengers, most of whom wore navy blue. With a banging of carriage doors, the *chirrup* of the guard's whistle and a high-pitched screech from the engine's whistle, the train resumed its journey.

As wisps of smoke and steam were carried away by the warm morning breeze Johnson searched the rapidly thinning crowd for a person fitting his concept of a lady reporter: someone tweedy, bespectacled, middle-aged, a bit frumpy perhaps. Nowhere was such a person to be seen and the platform was almost empty of passengers when, as Johnson himself described it, "I was accosted by a vision under a gaff topsail hat, brief silken skirt, silk stockings and high-heeled shoes (which was something in 1916). "I know you must be Lieutenant Johnson and I am Jane Anderson,' " announced his vision in delightfully feminine tones. Much to his delight he had found his journalist. During the short drive to the Admiral's residence Barney learned that she came from the American Midwest and was writing a book she intended to call "Britain at War."

When Johnson presented his attractive companion to the Admiral Superintendent that gentleman's attitude toward their previously less-than-welcome visitor changed dramatically. The steward was summoned, sherry sent for, comfortable seating arranged and cigarettes proffered all around. After a brief conversation with the engaging American visitor, the Admiral decided that Miss Anderson and her escort were to be his guests for luncheon; the humble submariners could entertain her to tea. "Had she not been such a pretty girl the submariners could have had her for lunch too," remarked Barney wryly.

After lunch he took his charming guest on a tour of *H8*, inspected the *G3*, one of the latest types of submarine under construction in the dockyard, and then enjoyed a cheerful tea with the submariners. After a delightful day Jane Anderson was put aboard her train on schedule and returned to London. Some time later she mailed a clipping of her article* to Johnson. Her bright personality brought to his mind the refrain of a musical comedy song that was popular at the time, "Yankee, swanky, full of hanky panky with an R.S.V.P. eye." Thus ended a bright interlude in what was destined to be a depressing time for Barney.

The survey determined that *H8* would need extensive rebuilding before she would be fit for action again and it was decided to pay off the boat and send the crew back to Harwich to be dispersed to other submarines in the flotilla. Cap' Johnson had pleaded for them to be kept together and given a new submarine, but this was impossible to arrange. The men soon cleared their possessions from the home they had shared for nine hectic months and marched off to the railway station in a heavy silence. Leaving one's ship, especially a happy ship, is a hard thing for sailors, and more so when they know that the special bond of being a crew is also going to end. None was sadder than their captain, for *H8* had been his first submarine command and against all expectations he had won the right to take her into action and had brought her home safely against tremendous odds.

---

* See Appendix 2 for transcript.

Boats of the Harwich flotilla, summer 1916. – RN Submarine Museum

This photo of Barney Johnson was taken around the time he assumed command of D3.
– Vancouver City Archives

A few days after the return of *H8*'s crew to HMS *Maidstone*, the ships' companies of all the boats alongside were mustered on the depot ship's quarterdeck by the order of Captain (S). When all were fallen in, Captain Waistell addressed the assembly and read out a letter from the Admiralty commending the crew of *H8* for their "steadiness and splendid behaviour under trying circumstances." For his part Cap' Johnson was promoted to lieutenant-commander and sent on indefinite UK sick leave, not that there was anything particularly wrong with him except that he needed, and deserved, a good rest.

Johnson's mother and two spinster sisters were still living in Birkenhead and it is likely he paid them at least a short visit, but for most of his leave he remained in the Harwich area. With little of vital interest to occupy his time he soon became bored and, what was worse, depressed. This unhappy situation persisted until the Flotilla padre took a hand and introduced him to the game of golf. Within a short time he had bucked up considerably, although he soon tired of his enforced inactivity and longed to get back into action.

Returning aboard *Maidstone* about three weeks later, Johnson called on Captain (S) and requested he be given a new command. Captain Waistell welcomed him and, explaining there were no H-class boats available, asked if he would consider taking over the *D3*, a boat with a good reputation and an experienced crew, which was then in refit at nearby Ipswich. Johnson accepted gladly and his appointment took effect from April 19, 1916.

D3's previous captain and first lieutenant had both been re-assigned and a new first lieutenant would have to be found before the end of the refit, sometime in mid-May. The third hand, Lieutenant Sam Champion, RNR, remained for the time being and Barney managed to bring Chief ERA Fletcher with him from *H8*. He would liked to have brought as many of his old crew as possible, but this was ruled out, as many had already been drafted to other boats and *D3* had a nearly complete complement.* Johnson now had a new set of goals and his depression vanished as he was caught up in the activities and responsibilities of a new command and all that it entailed.

The surviving six of the original eight D class — *D2* and *D5* having been lost early in the war — were considered old boats by the standards of the day. Built by Vickers at Barrow and commissioned between 1910 and 1912, they were the first RN submarines to be rated suitable for overseas patrol. The "Ds" had a displacement of 600 tons surfaced and 620 tons dived, were the first class of British submarines to be powered by diesel engines, the first to carry a wireless set and the first since the original Holland boats to be fitted with a proper head and a waste tank. The twin 600 h.p., six-cylinder, blast-injected diesel engines and 275 h.p. electric motors gave these boats a speed of 16 knots on the surface and 9 knots dived. They were armed with three 18-inch torpedo tubes, two forward arranged one above the other on the centre line and one in the stern. The "Ds" carried a total of six torpedoes, one "up the spout" (loaded) and one reload for each tube. Soon after the war began *D3* had been fitted with a high-angle six-pounder gun on the fore-casing; there was no magazine for the ammunition and this had to be stowed inside the boat wherever space could be found for the stowage boxes.

Internally these boats were open throughout, there being no complete subdividing bulkheads. They were the first class to be provided with external as well as the usual internal ballast tanks and were provided with underwater listening hydrophones. In wartime the "Ds" carried a crew of 3 officers and 26 men; there were bunks for captain and first lieutenant (shared by all three officers on a "hot-bunk" basis when at sea) in the

---

* See Appendix 3 for a reproduction of a letter Johnson wrote to Petty Officer Fred Wall on the subject.

tiny curtained-off wardroom which also featured chart drawers, a desk cum chart table, a few cupboards, a folding hand basin and the usual collapsible table and canvas folding chairs. A few of the senior hands slept in hammocks slung from the deckhead, while the rest of the crew dossed down on the decks forward and aft. The decks themselves (planked over the battery tank, steel plate elsewhere) were normally covered with painted canvas runners, commonly referred to as "deck clothes." These served to keep dirt from getting into the battery underneath, to assure good footing on an otherwise slippery bare steel deck, and to reduce noise. Electric hot-plates were provided forward and aft for cooking, while the fresh water tank held enough water for about four days consumption if carefully rationed.

The D class were bigger and, despite their age, were faster and more complex than the H class. *D3*'s new captain had a lot to learn.

While Johnson tackled the problems of an unfamiliar boat in refit, young Sub-Lieutenant Maitland-Dougall was still third hand aboard the *H10*. With three war patrols to the Bight under his belt he was now considered to be a seasoned submariner. So far the operations had been fairly routine and *H10* had not encountered any serious enemy activity. After returning from her third patrol on April 14, the submarine settled down alongside at Yarmouth for the usual leave and maintenance routine. Ten days later this was to be rudely disturbed.

In the wee hours of the morning of April 25, the narrow confines of the River Yare came alive with the movements of the submarines stationed there. The crews of the four serviceable boats had been standing by since late the previous evening. The "buzz" on the lower deck was that it was another big exercise; those in the know knew they were going out to meet the High Seas Fleet. Even at Whitehall the objective of this German foray was not apparent, although a coastal raid was considered most likely and the East Coast ports had been alerted. At 2 a.m. the submarines started to leave in line astern, *V1* leading, followed by *H5* and *H7*, with *H10* in the rear about 20 minutes behind the leader. Two more boats, *E53* and *E37*, were sent from Harwich to reinforce the Yarmouth flotilla. These and the four *Alecto* boats had been allotted defensive positions along two easterly lines off the harbour approaches so as to be on the line of advance of the High Seas Fleet as it continued north or on its flank when it turned eastward to avoid the shallows and head for its bases. *H10* had been given an area halfway between Smith's Knoll and Cross Sand, where she arrived at about 3 a.m. Her neighbours were *V1* at Smith's Knoll and *H5* in the vicinity of Cross Sand. First light was beginning to streak the eastern horizon as the submarines took up their positions, double lookouts straining to see something, anything. The ether was alive with the dot-dashing of Morse code messages from the light forces to the south, some of whom were already in action, and the wireless operators waited expectantly for orders and messages from *Alecto*. Everyone by this time knew it was no exercise, the Huns were loose and the Grand Fleet was on the way from its bases in the north to teach them a lesson they'd never forget, or so everyone hoped.

H10 followed Flotilla standing orders for surface running and made frequent alterations of course while she cruised her billet as the eastern horizon lightened. At about 3:30 a.m., while off the Cross Sand light vessel, the first sign of the enemy was spotted in the dark sky, the ominous shape of a Zeppelin headed southeast. *H10* immediately dived and followed the intruder for as long it remained visible through the periscope, then surfaced to resume her patrol. *H5* also spotted the Zepp, which hung around for about a half hour, and reported its presence to *Alecto*, adding that it appeared to be shadowing the submarines.

Typical D-class sub's control position. – RN Submarine Museum

At 4:10 all doubts as to the presence of German capital ships were set aside when the sky to the south was illuminated by the rippling flashes of big guns firing, flashes that preceded the dull thunder of gunfire by many seconds. The area from Yarmouth to Lowestoft was the target. "Full speed on gas engines" was ordered and the course altered to the southeast, toward the guns, with *V1* in sight astern following suit. Forty minutes later the two boats were making good time, the crews eagerly anticipating getting in a tin fish or two at the Huns when their plans received a sudden, and unexpected setback.

From out of nowhere two aircraft whose markings could not be discerned in the darkness suddenly swooped on the submarines and *H10* found herself the target of four bombs, all of which exploded between 50 and 100 yards away as she plunged to the safety of the depths, the klaxon screeching its raucous alarm in the crew's ears. This sudden change of fortunes notwithstanding, *H10* continued her course toward the enemy's position at a conservative six knots, this to ensure there was some battery left for an attack. At 5 a.m. excitement aboard the boat was running at fever pitch when Byron Cary ordered "action stations" and announced he had the enemy battlecruisers in sight formed in two lines heading north, toward them. Five minutes later their hopes were rudely doused when the German ships, which were then only two to three miles distant, made a radical turn to the east. Twenty minutes later it was all over for the submariners. The Germans were gone, their flight marked by a huge pall of black smoke on the eastern horizon and the glow of fires ashore to the west. *H10* surfaced and zigzagged back to her billet, alert for aircraft, Zeppelins and U-boats, and bitterly disappointed at having missed a chance at the big ships.

By tea time the submarines were back alongside *Alecto*, the men excitedly exchanging stories with their mates from the other boats. Although *H5* came the closest of all the Yarmouth boats, none had managed to get off a shot. The German battlecruisers were in full retreat by the time they were in a position to attack. An opening target making well over 20 knots was an impossible shot.

The daily newspapers soon provided the nation with all the details of the damage at Lowestoft and Yarmouth, which would have been far worse had not Commodore Tyrwhitt's Harwich-based light forces, of which the Yarmouth boats were considered an integral part, made such a show of determined resistance — which was just as well, for the Grand Fleet missed the enemy altogether. The submariners, however, were sobered by the loss of *E22* from the Harwich flotilla, which had been torpedoed by the lurking *UB-18*. The aeroplanes that had attacked them turned out to be British, and from that time onward the submarines sported distinctive air-recognition devices painted on their upper decks. Ten days later a jubilant Sub-Lieutenant Maitland-Dougall was posted to the *D3* to take over as first lieutenant under Barney Johnson.

9 EAST COAST PATROLS

While Cap' Johnson and his new first lieutenant attended *D3* through the final stages of her refit, two more Canadian submariners arrived on the scene. The first to finish his course at *Dolphin* was Fredrick Lawson, who on June 5 was confirmed as a sub-lieutenant and appointed to *H10* to fill the gap left by Maitland-Dougall's promotion. Lieutenant John M. Mansfield, *H10*'s first lieutenant since *H8* had paid off, also left the boat, and the young Canadian submariner was given the number one's billet. This was a big step upward for the 21 year old from Chesterville, Ontario, one he was going to find difficult to handle. Within a fortnight his new boat was off to sea to begin another round of patrols in the Bight, the proving ground, or otherwise, of so many submariners.

Three weeks after Lawson's departure the fourth RCN officer, Acting Sub-Lieutenant Ronald Watson, arrived at *Dolphin* to begin his training, having already completed a nine-month apprenticeship in the Esquimalt submarines. He experienced little difficulty with the course and on completion in August was sent to HMS *Adamant* at Brindisi, on the Adriatic side of the heel of Italy.

Adamant, sister ship to *Alecto*, was the depot ship for the handful of British submarines — at that time three Montreal-built H-boats and four B class — that formed part of an Allied submarine flotilla formed to assist the Italian Navy in its efforts to contain the powerful Austro-Hungarian fleet. Operating from their main base at Pola and a secondary base at Cattaro, the Austrians controlled the entire length of the island-studded Dalmation coast from Trieste to the Albanian border. Watson would see a great deal of the Mediterranean and Adriatic in the years to come, but in the beginning he occupied a billet in *Adamant*'s spare crew.

Lawson and Watson had both been members of Maitland-Dougall's term at the Naval College and it is interesting to note that three out of that first class of 20 cadets chose to serve in submarines. As the midshipmen left Canada to go overseas, their places in the Esquimalt submarines were taken by two midshipmen from the second class, both of whom would be sent overseas in their turn. The RCN was actually producing a tiny but keen crop of junior submarine officers for service with the Royal Navy.

At the end of April there was some excitement in the Harwich Command when the German mine-layer submarine *UC-5* went aground on Shipwash Sands and was captured by HMS *Firedrake*. The U-boat, commanded by Oberleutnant Ulrich Mohrbutter, had a dived displacement of only 183 tons and carried 12 mines.

She left Bruges on April 26 intending to lay her "eggs" in the approaches to Harwich. Early the following morning she was forced by a patrol vessel to dive in the vicinity of Galloper Sand. She evaded the British ship but ten minutes after surfacing ran aground. Working clear of the sandbank Mohrbutter pressed on inshore and dived around 8:00 to continue his approach submerged. Two hours later he grounded again while at periscope depth and with all of his mines still aboard. Unable to get off, *UC-5* was uncovered by the ebbing tide and spotted by *Firedrake*, which was returning to port after participating in some night exercises. The destroyer's CO, Commander Aubrey T. Tillard, soon determined it was an enemy submarine and he closed to 500 yards, fired a shot past her bows and sent a boat to investigate. The German crew abandoned their U-boat while her captain tried to detonate the mines. In this he was unsuccessful and Mohrbutter was forced to surrender his command more or less intact.

The little U-boat was eventually salvaged and put into the floating drydock at Harwich. At the same time, Johnson's *D3* was carrying out her post refit trials, and when it was found that one of the propellers was defective, she was put into the same dock alongside the German boat. Examining the tiny but deadly German submarine provided an interesting diversion for the British submariners. *D3* entered the dock on May 24 and came off again five days later.

During this same period the greatest naval battle the world had ever witnessed, the Battle of Jutland (or Heligoland, as it was known to the Germans), took place in the mist-shrouded North Sea off the Danish coast during the afternoon and evening of May 31, 1916. Submarines on both sides took little part in this, the contest of the behemoths. The speed of the combatants was much too high for any submarine to keep pace and a fleet action was no place for a boat of that era; she would have been everybody's enemy and in everybody's way. The three British boats in position to cover the return of the German ships to the Jade had been ordered to lie "doggo" until June 2 and thus missed a golden opportunity as the enemy ships, some of which were very badly damaged, limped homeward unobserved.

In conjunction with the sweep conducted by the High Seas Fleet that culminated in the famous battle, 16 U-boats had been deployed, some to watch and report, others to lay in ambush for the Grand Fleet as it left its bases. Those assigned to the Firth of Forth and the Tyne estuary arrived too late to witness the departure of the British ships, and as they only had orders to remain on their stations until June 1, orders which no one thought to change, they headed for home in time to allow their somewhat battered enemy to return to base unreported and unmolested.

Shortly after the return of the High Seas Fleet to its harbours, submarine anti-shipping operations around the British Isles were reinstated under the restrictions of the Prize Regulations. These attacks had been suspended since the loss of American lives in the torpedoing of the French cross-Channel steamer *Sussex* at the end of April. At the same time a new U-boat offensive was opened off the east coast of North America, a campaign which, in time, was to prove particularly devastating.

This was not a renewal of the unrestricted warfare as desired by the U-boat arm and so feared by the Allied maritime community but, even so, would prove damaging enough. As events were to show, these limited offensives that began in mid-1916 were but the first steps in a rapidly escalating U-boat campaign designed to bring Britain to her knees through economic strangulation at sea.

On June 1, 1916, the day after the Battle of Jutland, *D3* left Harwich for her first patrol under Barney Johnson's command and, in company with two old "chummy" boats from Yarmouth, *H10* (Lawson would join upon her return) and the *V1*, headed towards familiar seas off the coast of Holland. The three submarines took up their billets off Terschelling and settled down to a week of watch-and-report routine. Two days later *D3* was forced to return to harbour with defects on her port main motor, which would keep

D3 *in dock with the German minelayer* **UC-5.** – author's collection

her tied to *Maidstone* for the next two weeks. Once repairs were completed she was off again, this time to the Dogger Bank, where Johnson and his crew kept watch for a week.

Because of the very long summer days experienced in those northern latitudes, the submarines often spent upwards of 20 hours a day dived. Under those circumstances some sickness among the men was expected, but when *D3* arrived alongside on June 28 with no fewer than 13 of the crew taken seriously ill, there was cause for some alarm. Five members of the crew had to be hospitalized for treatment, including the coxswain, and Johnson was chided for remaining on patrol while his crew fell ill around him.

The cause of the sickness was attributed to the effects of breathing the gases produced by the battery during charging. The ship's company was turned to, taking up the battery, giving it a thorough inspection, and cleansing and stopping up any leaks in the battery ventilation system that could be the cause of the gases getting into the boat, something they had already done during the refit. With the standard of battery ventilation provided in the D-class boats and a battery-tank deck made up of wooden planks, there was little real chance of preventing at least some of the fumes from getting into the boat's atmosphere, but the effort had to be made.

By July 21 the submarine was judged fit for sea again. Two of the invalids had returned aboard and three new stokers joined a few days before sailing to complete the crew. *D3* slipped her lines that afternoon for a patrol off Terschelling.

By the following morning almost the entire ship's company was deathly ill, most of the men suffering in varying degrees from nausea, vomitting, abdominal pains, shortness of breath and severe headaches. Barney Johnson had no choice but to return to harbour while there were still men fit enough to run the boat. Upon arrival they joined the *D4*, which had also been forced to a standstill by the same symptoms. The unexplained illness had been experienced by that ship's company in increasing severity over their last three patrols.

Between the two crews, a total of 56 officers and men were affected, of whom 30 were admitted to the Royal Naval Hospital at Chatham for diagnosis and treatment, 15 others required treatment in *Maidstone*'s sick bay, while the remaining 11 were able to continue with their duties. Many of the men recovered with little treatment other than rest and fresh air, but blood tests carried out at RNH Chatham showed all of the victims to be suffering from pernicious aenemia, a condition characterized by an alarmingly low red cell and hemoglobin count. In simple terms, they were suffering from a form of blood poisoning.

Two days after *D3*'s premature return a team of distinguished scientists under the leadership of Dr. J.S. Haldane, F.R.S., an expert in respiratory illnesses and pulmonary diseases as experienced in the mining industry, was called to investigate the problem, and it was these scientific gentlemen who provided the clues for determining the real source.

It was readily confirmed that the problem originated with the battery, as had already been deduced by the 8th Flotilla staff, but nobody had been able to pinpoint what it was in the battery that was poisoning the atmosphere. Once Haldane's investigations determined that arsenic was the cause of the illness, it did not take the experts long to come up with the cause.

The battery cells were of an old type, having plates made of antimonial lead, which contained arsenic. During charging the plates had begun to break down, releasing arsenic into the hydrogen gas normally produced during charging, to form arseniurretted hydrogen. Given the opportunity to ventilate properly after the charge was finished, there was little danger of serious atmospheric contamination. However, with the lengthy charges made necessary by having to remain dived for such prolonged daylight periods, there was seldom sufficient time in which to ventilate before the ending of the short night forced them to dive again. Once dived, no further ventilation could take place and the gases, which would continue to escape from the cells and the ventilation tubing for some time, became trapped in the battery tank, there to seep through the deck planks and into the boat itself to be breathed by the crew. No amount of cleaning and leak-stopping was going to prevent this from happening.

During the investigation Barney Johnson was asked to attend a fact-finding conference aboard the *Maidstone*. Because of his condition he found it very difficult to stay awake and had to be prodded into awareness by his fellow captain whenever the committee required his attention. The outcome of this investigation was the institution of rigid standards for the timely maintenance of submarine batteries and for periodic monitoring and analysis of the gases produced during charging, particularly in the older boats. Both *D3* and *D4* were ordered to Portsmouth for a battery refit and overhaul. On August 2 the two submarines reached "Pompey" dockyard, where work on lifting their batteries commenced.

Neither Barney Johnson nor Maitland-Dougall had escaped the effects of the toxic gases. Barney, who spent much of the time during battery charging up on the bridge, had been less exposed but because of his age was nevertheless badly affected, and the medical officer insisted he take a month's sick leave. He was advised that the best antidote for his condition was to get plenty of sunshine, eat lots of good food and to drink plenty or port wine, and he remarks, "I got saturated with all three during the month of August." His first lieutenant, whose station was below during charging operations, should have been more severely afflicted, but having a strong constitution and being 14 years younger was actually less affected in the first place and able to recover much more quickly.

Young William Maitland-Dougall wasted little time in beginning his convalescence and sought the best possible care for his condition. To recuperate he went to "Fryern," the home of his paternal great-aunt, where he arrived on August 4. There, under the care of the capable Mrs. King and her household, the young submariner mended swiftly.

Also staying at "Fryern" was his aunt Sissy from Scotland, who had returned to her childhood home to be with her mother following the death of her husband, who had passed away on June 3 at the age of 64. It is said that during his final delirium the old Commander had described a great naval battle in amazing detail at about the time Jutland was in progress. After his death it had been necessary to dispose of "Scotscraig," and the family, headed by Aunt Sissy and accompanied by Arnold and Clare, moved to Storrington. After three days of solicitous care William, or "Billie," as the ladies called him, was back on his feet and taking a keen interest in his surroundings and relatives. "Fryern" was soon to play host to another family visitor from Canada.

The war had been raging for two years and during that time it had become common practice for the many thousands of soldiers joining the Canadian Expeditionary Force to pause in Britain for a few weeks on their way to the Front. Lance-Corporal Hamish Kinnear Maitland-Dougall, William's younger brother, was one of these and his regiment had arrived at Camp Borden, near Witley in Surrey, early in July as part of the 102nd Battalion. Having discovered his brother's whereabouts, William paid a visit to the camp on August 7. The authorities were persuaded to give Hamish some leave and the following day both boys arrived back at "Fryern" to the delight of the family.

The brothers had not seen one another for almost 18 months and Hamish had never met his English relatives; there was a lot to talk about. This was a memorable occasion for the Kings, who asked the local chemist, Mr. Fordham, to come up from Storrington to take photographs of the two Canadian boys. Time was all too short,

D3 at Harwich, June-July 1916. – RN Submarine Museum

William and Hamish at Fryern, August, 1916. – Maitland-Dougall family collection

however, and Hamish had to take his departure on the 14th, as his unit was embarking for France. He was driven down to Portsmouth in one of the King automobiles, accompanied by Billy and a handful of well-wishing young relatives.

Two weeks later a healthy, well-rested first lieutenant returned to his submarine as it was preparing to leave the dockyard basin and cross the harbour to the submarine base at Fort Blockhouse. The move took place on a Thursday. That weekend *D3*'s captain returned. On Monday they embarked a new outfit of torpedoes and carried out engine and diving trials in Stokes Bay. The comforts of "Fryern" and other personal refuges had to be relegated to memories as the realities of war once again caught up with *D3* and her ship's company.

During their refits both *D3* and *D4* had been assigned to the 3rd Flotilla based on HMS *Vulcan* at Immingham in the Humber estuary. In the reorganization of the flotillas that had taken place that June, *Vulcan* had been allotted the six surviving D-class boats for employment on East Coast patrols and in training duties. The two submarines arrived at their new base on September 8 and two days later *D3* was inspected by *Vulcan*'s new Commander (S), Cdr. R.F. White, who complimented Johnson on the boat's fine appearance. His remarks, however, did not reflect the true condition of the submarine and Johnson, who was well aware of the shortcomings engendered by a month's idleness, lost no time in getting his boat and its crew back into shape.

Coastal patrols were usually short two- or three-day trips, sometimes spent moored to a buoy in Spurn Bay in the harbour approaches, at other times cruising offshore waiting for an enemy sighting or for orders to be passed over the wireless. Time was almost equally divided between patrolling, such as it was, and practising attacks on the exercise grounds with the flotilla destroyers or tied up alongside doing maintenance.

On their first practice emergency dive, that is a dive initiated by sounding the klaxon alarm without any prior warning or preparation, it took almost five minutes to get the boat down, when between one and two minutes was the standard. Needless to say, the crew of *D3* continued to be subjected to a seemingly endless series of drills and exercises. Having experienced an intensive work-up in *H8*, Cap' Johnson knew what he was about. By October 4 the same evolution was taking 2½ minutes; an improvement to be sure, but nothing to boast about. Johnson and his crew had their work cut out for them.

Early in November 1916 a pair of acting sub-lieutenants presented themselves to the commanding officer at HMS *Dolphin* to bring the Royal Navy's Canadian submarine contingent up to a total of six officers. W.J.R. "Roy" Beech and Rupert Wainman Wood seemed to be inseparable: both hailed from the West Coast, Beech from Salt Spring Island and Wood from nearby Cowichan, where he had been a schoolmate of Maitland-Dougall; they had joined the RCN at the same time, if not together; early in January 1912 they commenced their training at the Naval College in the same term, completed their course and were promoted to midshipmen aboard HMS *Berwick* in February 1915, both with first-class certificates.

They volunteered for submarines while still aboard *Berwick* and at the end of February journeyed west to join the CC-boats at Esquimalt, where they replaced Robert Lawson and Ronald Watson. Here the two new midshipmen commenced a seven-month training period, during which they requested overseas duty in submarines and were accepted. While at Halifax on their way to England in October the pair were examined and passed for proficiency in seamanship by Commander Nixon, commandant of the Naval College, after which they boarded the troop ship *Corsican* for a fast run to the UK. At *Dolphin* they made second-class passes in the course and were posted to their submarines as first lieutenants: Beech to *H9* at Yarmouth, which he joined in January 1917; Wood to

D4 at Immingham, where he also reported early in the new year. After five years in the navy together the two were now separated, each to make his own way.

During the autumn of 1916 Barney Johnson and Maitland-Dougall discovered there were a few consolations in having been sidelined to coastal patrols and training duties. One was the availability of some good golf courses, a game they were both fond of. Another was the plentiful duck hunting along the banks of the Humber. As a bonus, the two Canadians were able to renew their acquaintance with Adrian Keyes. Since leaving Esquimalt, Keyes had spent most of his time in the Aegean, where he commanded the destroyer HMS *Wolverine*, and had been awarded the D.S.O. for his daring during the Gallipoli landings. After the withdrawal of the Expeditionary Force from that unhappy place early in 1916 and the subsequent reduction of naval forces in the Dardenelles, Keyes returned to England. Here he was promoted to commander, given command of the destroyer HMS *Ness*, married a colonel's daughter, and took up residence not far from Immingham. Many an idle evening was spent at the Keyes' household or in the mess recalling the excitements of the early days at Esquimalt and sharing their subsequent adventures.

For *Vulcan*'s submarines not all patrols were short coastal trips. *D3* made two trips that qualified as overseas patrols during her sojourn at Immingham, both to Dogger Bank. The first of these was carried out at the beginning of December, when she slipped from *Vulcan* at 8 a.m. on the 8th and returned on the afternoon of the 12th. There was little in the way of excitement, but it was a good shake-down trip for the crew and proved they were up to 3rd Flotilla standards at least. During this patrol it is interesting to note that the submarine was spending up to 17 hours a day continuously dived and that Barney Johnson made frequent use of the echo-sounder for navigational purposes. After returning to Immingham they carried on with the usual short trips to Spurn Bay and the local exercise areas, kept their maintenance up to date and took some Christmas leave.

New and innovative ideas were often tried out by the submariners and one of these, which made an appearance in most navies from time to time during the war, was the kite aerial. Even when there was no breeze the movement of the boat at cruising speed on the diesels was sufficient to get a fair-sized box kite launched, and this would be used to carry a long aerial wire aloft so as to increase the operating range of the wireless sets. Any kind of a wind was enough to carry the kite off or to tear its fabric to shreds and send it into the sea, and they were seldom used successfully. *D3* tried out a new kite early in January, but the experiment failed when the tether line parted and the kite sailed off into the North Sea, never to be seen again.

Recognition from the air was another problem for which many solutions were tried. One of these was the "water jet." The idea was that a submarine, upon sighting a friendly aircraft, would release a column of water vertically into the air to identify itself as an Allied boat. To accomplish this a pipe with a nozzle on the end and controlled by a valve operated by the officer of the watch was fitted to the fridge. The pipe was led to one of the internal water tanks that could be pressurized quickly with compressed air in order to give the desired jet at short notice. Although a fine column of water could be produced, the idea was not a success, as it was difficult for the aircraft to see the water jet from above. The idea was not popular with the submariners either, for in their philosophy there was no such thing as a "friendly" aeroplane and they preferred to dive at the first sign of any aircraft. In any case, the blowing overboard of water from a tank was a waste of compressed air and only upset the diving trim.

Early in January there were some flotilla personnel changes which affected the two Canadians aboard *D3*. The arrival of Acting Sub-Lieutenant Rupert W. Wood, who was posted to *D4* as first lieutenant, was an exciting event for Maitland-Dougall. The two were old friends from schooldays at Quamichan Lake School, while Wood had graduated from the term behind his at the College. The two chums would find much to talk about in the days that followed.

Prior to *D3*'s next trip a new third officer, Lieutenant Andrew Barlow, RNR, joined to complete the officer complement. Since finishing her refit the boat had not been assigned a permanent third hand, Johnson and Maitland-Dougall frequently taking the boat to sea on their own. The bearded Andy Barlow fitted in well with the two Canadians and would remain with *D3* for some time to come.

By the end of the month Cap' Johnson's boat was ready for another trip to the Dogger Bank and this patrol was to be an augury for things to come. The Bank is no place to be in the middle of winter, especially when the weather is bad, which is much of the time. When *D3* arrived on station around sunrise on February 2 it was already blowing hard, but she dived for the day, surfaced after sunset to charge the battery, then went to the bottom in 20 fathoms for a quiet night's rest.

At five the next morning they surfaced into a moderate southwesterly gale accompanied by heavy snow squalls. They carried out the mandatory wireless listening watch and an hour later dived for the usual periscope and hydrophone daylight routine. Under the circumstances, there wasn't much chance of seeing and even less of hearing anything, and one wonders if Barney didn't just want to get below for a bit of peace.

While dived the coxswain issued "war comforts" to the messes to augment the "pusser" rations. On this occasion he gave out 8 tins of bully beef, 6 tins of sausages, 4 tins of bacon and 4 bottles of fruit preserves.

By late afternoon the seas were running at between 12 and 14 feet, while the wind had freshened, bringing intermittent snow squalls. At 5:30 p.m. Barney surfaced the boat and ordered a charge using both engines. Despite the best efforts of the chief ERA and his men, both diesels were completely flooded out through the exhaust system during efforts to get them started. This was an engineering disaster of the worst kind. Both engines would have to be purged of salt water, examined for damage, repaired and re-assembled before they could attempt to start them again. The chief ERA and his crew had their work cut out for them.

All the while the steep, white-crested seas smashed relentlessly onto the 600-ton submarine, so much so that without the need to supply air to the engines the tower was shut down to keep the seas from flooding into the boat. No one knew how long it would take to make repairs; piston heads were almost certainly cracked, connecting rods could be bent and cylinder liners split. The battery, which was already low, had to be made to last as long as possible, which meant slow revolutions, no cooking, minimum lighting and no electric heaters.

The interior of the submarine was soon a scene of utter misery — a heaving, cold, foul-smelling, sodden length of pipe packed with 20-odd half-frozen, hungry, frustrated humans. Those who manned the bridge, muffled to the ears in lammies and oilskins to keep out the elements, were almost happy to be clear of the chaos that reigned inside.

Ordinarily the diesels occupied a good quarter of the vessel, but when stripped down, large, heavy, greasy parts of the engines littered the interior compartment from bow to stern, the stink of diesel oil permeated everything, and the decks were soon covered in a thick, slippery sludge compounded of sea water, oil, grease and carbon. At least the engines hadn't had a chance to heat up. It was bad enough having to work on them in a gale when they were cool, but hot engines meant much slower progress and certain burns. Despite the cold and the wet the ERAs and stokers slaved like demons. By midnight the

D-class boats at sea, winter 1916-17.
– RN Submarine Museum

D-class engines with stern torpedo tube in centre.
– author's collection

port engine was running again, "bumping amps into the box" as hard as it could be made to go. The hands anxiously anticipated that moment when the battery was "up" and they would be able to dive out of the weather.

By 2 a.m. Barney had had enough and took the boat down to the bottom for what was left of the night. This respite from the effects of the weather gave the engine-room staff considerably better working conditions, but there would be no sleep for any of them until both engines were restored to full working order. All through the remainder of that night and into the next morning the engineer's tools clanked and clattered in tune with the ERA's and stokers' cursing as the recalcitrant engines were repaired.

By 10 a.m. *D3* was back on the job at periscope depth keeping her watch. The seas were falling, visibility had improved considerably, and with two good engines the patrol continued until they finally surfaced 48 hours later and set course for Flamborough Head. Some patrols were definitely better than others and that had been a bad one. It is interesting to note that despite their nearness to home port and the state of the weather there was never any thought of breaking off the patrol and heading for base. That was not Barney Johnson's way of doing things.

Upon arrival only a "make-and-mend," or afternoon off, was granted to the crew, and the customary three days patrol leave was not extended to the watch, whose turn it was to take it. Exciting things were happening all around the *Vulcan* and the boats had been ordered to hold themselves in readiness to go to sea at short notice. The most significant event, and that which heralded everything else that was about to happen to *Vulcan* and her charges, was the arrival of Captain M.E. Nasmith, VC, one of Britain's foremost submariners, who had relieved Commander White in command of the 3rd Flotilla during *D3*'s absence. The rumour soon reached the mess decks: they were headed overseas, the whole flotilla.

On February 1, 1917, Germany, despite the direst predictions of the government's critics and the opposition of many within the government itself, declared unrestricted U-boat warfare in the English Channel, North Sea, Western Approaches and the Mediterranean, and would later extend this to cover the American eastern seaboard as well. This declaration was predicated on the Naval Staff conclusion that a total U-boat blockade of Britain was feasible and that the war could be concluded in Germany's favour before the entry of the United States, which now seemed almost a foregone conclusion. The decimation of the mercantile fleets of Great Britain and her allies had been resumed in deadly earnest.

Since the beginning of the war submarines had enjoyed some success against U-boats, five having been sunk by RN submarines prior to January 1917, and the decision had been taken at the Admiralty to deploy one, and later two, flotillas on anti-U-boat patrols in the Western Approaches. These boats would be positioned on the routes used by U-boats making the passage to and from the Atlantic shipping arteries, as well as those attacking shipping along the west coast of Ireland and in the confined waters to the north and south of the island. The first flotilla to take up its station on this new assignment was *Vulcan*'s 3rd Flotilla, and their new base of operations was to be at Queenstown, under the overall command of Vice-Admiral Sir Lewis Bayly.

At the beginning of November 1916, in the distant Adriatic, Ronald Watson had been appointed to *H2* as first lieutenant. His captain was Lieutenant David Fell, who had continued in command of the boat since her commissioning at Montreal. In October the flotilla had moved to Venice, where *Adamant* had undergone a short refit. In November she departed for Brindisi, leaving the H-boats and the B-class submarines behind at a temporary depot in the naval dockyard where *H2* went into refit at the end of December.

Watson, it would appear by his commanding officer's remarks, was quick to acquire a knowledge of the Italian language, an asset that was to stand the young Canadian in good stead with his seniors and contemporaries alike. He remained with the boats at Venice until the beginning of March, when *H2*'s refit was completed, and was then posted to the famous *E11*, at that time under the command of Lieutenant Henry F.M. Peto.

This boat had gained an honourable place in the annals of the Royal Navy when she made several outstandingly successful patrols in the Sea of Marmara under the command of Martin Nasmith, in the course of which she had to fight her way through the heavily defended Dardenelles in both directions. It was Nasmith's exploits during the first of these patrols that had won *E11*'s captain the Victoria Cross. When Ronald Watson went aboard, *E11* was based at Malta and engaged in conducting patrols on the Mediterranean side of the Straits of Otranto.

On the morning of Sunday, February 11, 1917, *Vulcan*, trailed by the two flotilla destroyers, left the Humber and soon disappeared beneath a cloud of black coal smoke to the southward, intending to arrive at their new base at Queenstown, on the southeast coast of Ireland, well in advance of the slower submarines. The five submarines, *D3, D7, D8, E32* and *E54*, accompanied by the sloops *Mignonette* and *Gladiolus*, set sail in convoy to follow in *Vulcan*'s wake in easy stages. *D4* remained at Immingham, as she was due for a refit, and would stay behind until this had been completed.

After a rough passage around the southern tip of England and across the Celtic Sea, the submarines and their escort came to anchor opposite Queenstown in Cork harbour during the forenoon of Friday the 16th. The next morning the five submarines congregated alongside *Vulcan*. On arrival the captains went inboard to attend a pre-sailing conference, while the crews turned to, storing ship and preparing to go on patrol.

The five COs gathered about the great, round table in Captain (S)'s office, where they were greeted by Captain Nasmith's staff officers. The group was soon joined by the legendary submariner himself. Formalities were few; he already knew most of his captains and had been introduced to the others before leaving Immingham. Barney Johnson, never easily swayed by reputation alone, took an instant and respectful liking to his new "Gov'ner."

It was quickly apparent that the new Captain (S) took his assignment very seriously. He obviously knew what he was talking about, and it was equally obvious that he expected a very high standard of performance from his submarines. The briefing was thorough and professional. There wasn't going to be any "hanging about the buoy" with this fellow; they had a real job to perform and nobody was fooled into thinking it was going to be easy.

Late on Sunday afternoon all five submarines slipped from *Vulcan* and headed for sea with one of the decoy ships, the *Q13*, acting as command ship for the patrol. She was in fact HMS *Aubrietia*, a naval sloop rebuilt to resemble a small merchant ship and provided with concealed armament. *Q13* was commanded by Admiral John L. Marx, MVO, who had come out of retirement to accept a temporary commission as a captain, RNR.

Sailing as a flotilla, with *Q13* in the lead, the six ships, each steering its own zigzag course, set course southward around the southern tip of Ireland, bound for the Atlantic. After rounding Dursey Head and clearing the Blasket Islands, the flotilla headed north for its patrol area off Eagle Island, on the westernmost tip of Ireland, which they reached about noon on the Monday. At a signal from *Q13* the submarines struck out to the westward, where they took up their pre-assigned billets spaced 20 miles apart.

Once in position the five boats patrolled inside the limits of their individual

H2 *in the Adriatic. David*
Fell, captain, in centre,
Ronald Watson on his left.
– author's collection

A panoramic view of Queenstown Harbour taken from HMS Vulcan, *February 1917.* – RN Submarine Museum

rectangular areas. The command ship, meanwhile, behaved like an independent merchantman and steamed at a leisurely rate along a course that took her across the patrol lines, live bait in a trap of submerged adversaries.

The submarines were required to surface briefly early each morning, again around noon and during the late afternoon to receive wireless messages from the command ship, and they remained up throughout the night. During the hours of darkness the men on watch had to remain at full alert; there could be no more comfortable "all-nighters" spent on the bottom. The U-boats, too, could be expected to be on the surface, either hanging about in the approaches area or making their overnight passage outward or inward bound from the lucrative Atlantic trade routes. Special precautions had to be taken during darkness to prevent submarines in adjoining billets from accidently attacking one another.

This first patrol lasted five days, during which no surfaced U-boats were spotted and none rose to the bait. It took another day and a half to return to Queenstown, where *D3* made fast on *Vulcan* just before noon on February 27. They were given a week in which to get ready for the next trip, and during that time all defects had to be corrected, the lessons they'd learned analyzed and solutions to new problems found.

A D-class submarine receives torpedoes embarked from the depot ship.
– RN Submarine Museum

One pressing deficiency in the D-class boats was the inadequacy of the freshwater supply, and to overcome this the "water-round-torpedo" and the forward-most compensating tanks were refitted for use as additional freshwater tanks. Using the WRT tanks presented something of a problem when it came to flooding the torpedo tubes during an attack. Maintaining the trim was already enough of a problem and an alternate source of water had to be found so the tubes could be flooded up without upsetting the delicate trim at what was invariably a critical point in any attack.

With defects made good and the water supply problems sorted out, *D3* along with the rest of the flotilla was prepared to sail on the morning of Sunday, March 4. A new addition to the flotilla, the *H5*, still under the command of Cromwell Varley, was scheduled to join the other five submarines before they left Queenstown. The command ship for this patrol was the light cruiser HMS *Adventure*.

Torrential rains prevented the flotilla from sailing that morning and a "Sunday routine" was given to the ships' companies. The weather also delayed *H5* and she would be forced to join the rest of the group at the dispersal point.

Heavy rain, like fog, was a severe handicap to navigation in the days before radar, and under the circumstances it was better to wait out the weather than to leave harbour and attempt the dangerous passage around the southern tip of Ireland without sight of land. Poor visibility made life particularly dangerous for the submarines, as any Allied ship blundering onto one of them in the murk would at least call up the patrol ships and, if fitted with a gun, would probably open fire too. At worst the merchantman would try to run them down without challenging. This hostility toward all submarines was a fact of war that had to be taken into account by the submariners at all times.

By Monday the rain had cleared off and *Adventure*, with her five charges in line astern, cleared the harbour at 7:30 a.m., headed for a position off the west coast about 25 miles to the northwest of Slyne Head. The passing storm had left the seas rolling in huge swells, which caused some difficulties for the small submarines. Aboard *D3* the violent motion caused the gyro compass to wander so badly it was useless for navigation, while the force of plunging through the heavy seas at speed imparted a severe strain on the forward hydroplanes, which in this class were located underwater near the bows and permanently fixed outwards, causing damage that would not be apparent until later. Keeping station on the cruiser became impossible and the boats were ordered to proceed to their patrol billets independently, thus bypassing the rendezvous.

By evening, conditions had moderated sufficiently to carry out a trim dive. All that night speed was well maintained, and *D3* reached her billet and commenced patrolling at first light on the 7th. Johnson's billet, about 125 miles northwest of Eagle Island, was the furthest to seaward but one, and that one was occupied by *H5* when she succeeded in catching up during the first day. Once dived the problems with the foreplanes became apparent and the ERAs were faced with keeping them operating while Johnson patrolled as slowly as conditions would allow so as to ease the strain.

Storm-related damage forced *D7* and *D8* to take shelter. *D7* had electrical problems with a main motor which resulted in two electrical fires, while *D8* suffered a fractured main shaft. *D3* and *H5* were ordered to close up the gaps left by the two casualties.

Adventure, unlike *Q13* on the previous patrol, had to remain out of sight of the submarines, as no U-boat would show herself with a warship nearby, and the cruiser remained invisible in the shelter of a convenient bay. The submarines and their command ship maintained a pre-arranged schedule of wireless contact, the submarines surfacing as before for receiving routine messages but otherwise remaining dived during daylight and maintaining wireless silence except to report a U-boat sighting. Able to make 25 knots, the four-funnelled cruiser would not be far from any of the boats on station if her assistance was required, and during the 7th and 8th was able to give technical help to the incapacitated *D7* and *D8* while anchored in Broadhaven Bay awaiting developments.

Late on the afternoon of the 8th *E32*, commanded by Lieutenant E.E. Whitehouse, sighted a surfaced U-boat, dived, carried out an unsuccessful attack, then lost sight of the target because of the high seas and failing light. An hour after the first sighting *E32* again spotted her quarry heading north-northeast at full speed. *E32* surfaced and shaped a course to intercept the U-boat at daybreak, but dawn revealed nothing but an empty sea. Whitehouse took a chance and patrolled on the surface, hoping for a sighting, but gave up early in the afternoon and returned to his billet.

No further contacts were made with the enemy during the remainder of the patrol. At twilight on the 11th the four submarines left their stations and steered for a pre-arranged rendezvous with *Adventure* the next morning. The submarine crews were looking forward to a two-day break in Galway Bay.

The boats had been instructed to wait off Slyne Head, spaced along a north-south line, where *Adventure* would pick them up one at a time and then escort them as a flotilla into Galway Bay, once again care being taken not to expose the submarines to other shipping except when under escort. That Monday morning the seas were calm but visibility was poor due to a heavy mist which developed with the rising sun. *Adventure* successfully rounded up *E54*, *E32* and *D3* but could not locate *H5*. Leaving the three boats stopped in a group within sight of one another in the mist near the rendezvous, the cruiser steamed off to find the fourth boat.

Adventure had no sooner disappeared into the mist when the steamer *Tuskar* came across the three stopped submarines and immediately opened fire on *D3* and *E32* with her four-inch gun. As soon as the *Tuskar*'s intentions were appreciated, the submarines got under way on their motors, steering away from the merchant ship, but *Tuskar*'s gunners scored a hit on *E32*'s conning tower with their second round before the changing range threw them off aim. Fortunately no one was injured and the damage was superficial.

When *Adventure* heard the commotion she turned back to investigate. Raising *Tuskar* with the signal lamp, the cruiser's captain ordered a cease-fire. Once calm was restored he apprised the merchantman of the results of their impromptu gun-shoot and suggested ways in which to improve their aim. Despite unspoken hard feelings, no blame could be attached to *Tuskar*'s actions; for merchant seamen there was no such thing as a friendly submarine and the *Tuskar*'s crew had only acted out of self-preservation.

H5 was located shortly afterward and the flotilla formed line and steamed toward Galway. A few hours later they stopped while the cruiser's boats were sent to the assistance of a lifeboat, in which were found 17 survivors and one corpse, all belonging to the S.S. *Dunbarmoor*, which had been sunk by U-boat gunfire 180 miles to the west five days before. The flotilla finally anchored in Galway Bay during the middle of the afternoon.

D7 and *D8* were both unfit to continue the patrol and were sent back to Queenstown for repairs. With the help of *Adventure*'s engineers and the limited workshop facilities found ashore, the remaining four boats set to work making good their defects. By noon on Wednesday the 14th, *E54*, *E32*, *H5* and *D3* were patched up, cleaned up, stored and ready for sea.

The four submarines left Galway Bay together just before sunset and once clear of the harbour split up to make for their billets, spaced 20 miles apart along a line to the west of Slyne Head. *D3* had been allocated the station nearest the coast and by first light she was dived and on patrol. At 10:20 a.m., during the forenoon watch, a small sail was sighted to seaward and Cap' Johnson surfaced to investigate. It was a lifeboat from the *Q27* and contained 27 survivors, who were hauled aboard and hustled below. The decoy ship had formerly been the S.S. *Warner*, a small freighter of 1,273 tons, and she had been torpedoed by the *U-61* around sunset on March 13. At 2 p.m. a second boat was found from *Q27*. This one contained 21 survivors, who were also sent below.

D3 now had 72 souls on board, three times the number she was designed to accommodate, and conditions inside the boat were desperate. Johnson wirelessed his situation to *Adventure* and headed back to Galway Bay. Taking no chances, and wanting to be prepared for anything that might happen, he made a quick dive to adjust the trim so they could dive out of trouble if that became necessary. Just what their "passengers" thought of all this is not recorded, doubtless many would have preferred their chances in the open boats. *D3* pulled alongside the sloop *Q15* at 1:30 a.m. on the 13th, where she landed her unhappy cargo and remained working on engine and hydroplane defects until 5 p.m., at which time she headed seaward once again.

Johnson reported *D3* back on station at first light the following morning. A strong gale was blowing, the Sperry gyro was wandering because of the severe rolling, and the Forbes log had quit. For the next three days the foul weather persisted, the wind increasing on the third day to a full gale out of the north-northwest at force 8-10. *D3* remained on station, patrolling on the surface until sunset on the 20th, when she turned her bows southward and made a run for Galway Bay, which was reached just after midnight.

The oiler *Alchymist* arrived the next morning to refuel the submarines. *Adventure* and her four charges sailed for Queenstown that afternoon and the boats made fast on *Vulcan* around 8 a.m. on Thursday, March 3, eighteen days after leaving.

Aboard *D3*, the following two days were spent preparing for a three-week refit, to be carried out at Haulbowlines yard in Cork harbour. Both boat and crew were ready for the respite. The foul weather and hard running of the past month had been hard on the machinery, and the crew had not had a decent break since the end of January.

D3 picks up survivors from the sinking of the Q27 off the west coast of Ireland, March 15, 1917. – RN Submarine Museum

Clockwise: D4 *in dock.*
– RN Submarine Museum

Stern view of a D-class in dock.
– RN Submarine Museum

Ship's company of HMS/M D3, Ireland, circa March 1917. Sub-Lieutenant Maitland-Dougall, RCN, seated, with Coxswain W.C. Osborn on his right and Chief ERA R. Turbett on his left. – RN Submarine Museum, C.F. LeMesseurier collection

10 THE IRISH FLOTILLA

Sometime on March 30, 1917, the newly completed submarine depot ship, HMS *Platypus*, steamed out of the Firth of Clyde and into the North Channel heading north by northwest. Started two days before war was declared, the 2,460-ton vessel had been built by John Brown of Clydebank for the Royal Australian Navy, hence her uniquely "down under" name. With the loss of both of the RAN's new submarines early in the war, there was no longer any urgent need for the ship in the Pacific and by an arrangement with the Australian government *Platypus* was commissioned into the Royal Navy for the duration of the war with an RN crew under the command of Commander (S), Charles G. Brodie, RN.

Her course that day took the new ship to the northern tip of Ireland and well into the narrow waters of Lough Swilly, where she anchored off the town of Buncrana on the eastern shore of the ruggedly picturesque fiord. Here *Platypus* practised the drills and evolutions that all new ships must to become efficient and waited for her brood of submarines to arrive. The second submarine flotilla to be assigned to anti-U-boat operations in the Western Approaches was beginning to take shape and was to be known as *Platypus* Flotilla.

Two days earlier six submarines had sailed from Harwich also bound for Ireland. The group consisted of *D1, D4, D6, E23, E35* and *E56*. These boats took the southern route via a brief stopover at Plymouth, where *D1* was left behind with engine trouble, then around Land's End, across the Bristol Channel and the Celtic Sea, reaching Queenstown on April 2. As soon as the boats had made good their defects they were sent out on patrol with instructions to return to their assigned depot ships, the E-class boats to *Vulcan* at Queenstown, the D-class to *Platypus* at Buncrana. *D4*, however, was in need of extensive repairs and went into dock at Haulbowline, where she joined *D3*. The two Canadian West Coast school chums, William Maitland-Dougall and Rupert Wood, were given a fortnight in which to share their latest adventures and explore the delights of County Cork before *D3* was ready for sea again.

On April 6 America declared war on the Central Powers. In time this momentous event would change the pace of the war entirely and eventually a million American "doughboys" would be brought across the Atlantic to take the field on the Western Front against Germany and her allies. The vast army, however, had yet to be recruited, trained and equipped, and in the meantime there was little physical evidence of direct American participation in the war except at sea. There, the mass-produced "Woolworth" merchant ships had already made their welcome debut and a number of destroyers of the United States Navy had been hard at work for some months, ostensibly to ensure the safety of

American neutrals, but also to gain valuable experience before the "balloon went up" for the American Navy. Very shortly afterward the command of Queenstown Force was created under Vice-Admiral Sir Lewis Bayly to include both British and American escort forces operating on the transatlantic routes and in the Western Approaches.

Cap' Johnson, Billy Maitland-Dougall and Andy Barlow, with a full ship's company aboard, undocked their boat at 10:30 a.m. on Saturday, April 14, 1917. The tall, young RCN first lieutenant, however, was uncharacteristically subdued. Only five days before, on Easter Monday, four divisions of the Canadian Corps had moved to the attack along a four-mile front against heavily defended German positions on Vimy Ridge. This was one of the most successful assaults carried out by the Allies during the prolonged slogging match in France and was ultimately to prove a landmark event in Canada's efforts to assert her nationhood. Following 20 days of continuous bombardment, the strongly contested ridge was secured after a brief two days of fierce and determined fighting by the Canadian infantry. Heralded as the greatest "British" victory of the war up until that time, the cost of taking those few critical acres was low by the standards of the times, *only* 3,598 Canadians having been killed and nearly twice that number wounded. Included in that awful list was Corporal Hamish Kinnear Maitland-Dougall, who had celebrated his twentieth birthday but five days before. Severely wounded in the initial assault, he died of his wounds at the dressing station.

There were many among those serving in the flotilla who had already been brushed by the hand of death during the 32 months of the war. Some had lost a father, a brother, or other close relative, while many one-time shipmates would never set foot ashore again. William Maitland-Dougall had already experienced the loss of four of his friends and term-mates when the *Good Hope* had gone down in 1914. Having lived in the midst of violence and tragedy for 18 months the young officer had his own awareness of death in war. He also had the comradeship and understanding of his companions to support him and could share his grief and ease the pain of his loss to a degree. They were all in the war together, were taking the same chances that Hamish had accepted, and could comprehend what had happened and appreciate why.

For Hamish's mother and father back at Duncan, there would have been little comprehension or appreciation for the tragedy that had taken place. Despite their patriotism, the war in France was a terrible and alien thing. Their very worst and most secret of fears had come to pass, and even their other son was too far away to comfort, or to give comfort. When the customary black-edged telegram arrived, the grief-stricken parents turned to their relatives and friends for solace and, as they were to find, there was sympathy, understanding and support to be had from the community. British Columbia may have been a long way from the Western Front, but thousands of West Coast Canadians were in the Corps and Canada as a nation was learning fast about how to cope with the tragic cost of modern warfare.

For James this was a particularly trying time, as he had lost both his brothers the previous year — William, the eldest of the three, had died in Scotland in June, while Fred, with whom he and Winnifred had been particularly close, died at home in Duncan that October. For the Maitland-Dougalls, however, even the death of Hamish was to bring no relief from the anxiety they had endured since William had first gone overseas. It was not enough that they had lost their youngest son on a distant, blood-soaked battlefield in France, but their first-born was still at risk almost daily on a different, truly sinister battlefield.

There was plenty to be done in getting *D3* put back together and off to sea again, and with only six days in which to do it the entire crew was soon fully occupied preparing for their next patrol. This would take them to a billet on the northwest coast of Ireland and finish at Lough Swilly, where they would join *Platypus* Flotilla. Late on the afternoon of the 20th *D3* slipped from the trot alongside the old *Vulcan* for the last time and headed seaward.

Johnson commenced his patrol on the 21st at a position in the Atlantic near 57° N latitude, 11° W longitude, and slowly worked his way southwards across the approaches to the North Channel. They had sighted one distant U-boat periscope on the first day but were unable to make an attack. On the morning of the 23rd he was keeping a surfaced watch about 14 miles due west of Eagle Island, off the northwesterly tip of Ireland, when a barque under all plain sail was sighted steering south-southeast. Johnson dived his boat and followed the three-master, reasoning that the sailing ship was a prime target for any U-boats in the area and he might be able to catch one in the act of attacking the merchantman. Having first gone to sea in sailing ships, Barney must have appreciated both the beauty of the tall-masted ship and the irony of a British submarine using her as bait to trap a German U-boat.

The barque was the iron-hulled S.V. *Arethusa* commanded by Captain S.W. Burnley. Registered at Greenock, she was making for that port, having successfully crossed the Atlantic with a cargo taken aboard at Gulfport, Florida. She was fitted with a wireless set, but this was not continuously manned.

As expected the *Arethusa* did attract a German submarine, the minelayer *UC-66* captained by the U-boat ace Kapitän-Leutnant Herbert Pustkutchen. It was Pustkutchen who, while in command of the *U-29*, had torpedoed the French cross-Channel packet *Sussex* 12 months before. The steamer had survived her ordeal but several American citizens were numbered amongst the 50 men, women and children killed in the blast. The diplomatic reactions from an outraged United States government caused the Germans to halt the unrestricted U-boat offensive then in progress.

Carrying a load of 18 mines, *UC-66* had set out from Zeebrugge eight days before on the first-ever mine-laying cruise to Belfast Lough, where a small field was laid which claimed one minesweeper and shut down the port. *UC-66* laid a final clutch of her deadly "eggs" off the Mull of Kintyre, causing the closure of the Firth of Clyde. In a gunnery duel off Tory Island she had engaged, and almost sank, the decoy ship *Q4*, only to be chased off by two patrol vessels. Rounding the northern tip of Ireland, Pustkutchen set out to circumnavigate the island before heading home. It was while steaming southward along the Atlantic coast that he too sighted the *Arethusa*.

For reasons known only to the German submariner, he decided to board the sailing ship rather than torpedo her without warning or destroy her by gunfire. Perhaps, as the weather was calm and the ship unarmed, he wanted to give his crew some exercise, a chance to do a little looting and avoid wasting an expensive torpedo, of which he only had three, or expending ammunition that might be needed later.

Making a dived approach so as to effect surprise, Pustkutchen surfaced a few hundred yards ahead of his victim, fired two shots across her bow, ordered the captain to heave to, then went alongside, boarder her, ordered the crew into their boats and set about planting scuttling charges in the barque's pump wells. The whole operation was accomplished swiftly and professionally. The shadowing British submarine had no inkling of these events except that the two warning shots from the Germans' 8.8 cm gun had carried clearly through the water and were picked up by *D3*'s hydrophone operator.

Johnson could see nothing of note through the periscope except that the barque had heaved to and come to a stop. This he could tell by the set of her yards, but at three miles it's doubtful he could have made out the ship's side clearly even with the high-power periscopes then in use. Sensing something amiss he decided to investigate but chose to make a cautious approach lest he startle the barque or alert an unseen enemy. By this time the sea was flat calm with only a soft swell to hide the stealthy attacker. To be on the safe side Johnson called his crew to action stations as he turned his boat toward the barque.

It took nearly an hour to close the stopped ship and *D3* was still 1,500 yards off her stern when Johnson saw the *UC-66* in silhouette alongside the black-hulled vessel. To avoid the risk of torpedoing the *Arethusa*, Johnson had to wait until the German submarine was clear of its victim before he could attack. Staying deep and using the periscope as little as possible he started to close the U-boat, hoping to get within 500 yards before firing, but when the submarine began to pull away he was forced to shoot at 1,200 yards, a long shot in those days. He fired both bow torpedoes in rapid succession.

At about the correct time for the first weapon to strike, an explosion was heard which was taken as confirmation of a hit. Unfortunately *D3*'s bow planesman misheard the order to come shallow to 18 feet, an action that would have given her captain a good view of the results of his shooting. Instead, he set his planes hard to dive and headed the boat for 80 feet, the depth that had registered in his mind, otherwise Johnson would have seen that it was the charges aboard the barque going off and not a torpedo hit that had made the explosion. *UC-66* had safely avoided both torpedoes and rounded the doomed sailing ship's bows before *D3* regained depth and turned to round the stern of the barque.

Johnson, having passed astern of the sinking ship and assuming he'd sunk the first U-boat, thought he was encountering a second when he sighted the oncoming German submarine. He ordered the helm hard over and began turning on his screws in an attempt to bring the stern torpedo tube to bear, but while doing so the U-boat dived. To avoid becoming a target for the Germans' torpedoes, *D3* went deep, where she circled for over an hour trying to pick up the enemy submarine on her hydrophones, but without success.

Surfacing at 5 p.m. Johnson sighted the *UC-66* on the horizon far to the south, almost hidden under a cloud of its own diesel exhaust, too far off for him to make another attack before dark. While reloading the torpedo tubes and transmitting details of the encounter to *Platypus*, Barney searched the area of the attack for evidence of their kill but found only some nondescript wreckage and a patch of oil. There was no sign of the barque or her company. The following day *D3* put into Lough Swilly and made fast alongside *Platypus*, where Johnson entered his claim for possibly sinking a U-boat. Ultimately this was disallowed when examination of the records proved there was only one U-boat in his area at the time of the incident. Dismayed at his failure to protect the barque, he was relieved to find that Captain Burnley and his crew had made it safely to shore in their boats.

The *UC-66* continued her voyage back to Zeebrugge, where she arrived ten days later, having sunk two more small ships on the way. That was Pustkutchen's last successful patrol, for shortly after the commencement of her next trip *UC-66* was sunk with all hands off The Lizard by the armed trawler *Sea King*, commanded by Commander Godfrey Herbert, DSO, a submariner turned U-boat hunter.

D3's next patrol took her to an area about 120 miles due west of Malin Head. Dawn comes early during May in the northern latitudes and Johnson submerged his boat at 1:30 a.m. on the morning of the 8th in order to be dived and settled by first light. The wind was blowing out of the northwest at about force six, the seas were choppy and visibility generally poor. Having satisfied himself that there was nothing in sight and little to be gained in remaining dived, *D3*'s captain brought his boat to the surface at 7 a.m. Fifteen minutes later the lookout sighted a surfaced submarine three miles off to the west-southwest and heading east. The target was well within his patrol boundaries and Johnson dived to attack.

A UC-boat of the same type as UC-66. – author's collection

D3 *off Rathmullen in Lough Swilly circa April-May 1917.* – RN Submarine Museum

HMS/M D3 *alongside HMS* Platypus *during the summer of 1917.* – RN Submarine Museum

A very lucky E48 *coming alongside an equally fortunate* D3. – author's collecton

The choppy seas and poor visibility made the approach difficult. Johnson had to expose the periscope in order to see his target, but he was determined to succeed this time. By 7:40 *D3* was making full speed, "grouper switch up," boring in on the target's starboard beam at nine knots. The coxswain and his companion on the bow planes had a nerve-wracking time trying to keep the boat on depth at that speed, but they managed and the whole attack went like clockwork. At 7:42 the lower bow tube was fired and 15 seconds later the upper torpedo was sent on its way. As luck would have it the first torpedo, which was headed directly for the target's beam, suffered from a defective depth-keeping mechanism and within a hundred yards of beginning its run began skipping along the surface, alerting the U-boat to its danger and causing her to dive. The second torpedo made a good run but passed just ahead of the enemy as he dipped below the surface. With the failure of the attack Barney had no choice but to go deep and avoid becoming a target himself. The crew was bitterly disappointed by the failure, particularly the torpedomen, who had completed weekly maintenance routines on the torpedoes that very morning.

By noon they had surfaced and reloaded. The rest of the patrol passed without incident except for running out of fresh water the night before returning to harbour. Whether the entire supply was consumed or some of the temporary tanks had been contaminated by salt water is not known. Early on the morning of the 13th Johnson secured his boat alongside *Platypus*, which was now anchored off Killybegs in one of the short loughs that stretched inland from the north shore of Donegal Bay.

" 'Tis an ill wind that blows no good," so the saying goes, and this was indeed the case for HM Submarine *E48*, for it was a British boat that Johnson had attacked and fortunately missed. Her captain, Lieutenant F.H. Taylor, DSC, RN, sighted Barney's periscope at 7:40 a.m., two minutes before the first fish was fired, and had been able to swing his bows towards his attacker enough that the torpedoes passed astern and ahead, the former by a mere 10 yards, the latter by 20 yards. Taylor dived his boat at 7:45, confirming Johnson's observations exactly. It had been a close call.

E48 was one of *Vulcan*'s boats, and she and *D3* had unwittingly been assigned overlapping patrol areas by their respective flotilla commanders. Whether the two captains were ever told the truth of their near tragic encounter is not recorded. When the two patrol reports were compared at Queenstown Command, the dangerous arrangement of patrol billets became painfully apparent and the manner in which these areas were divided up and assigned was changed to prevent such an occurrence from happening again.

At the end of April the hitherto controversial system of merchant ship convoy was officially adopted by the Admiralty for all shipping in the Atlantic. It would be several months before transatlantic traffic was fully organized and sufficient escort vessels could be found and assigned to convoy duties, but the effect of convoying was immediate, merchant ship losses declined dramatically almost from the beginning. Coincidentally it was at this time that the U-boats became most numerous and, in July, their loss rate the heaviest yet when sinkings nearly exceeded production for the first time ever. Fortunately for the Allies the combination of convoys, the provision of air cover (including tethered observation balloons within the convoys themselves), aggressive anti-submarine tactics and a plentiful supply of heavier, more effective depth charges denied the U-boats the full extent of their spoils.

For *D3* two more patrols followed in June. U-boat sightings became more numerous as the numbers of German submarines increased and, frustrated by the convoys, were forced to expose themselves more than was prudent. The U-boats, however, were very difficult targets and more often than not managed to dive before an attack could be completed. In the periods between patrols submarine-versus-submarine tactics, where a dived submarine attacked one on the surface, were frequently practised, including the actual firing of torpedoes to enhance the realism of the exercise. For these exercises the torpedoes were fitted with cork-filled collision heads and, as a further precaution, were set to run under the target, for even with a "soft nose" a 1,500-pound torpedo travelling at between 30 and 40 knots could prove destructive to a thin-skinned submarine. Early in June *D4* arrived from her refit at Haulbowline and toward the end of the month Nasmith's flotilla came north and worked from *Platypus* at Killybegs for a few weeks while *Vulcan* underwent repairs at Belfast. At the end of June *D3* made an 11-day patrol, during which another slippery U-boat was pursued until it disappeared into the night.

Early in April Rupert Wood added to his experiences off Ireland when *D4*, commanded by Lieutenant Eric Tufnell, attacked a U-boat around noon on the 5th. They had chased one elusive German for almost an hour on their previous patrol but never got close enough to get off a torpedo before it dived and slipped away. As on the previous occasion, *D4* spotted the surfaced German submarine while they were dived, an ideal set-up except that the enemy was zigzagging. Tufnell got into range, fired one torpedo, which missed, and prepared to fire his second. In the meantime the U-boat, which had not seen the first torpedo, made a large alteration of course causing *D4* to turn sharply and speed up to keep a favourable firing position. *D4's* planesmen were faced with the problem of keeping their boat down while making a sharp turn. As had been proven many times, the more rudder one applied the more the submarine wanted to surface as with the increasing angle so that the rudder acted like an upward-angled hydroplane surface. This time they didn't succeed, *D4* broached, the U-boat spotted her, dived and escaped.

During the summer of 1917 the US Navy sent a group of senior officers to Ireland, where they visited Queenstown Command and the various sub-commands to make preparations for receiving the large numbers of American ships and submarines that would begin arriving at the end of July. Barney Johnson was asked to take one of these officers, a Commander Boyd, USN, to sea for a four-day trip to give him some experience of what an anti-submarine patrol was like. In Johnson's own words, Commander Brodie instructed him to "bring him back alive, or else." The American was not a submariner, but he was game and, as the crew no doubt suspected, was going to be well entertained.

D3 sailed from Killybegs late on the afternoon of April 19. After carrying out a practice attack and firing a torpedo fitted with a collision head at *D1*, Cap' Johnson headed for his billet a few miles east of Rockall, about 24 hours steaming distance away to the north. At 3:45 the next morning they sighted their first U-boat and dived to attack, but the Germans had spotted *D3* and slipped beneath the sea before Barney could close her. A short time later *D3* surfaced and they continued on their passage. Around 9 a.m. a lone sloop was sighted which immediately opened fire and turned towards *D3* with obvious malicious intent. Johnson dived to get clear of their ill-intentioned and dangerous ally. Commander Boyd was certainly getting an active introduction to conditions in the Approaches.

Having avoided the sloop, Johnson resumed surfaced running and had their guest join him and the lookout on the bridge. The weather was worsening. The wind, blowing out of the southwest at about force five, was accompanied by frequent heavy rain squalls. During their conversation Johnson ascertained that their visitor had never made a "crash dive" and took the precaution of instructing him in the necessary drill, just in case. It was as well he did, for about an hour later the rain suddenly lifted to reveal a large, well-armed Allied convoy ahead.

Barney instinctively hit the klaxon alarm button. The lookout slipped down the tower with well-practised ease, followed with all the speed he could muster by the inexperienced American, on top of whom came Barney Johnson, sea-boots first and pulling the upper lid shut for all he was worth. Despite his best efforts the Commander was not quick enough and their flight down the tower was hastened by several gallons of cold, wet Atlantic. To complete his discomfort their American passenger had lost a brand-new "brass hat" over the side in his scramble for the tower. After that Barney kept his guest safely down below, *D3* dived much too quickly to clear three men off the bridge at once.

While on the surface just before noon-hour the following day, another U-boat was sighted, also on the surface. Johnson dived and went to action stations. An hour later he was manoeuvring to fire when the U-boat dived and disappeared. Barney observed in his log that "there was plenty of shipping about," something the Germans were undoubtedly well aware of. That night *D3* made the return trip to Ireland and arrived alongside *Platypus* early on the morning of the 23rd, in time to put Commander Boyd aboard the depot ship for a decent breakfast. That afternoon *D3* headed back to the same area to continue her interrupted patrol. Any observations the American officer may have offered are no longer on record, but he was certainly much the wiser for his experiences.

After the completion of the next patrol, during which two U-boats were sighted and pursued without result, *D3* returned to Killybegs and went alongside *Platypus* as usual. All of the following day was spent landing torpedoes, ammunition and stores in preparation for taking the boat into a much-needed refit at Belfast. On August 1, *D3* slipped from her parent ship and joined the sloop that would act as her escort for the trip to Belfast, and together they headed for the North Channel. *D3* reached her destination early the following morning. On arrival the boat went into the graving dock and would remain in dockyard hands until the last week in October.

While the submarine was in refit Maitland-Dougall left *D3* for a command of his own. On September 6 he was appointed to HMS/M *D1* as "lieutenant in command." With over two years of almost continuous sea time, most of it in a war zone, he had gained plenty of experience and had consistently received favourable assessments. As a result he had been highly recommended by both his flotilla commander and by Barney Johnson, his captain for the previous 15 months and long-time mentor in the submarine service.

This was the pinnacle of achievement for the young officer, the goal he had been striving for since first setting foot aboard *CC1* at Esquimalt. Although that had been just over three years ago, it seemed to him like a lifetime had passed. But he had made it. The new submarine CO was 22½ years of age.

In order for him to have been considered for command the young aspirant would have had to prove his abilities in submarine handling, seamanship and, most of all, in the attack. Whenever there was an opportunity he would have been required to make dummy attacks on every type of ship he could find, under every kind of circumstance imaginable, knowing that his performance would be carefully scrutinized by his captain at the time and by the staff inboard afterward. He would have spent many hours of his otherwise unoccupied time (a first lieutenant who was doing his job properly never had any "spare time") "swatting up" on the theory and mathematics needed to resolve the attacking equation, and in committing it all to memory. In those days there were no mechanical or electronic calculators with which to solve the complex computations. Some home-made slide rules had been devised to help with solving recurring equations, but the primary attacking instrument was still the captain's own brain and his interpretation of what he saw through the periscope. Many long hours would have been spent rehearsing attack drills with the other lieutenants, all as eager as he had been to make the grade. For the junior officers it was an ongoing game. For young Billy the game had ended, from that time on it was to be the real thing.

Although the new captain may not have realized it, he had become the first RCN officer to ever command a British warship of any kind, a unique distinction and one that was to pass unrecognized in his own Service. The RCN appears to have thought little of Maitland-Dougall's achievement; in Ottawa's books he was still a lowly acting lieutenant. The Royal Navy, although listing him correctly in the Nominal Lists, at least accorded him the pay status of full lieutenancy, giving him the extra shilling a day to which this entitled him. For the young officer his promotion to command also meant receiving three shillings and nine pence a day command pay ($1 a day Canadian). Not much of a bonus when he was already receiving six shillings ($1.50) a day in submarine pay. Still, every penny counted and having the notation of "in command" after his name was worth more to him than any amount of money.

When he took over *D1* the boat was in the process of being transferred from *Platypus* Flotilla to the 4th Flotilla attached to HMS *Thames*, which had only recently moved from Sheerness to Portsmouth. At the time *D1* joined, *Thames* was in the process of becoming the Submarine Service's commanding officers' training establishment and would become known as "The Periscope School." Maitland-Dougall's boat was assigned to "Special Experimental Duties" at *Thames*, but what these may have been is not revealed. Presumably they had something to do with establishing the Periscope School. The new Canadian CO brought his command alongside the familiar jetty in Haslar Creek on September 12.

When Maitland-Dougall left *D3* his place in the boat was taken by a young Irishman, Sub-Lieutenant Esme J.R. Wingfield-Stratford, a distant relative of the Viscounts Powerscourt. What Barney thought of this development is not recorded, but he was already aware that changes were in the wind for him and the rest of the Irish Flotilla.

Although things may have been going well for Maitland-Dougall, his one-time RNCC classmate Fredrick Lawson was having a hard job coping with his position as first lieutenant in *H10*. For him the winter of 1916-17 had proved to be something of a personal nightmare. Whether he was previously aware of it or not, it was soon discovered that he suffered from chronic seasickness. His condition led to a less than average performance, which resulted in a series of adverse assessments. When he fell ill with a mildly debilitating infection in the spring of 1917 and was invalided ashore, causing him to be absent from two patrols in the space of a month, 22-year-old Fredrick Lawson was recommended for release from the Submarine Service. He had stuck it out gamely for 14 months, but his wretched seasickness and other illnesses, coupled with the long periods at sea, the incessant demands of his duties as first lieutenant and the stringent assessment methods, had all served to defeat his resolve to remain in submarines. In the middle of August he was posted to the old cruiser HMS *King Alfred*, which was employed on transatlantic escort duties.

The other Canadian in *Platypus* Flotilla, Rupert Wood, was given a bit of a break when *D4* was sent to Fairfield's near Glasgow for repairs. It was taking a lot of work to keep the D-class boats at sea under the demanding conditions found in the Western Approaches, but until the newer submarines reached a fully operational state and relieved them, the older boats were going to have to bear the brunt of the North Atlantic patrols. It would be the end of September before she returned to the Irish Flotilla.

The spring of 1917 had seen the arrival of a familiar Canadian submariner when Jock Edwards reached *Dolphin* to begin his RN submarine training. Edwards by this time was not only an experienced submariner but also a well-qualified, seasoned naval officer. In order to compete for promotion to lieutenant he had spent six months aboard the *Rainbow* keeping bridge watches and studying for his examinations. While he was aboard the Canadian cruiser she was employed on patrol duties off the Central American coast. On his return to Esquimalt and the CC-boats he was made first lieutenant aboard *CC2*, and in April 1917 he requested to be allowed to serve in submarines overseas. His request was granted and later the same month he made the trip to England and HMS *Dolphin*. On completion of his course, in which he achieved a first-class pass, he was appointed to HMS *Alecto*, where he joined his shipmates from earlier Esquimalt days, Roy Beech, who was still in *H9*, and Fredrick Lawson, who was about to leave *H10*. Edwards would have to wait a few months before being given a permanent billet aboard one of the flotilla boats, and it was not until mid-October that he was appointed to *E55* as first lieutenant.

For Ronald Watson, meantime, service in the Mediterranean Theatre was proving to be something of a struggle within a struggle. It seemed at times that the bickering among the Allies, particularly between the French and Italians, who were uneasy comrades at the best of times, was almost as intense as the conflict between the Allies and the Austrians. Nevertheless, the stresses engendered by ally and enemy alike had to be endured while they all soldiered on in what, to the English at least, seemed a badly run, long, fruitless, and forgotten campaign.

There was some relief to be had in the mild climate and scenic delights, and Watson probably enjoyed his time ashore in Venice while *H2* underwent her refit. Sometime after February, while at Malta aboard *E11*, he met his future wife, Aimee Esther Fleury, an attractive Irish girl who was an officer ambulance driver in the Women's Auxiliary Corps. There were many dilettantes among the female units, but despite her attractiveness, Aimee Esther was not one of them. Watson's young lady already had a reputation for cool-headed courage, which she'd earned the hard way while driving her ambulance inside the range of enemy guns at the Italian front. Aimee was the sister of a British naval officer, Richard Fleury who was on Rear Admiral Ballard's staff in Malta.

In the Adriatic the weather had been cold that winter. The submariners were unable to get much help from the Naval Supply system in the way of warm clothing while replacement kit of any kind continued to be scarce. It had been a long, demoralizing winter for many.

The welcome return of warmer weather in the spring, however, brought with it the advent of the dreaded calms which left even dived submarines seemingly naked and exposed in the still, transparent, shallow waters along the Dalmation coast. The Austrians employed large numbers of aircraft on maritime patrol duties, and the Allied submariners were the first to admit that these were often skilfully and effectively handled. Enemy patrol craft, too, were plentiful, while the minefields laid by both sides multiplied monthly. Inshore reconnaissance work was notoriously hazardous.

That this was so had been tragically demonstrated the year before when HMS/M *H3*, Lieutenant G.E. Jenkinson, RN, attempted to penetrate the entrance to the Austrian anchorage in the Gulf of Cattaro during July 1916. Little is known of *H3*'s fate except that she struck a mine while dived in the harbour approaches. The boat had been spotted on the surface early that morning off Puerta d' Ostro and at about 1:30 p.m. an explosion was observed in the minefields covering the approaches to the narrow harbour entrance. All that was found was a large pool of diesel oil and some bits of wood, one piece of which had an English trade name on it. Such was the end of *H3*.

The standard of human comforts, recreation and entertainment had deteriorated quickly after the closure of the Gallipoli campaign and by mid-1917 had reached something of a low, a serious factor so far as maintaining morale was concerned. During the Great War there was no deliberate rotation of ships or personnel, and for officers and men alike, once in the Mediterranean Theatre, which included the Adriatic and Aegean, they were quite likely to remain there for the duration. Unless their ship was required elsewhere or they were lucky enough to be sent home on a course or were drafted to a ship on duty in home waters, the men could — and thousands of sailors actually did — spend years away from the United Kingdom.

The provision of cinematic equipment on the big ships helped ease the boredom and the picture shows ashore boasted a brisk business, while travelling entertainment groups began to make an appearance as well. Unfortunately there was no socially acceptable way to relieve the enforced celibacy of the sailors and this gave rise to a large prostitute population in the naval ports, with all its attendant problems. In the days before antibiotics, even a minor case of venereal disease could be devastating and some of the so-called cures were as painful as the effects of the disease itself and often completely ineffective.

Mail destined for the Mediterranean naval forces was held up for months, usually in a warehouse in Britain or deep in the hold of some steamer making the rounds of half the ports in the world. Relatives soon learned to send their men preserves and other long-lasting gifts to ensure they were still edible when they reached them. Traditional British rations were constantly in short supply. Local foodstuffs were available, though often poor in quality and unsatisfying to the "meat and potatoes" British sailors. The granting of long leave was the exception, though local leave was given and many of the more enterprising hands "went native."

The British submariners, outwardly at least, appeared to thrive on adversity and they took it all in their stride. The invaluable and very necessary task of keeping the Austrian and Turkish fleets contained and under observation was doggedly continued.

During that summer, far away in the Pacific off the North American seaboard, a drama of courageous endurance was beginning to unfold. With the entry of the United States into the war and the safety of British possessions in the Pacific assured, Whitehall, with the agreement of the Canadian government, decided to transfer *CC1* and *CC2* to the Mediterranean. The voyage of over 11,000 miles was to be made in stages and the *Shearwater* was to accompany the submarines throughout. With mixed emotions and hopes running high, the little flotilla sailed from Esquimalt without fanfare on the morning of June 21, 1917.

HMCS *Shearwater* and the flotilla were commanded by Lieutenant-Commander Bertram E. Jones, who had continued in this capacity since taking over from Adrian Keyes. *CC1* was commanded by Lieutenant Francis B. Hanson, RN, and *CC2* by Lieutenant Geoffrey Lake, RNCVR. The first lieutenants and third hands of the two boats were all RNCVR officers, while their crews, though mostly regular RCN, still contained a fair sprinkling of the original reservists. On this occasion *CC1* boasted a chief yeoman of signals, certainly the most senior signalman ever carried in a Canadian submarine.

All went well for the first two days and the flotilla, making good between 10 and 11 knots, covered a respectable 250 miles a day. On the third day the weather broke and the two submarines were forced to run in the shut-down condition, using only the bridge ventilator pipe to supply air to the engines.

With the severe pitching being experienced in the high seas, the propellers were frequently exposed, causing the engines to over-speed. Lacking any type of effective governor control, this would have caused severe damage if allowed to continue and the engineers had to devise a way to prevent it from happening. The normally accepted method was to load the generators and charge the batteries while continuing to propel. This procedure was known as a "running charge." To accomplish this the batteries had to be depleted, so the engines were stopped and the boats were propelled on their electric motors until the batteries were low. The engines were then started and a running charge was put on. A sequence of 20 minutes on the battery and 10 minutes on the engines was soon established. The conditions inside the boats quickly became intolerable, particularly while running on the battery when there was no forced ventilation. Temperatures of up to 140° F. were recorded in the engine rooms. The start-and-stop running of the engines began to cause problems with the ever-cranky machinery and, what was worse, with the batteries.

Stressed and overheated by the constant charging and discharging cycle, the lack of ventilation and a high ambient temperature, the cells in *CC2*'s battery began to break down. This resulted in short-circuiting, which ultimately caused the defective cells to catch fire. The only way to stop this was to open up the battery tanks and disconnect the damaged cells, much the same situation as was faced by Barney Johnson in *H8* in January 1916. Unable to open the hatches to get rid of the smoke and gases that escaped when the battery boards were lifted, the crew had a bad time of it, many being mildly gassed.

Problems aside, the *Shearwater* and her charges made port at Seattle in time for the Fourth of July celebrations and the Americans accorded the "British" submariners, as their newspapers proclaimed them, the position of honour at the head of the Independence Day parade. Two exhausting days later, worn out more from American hospitality than from overwork, the sailors reluctantly headed back out to sea to resume their voyage. Their destination was Balboa, at the Pacific entrance to the Panama Canal.

The weather was generally better so far as the sea was concerned, but as they worked their way south it became hotter, resulting in further stress on machinery and men alike. The engines, never known for their mechanical endurance, broke down with monotonous regularity. Aboard *CC1* it was seldom that both diesels were running at the same time and *Shearwater* was occasionally called upon to tow one or the other of the boats when things got beyond the capabilities of the overworked engineers.

CC2's engines behaved much better than her sister's, but her battery again caught fire during a storm off Salina Cruz, Mexico. On this occasion most of the crew became too sick to stand their watches and some of the men passed out altogether from the combined effects of the heat and gassing. During the night only the coxswain and a few others less ill than their companions remained at their stations. The only sustenance they could find was some bread and tins of sardines. That was the lowest point of the entire voyage. At times they thought of packing the whole thing in, but they persevered and the situation seemed less bleak in the light of another day. Stopping only when necessary and for as short a time as was needed, the intrepid trio made Balboa near the end of July. The submariners were well received by the authorities and it was agreed they would stay to rest up and make repairs before continuing on into the Atlantic.

On August 12, after 12 days alongside at Balboa, *Shearwater* and her two charges commenced the 51-mile trip through the famous Panama Canal. They were the first ships flying the white ensign to make the passage, and the British Minister to Panama and the Vice-Consul at Colon were embarked to mark the occasion.

At Colon, the Atlantic terminus of the canal, the *CC1* and *CC2* joined in exercises with some USN submarines before commencing the long eastern leg of their journey. During the exercise *CC2* made an uncontrolled dive for the bottom. Her sudden descent was reversed at the last moment only by the quick actions of her crew. Significantly, though it was only a Thursday, it was the 13th of August.

The Atlantic provided no better weather than had the Pacific, and a continuous battle against nature and mechanical failure was waged by the crews all the way to Halifax,

CC1 and CC2 passing through the Panama Canal in August 1917.

– Maritime Museum of BC

where they arrived on October 14 after an odyssey of 7,300 miles. Bertram Jones immediately signalled their willingness to continue and the Admiralty reaffirmed its need of the boats for employment in the Mediterranean Theatre. The staff of the Chief Engineer at Halifax, however, would have none of it — the boats, and particularly the engines, were in no fit state to go anywhere. The Admiralty was informed, the orders were rescinded, and the Canadian authorities made the decision to repair the two submarines and keep them at Halifax.

In relegating the submarines to what amounted to a harbour defence role, the RCN did not neglect to single out the extraordinary effort the engineering department had put into getting them that far. The tireless work of the flotilla engineer, Artificer Engineer Arthur J.S. Hunting, was particularly mentioned. As well as carrying out the duties of flotilla engineer he was also required to take over as chief ERA of *CC1* when the original chief had to be relieved part way through the journey. In recognition of his outstanding services he was promoted to chief artificer engineer before the month was out. Bertram Jones too was to have his reward and he was promoted to commander on November 1.

In time, accommodations would be found for the submariners in the dockyard and the *Shearwater* would be re-armed for patrol work. She would, however, retain the original officers and crew that had brought her east, at least as much as was possible with the normal changes that occurred among a ship's company.

The CC-boats on arrival at Halifax, October 14, 1917. Personnel on the bridge are, from left to right across the front: Art. Eng. A.J.S. Hunting, Lt. F.B. Hanson, Lt. A.C. Pitts, Gnr. (T) G. Briscoe, Lt. G. Lake. Standing behind Hunting is Ch. Yeo. H. Reading. The LH man in the far crew (CC1) is Sig. Astwood. The man on the right with the peaked cap is Cox'n Addison. The LH man in the near (CC2) crew is Stkr. Lee. The fellow with the mustache is LS Stapely.

– Maritime Command Museum

HMS Platypus' *Irish flotilla, Killybegs, July 1917. Submarines, inboard to outboard: unidentified D-class, E54, H8, H5, D3 and E35. This photo is of particular interest, as it has captured three of Barney Johnson's commands at one location, namely H8, D3 and E54. At the time the photo was taken, Johnson was in command of D3. E54 was a visitor to* Platypus. *She properly belonged to* Vulcan's *flotilla, which was also at Killybegs at this time. –* RN Submarine Museum

11 REWARD AND TRAGEDY

"Have you news of my boy Jack?"
Not this tide.
"When d'you think that he'll come back?"
Not with this wind blowing, and this tide.

"Has anyone else had word of him?"
Not this tide.
For what is sunk will hardly swim,
Not with this wind blowing and this tide.

"Oh, dear, what comfort can I find?"
None this tide,
Nor any tide.
Except he didn't shame his kind
Not even with that wind blowing and that tide.

Then hold your head up all the more
This tide,
And every tide,
Because he was the son you bore,
And gave to that wind blowing and that tide!

Untitled poem by Rudyard Kipling
from *Sea Warfare*, 1916

The war, as everyone knew by the late summer of 1917, would be won and lost on the Western Front. It was there, in the ragged lines of trenches stretching from the Alps to the Channel, that the fate of Europe was to be decided.

To the war-weary British public the fighting seemed interminable as a series of Allied offensives commenced in late spring were continued into the early autumn. These brought little in the way of real success. Great breakthroughs had been hoped for, but as nature assumed her sombre autumnal hues and the rains brought a halt to the fighting on the battlefields of France and Flanders, as no human agency could ever do, the Allied generals had to content themselves with having made only modest gains. In human terms the cost had been very high and the casualty lists grew more terrible with each victory.

Many on the home front began again to ponder the quality of the military leadership under which their men were fighting and to wonder if the war could ever be won.

At sea the unrestricted U-boat campaign launched in January 1917 against Allied merchant shipping continued unabated. In terms of tonnage destroyed, Germany should have been winning, and indeed very nearly was. Though it was unrealized by the British public, in the spring of 1917 Britain had been brought to the very edge of economic defeat by the depredations of the U-boats. Only the timely entry of the United States into the war and the imposition of the convoy system by a once-reluctant Admiralty had rescued Britain from the brink of starvation. Even with this reprieve conditions in the British Isles, as elsewhere in Allied Europe, were slipping from bad to worse.

The insatiable demand for war supplies engendered by the long summer of battles resulted in shipments of food and clothing for civilian consumption being severely restricted. There were no longer enough ships to satisfy all the demands and to deny the men at the Front was to condemn them. Although not identified as such, a condition of near "Total War" existed in Britain and Allied Europe, imposed by the enemy if not by choice. In the cities shortages of consumer goods and foodstuffs were chronic, even basic staples like white bread were becoming scarce. Rationing had been a way of life since early 1915 and the shop-door queue was rapidly becoming a national institution.

The U-boats were not having things entirely their own way. Sixty-three were destroyed during 1917, including 11 in the month of September alone, staggering casualties by Great War standards. This was almost a third more than had been lost from all causes between August 1914 and December 1916. For the first time losses threatened to exceed production and the expansion of the U-boat fleet suffered a serious setback. Shortages of strategic materials brought about by the Allied blockade made replacing the boats difficult for German industry, but these production problems were as nothing compared to the impossibility of finding experienced captains and crews.

In the final analysis the German Navy was never to have enough submarines to defeat Britain and her allies at sea, and as losses mounted, the shortage of experienced officers and men, particularly of submarine captains, was to dramatically reduce the effectiveness of those that did get to sea.

Not that all was shortage and depression in England. Although the older population felt the rationing badly and many viewed the cracks appearing in the fabric of their familiar social order with serious concern, for the youth of the country it was a time of high adventure and excitement. Everything, it seemed depended on *their* energies and endeavours. Not only in the Armed Forces but, just as importantly, in the burgeoning fields of science, engineering and industry. Never before in history had technological development taken place at such speed, nor had the young people of the country been so deeply involved in areas of national concern. The society of the young was intelligent, fast-paced, full of promise and bright with optimism for a better world order after the war.

For the submariners in *Platypus* Flotilla there was work to be done. During her refit at Belfast some welcome modernization of the old *D3* had been undertaken, including the installation of a permanent sheet-metal screen around the front of the bridge and an improved gun platform. No longer would the second coxswain be faced with rigging and unrigging the usually soggy canvas dodger that had hitherto afforded the bridge watchkeepers their only protection against the elements.

The gun's crew, who could be called upon to man the gun in any but the very worst weather, would be able to fire the little six-pounder with less fear of accidentally going over the side with a misplaced step. The new arrangement provided a large circular grating, which gave good footing and ample room to work the gun, in place of the little folding sponsons on the sides of the casing that had sufficed until then. The old boat was looking up.

For Barney Johnson there was a moment of deep personal satisfaction when, on November 2, he was Gazetted to receive the Distinguished Service Order, a singular honour indeed, especially for an officer of the Royal Naval Reserve. The citation read, "For gallantry aboard *H8* and for continued service in submarines." Barney was also heartened to see the name of one of his old *H8* crew on the same honours list when Petty Officer Fred Wall, then aboard another *Platypus* boat, the *H5*, was awarded the DSM. Ever since the mining incident he had been disappointed that none of his old ship's company had ever been decorated for the courage and devotion to duty they had shown on that occasion, despite his personal recommendations to Whitehall.

Toward the end of October the crew began getting *D3* ready for sea. The battery was re-embarked, the boat undocked and final touch-ups made in preparation for starting engine trials. On the 28th these got off to an inauspicious start when both diesels broke down and they had to be towed back to port. Perhaps the Old Man going off to London to "have a yarn with the King and collect his gong" had something to do with it. A week later, however, all was back in order.

On the 9th *D3* returned to *Platypus* and the flotilla at Killybegs. The remainder of that day and the one following were spent in storing, fuelling, topping up the fresh water tanks, embarking a new outfit of torpedoes, remounting the gun, which had been left behind in *Platypus*, and stowing the ammunition.

Two days after their arrival, on Sunday, November 11, Barney, or more properly Lieutenant-Commander B.L. Johnson, DSO, RNR, following an irregular zigzag course to confound any lurking U-boats, headed his command out into the familiar, steely grey waters off Rockall.

No enemy submarines were sighted, but on the fourth day, when the armed trawler *Vale of Lennox* fired a couple of rounds in *D3*'s direction, Johnson, following the recently revised flotilla standing orders, remained surfaced and hoisted his colours. Diving out of the way was no longer considered a safe procedure; the new British depth charges, with which most escorts were well provided, were proving highly effective and even a near miss could be very damaging. It was deemed better to take one's chances on the surface and to rely on the system of challenge and reply.

When two experienced ABs reported sick on the seventh day, Barney put into Killybegs, landed them, picked up their replacements and headed back out to sea to complete the patrol before finally returning to harbour three days later. Fearing that the problems of battery gassing had returned, the entire crew was given a medical check-up before the off-watch was sent on its three days patrol leave. There was no sign of the dreaded anemia, however, and the submarine was given a clean bill of health.

That was Cap' Johnson's last patrol aboard *D3*. When they arrived alongside *Platypus*, a jubilant and inwardly satisfied Lieutenant Maitland-Dougall was waiting for them. "Young Billy" had successfully completed his probationary period in *D1* and was to take command of *D3* as soon as he and Barney could complete the necessary turnover. Two days later, on November 24, 1917, Cap' handed command of the boat over to his young protégé and fellow British Columbian.

That Maitland-Dougall was appointed to command his "old ship" was somewhat out of the ordinary. Barney Johnson probably had a hand in it and the Flotilla Commander, Charles Brodie, certainly must have. Who else was pulling for the young Maitland-Dougall is not recorded, but his own abilities must have had some influence in the decision. It was Commodore Hall who gave de facto approval for commanding officers' appointments within "The Trade," and although the Admiralty was the true arbiter, it's doubtful Their Lordships ever interfered.

Barney Johnson was ordered south to join Nasmith's flotilla at Berehaven, where he was to take over one of the E class. He went alone but before going arranged with Commander (S) and Maitland-Dougall for Andy Barlow to join him in his new boat as soon as a suitable replacement could be found for *D3*.

When he arrived at Bantry Bay Barney found that Captain Nasmith's headquarters had only recently been moved from the old *Vulcan* to the newly arrived HMS *Ambrose*, a 6,600-ton converted liner, and the flotilla was in something of an upheaval. It was widely rumoured that a flotilla of American submarines complete with depot ship were going to join them early in the new year, as well as some of the new British L class. Berehaven was to become headquarters for anti-U-boat submarine operations for the entire Western Approaches area and the only submarine base in Ireland.

Near the end of December Johnson was appointed in command of HMS/M *E54*, where he succeeded Commander R.H.T. Raikes, DSO, who was slated to take over the brand-new *L3*. Under that very successful submariner *E54* had torpedoed two U-boats, the *UC-10* in the North Sea during August 1916 and the *U-81* off Ireland on May 1, 1917, in circumstances very similar to Johnson's encounter with *UC-66*.

In the wardroom aboard *Ambrose* Cap' Johnson found himself mingling with the elite of the Submarine Service, for Captain M.E. Nasmith, VC, had gathered a very successful group of submariners under his command. Of the 11 COs in the flotilla, five, including Barney Johnson, wore the scarlet and deep-blue ribbon of the DSO. One of these, Lieutenant Guy D'Oyly Hughes, who had been on some of the early Dardenelles patrols, had won a DSC as well as a DSO. A sixth CO had earned himself a DSC, as also had one of the first lieutenants.

On November 30 Maitland-Dougall took *D3* to sea for his first patrol as captain. They kept watch for six days off the western approaches to the North Channel without incident and returned to *Platypus* at Killybegs on the 5th. Shortly after his arrival the Canadian captain was called to Commander (S)'s office, where Brodie informed him that the old flotilla was to be broken up. At the end of December *Platypus* was bound for Campbeltown in the Clyde, taking *E38* and the three newer D class, *D6*, *D7* and *D8*, with her. From the new base these boats would patrol the North Channel and the Irish Sea. *D3* and *D4* had been ordered to join the 6th Flotilla at Fort Blockhouse for English Channel patrols and were to begin their journey to Portsmouth the next day by way of Belfast. In the mess that evening William learned that his friend Rupert Wood was to transfer to *E38* when they arrived at Belfast. The flotilla that he and Johnson had helped to create and had called home for 16 wearying, exciting months was fast dissolving.

With the redisposition of *Platypus* Flotilla, the three Canadians who had formed a small community in Ireland for the best part of a year were now separated. Johnson was at Berehaven, Maitland-Dougall at Fort Blockhouse and Wood at Campbeltown. Of the remainder, Jock Edwards, who had been first lieutenant aboard *E55* since October, was running out of Harwich on North Sea and Heligoland Bight patrols, as also was Roy Beech aboard *H9* but working from the *Electo* at Yarmouth. Watson remained in the Mediterranean, where he had left *E11* to continue his duties aboard *E2* when *E11* had gone into refit in September. At the same time, he was confirmed in rank as a lieutenant. *E2* was attached to HMS *Adamant* and engaged in patrols in the Adriatic and the approaches to the Straits of Otranto. With the two CC-boats *Hors de combat* at Halifax following their odyssey from the West Coast, there was little expectation of any new Canadian-trained additions to the group of RCN submariners serving overseas.

Maitland-Dougall's D1 *alongside HMS* Platypus, *September 1917.* – author's collection

Lt. Maitland-Dougall and unidentified ladyfriend.

– Maitland-Dougall family collection

Travelling together *D3* and *D4* arrived at Fort Blockhouse on December 10, 1917. Here they joined the 6th Flotilla, where Alexander Quicke was soon to succeed Commander Crowther as flotilla commander. In this flotilla Maitland-Dougall was among many acquaintances from his own early days in boats. Well known to him were Wilfrid Pirie, who had commissioned *H1*, and Cromwell Varley, who had left *H5* and was on his way to the United States to take over *H11*. John Mansfield, Cap' Johnson's number one in *H8* when she hit the mine, had won himself the DSC and was in command of *C20*, Frank Busbridge from Yarmouth days had command of *C18*, while others he knew from Harwich and Immingham were on the staff. For the new arrivals there was time for one six-day patrol in the Channel before putting alongside for the Christmas period.

The fifth Christmas of the war was for many a lean and sombre Yuletide. Supplies were at their lowest and the casualty lists at their worst. The war was hitting home all over the British Empire and the brightest star in the sky of the future was the fact that America had finally come in with her vast reserves of material and manpower. For many this fact added some excitement to the season, for it meant there might be a quick end to the war, while the advent of the Americans themselves was anticipated with great curiosity.

The young Canadian officers were all in receipt of generous parcels of hard-to-get items sent from home and these they distributed among families of their acquaintance ashore. Tea and sugar were particularly welcomed. In a letter to his mother penned around that time, Maitland-Dougall thanks her for copies of the local papers and recounts that he shared a fruit cake she'd sent to him among his messmates while on patrol.

On January 6, 1918, Maitland-Dougall took *D3* out for an eight-day anti-U-boat patrol in a Channel billet almost midway between Brighton and Le Havre. These patrols, though not as demanding as those in the Atlantic and North Sea, presented some unique problems of their own. The Channel had been divided into submarine patrol areas, where British boats were positioned to intercept U-boats leaving and approaching the Dover Strait. Allied shipping traffic in these billets was heavy, mostly armed, almost always escorted and had long ago learned to keep a very sharp lookout. For these ships any submarine was an enemy and their gunners could be expected to shoot on sight; to them it was a matter or survival. Because of this, British submarines were provided with surface escorts when passing through heavily trafficked areas.

Allied patrol vessels, manned almost exclusively by reservists, were nearly as quick on the trigger as their mercantile counterparts, as *D3* was to learn on her first patrol in the New Year when a French armed trawler sent a couple of rounds her way to speed her return to Fort Blockhouse on the last day of the patrol. There was also some risk of attack by German aircraft and *D3* exchanged her outfit of Canadian-made Ross rifles and sword bayonets for a Lewis machine-gun shortly after arrival at *Dolphin*. The Channel was too far west of the Front and too close to French and British airfields to be bothered by Zeppelins, although these were fairly common in the North Sea. Stray mines, set adrift in minesweeping operations or torn loose by gales, presented an ever-present hazard to all Channel shipping, including submarines. When encountered these were generally sunk or exploded by rifle fire.

While on patrol the familiar routine was followed: daylight hours were spent dived, keeping an alternating periscope and hydrophone lookout; surface for a charge; wireless routines and domestic purposes once full darkness had descended; then dived resting on the bottom overnight to begin again at first light. With merchant vessels frequently passing through the area, great care had to be taken in coming to the surface and while on the surface at night lest the boat be accidentally run down.

For reasons known only to himself, Maitland-Dougall had taken a formal last will and testament form with him to sea, and it was during this patrol that he filled it out, signed it and had it witnessed by Andy Barlow and Chief ERA Turbett. The will was dated January 11, 1918, and the beneficiaries were his parents.

In mid-January *D3* commenced a three-week maintenance and leave period. Toward the end of the month Andy Barlow bade farewell to his old boat and left for Ireland to rejoin Barney Johnson. He was relieved in *D3* by another RNR officer, Alfred A. Hall.

Returning to sea on February 5, Maitland-Dougall and his crew were afforded a dramatic demonstration of what it was like to be the enemy while on patrol midway between Portland Bill and the island of Guernsey. At 9:15 a.m., while surfaced in misty weather, the young captain sighted a large merchantman to the west. She was being escorted by two destroyers and steering an easterly course. The ships were a good five miles away and, assuming he had not been seen, the submariner decided to dive and alter course away from their approach. Ten minutes later, having reached 70 feet, the crash of a depth charge exploding about 500 yards away told him they had indeed been spotted. It was too late then to try and surface to exchange identities. Continuing its descent the boat was shaken by a second blast at 90 feet and a final pair of light-bulb-shattering explosions at 110 feet. After these there was silence.

Three-quarters of an hour later, having heard nothing on the hydrophones for some time, *D3* cautiously ascended to periscope depth for a look around, but her captain could see nothing through the instrument. Surfacing, Maitland-Dougall spotted a lone destroyer about five miles to the west, which by its behaviour did not appear to see the submarine. The merchant ship and the other escort were visible in a clear patch in the mist eight miles away, continuing their journey northeastward. These soon disappeared into the murk, at about which time the lone destroyer turned towards and exchanged identities with the submarine, which had taken the precaution of displaying a large white ensign. No one in *D3* was surprised when she flashed a message that her companion, HMS *Achates*, had spotted a U-boat and dropped a pattern of depth charges. The signalman was instructed to pass the reply that it had been *D3* and that no harm was done. Half an hour later the mist cleared and *D3* dived to continue her hydrophone and periscope watch. She returned to Fort Blockhouse five days later.

The depth-charging of an Allied submarine was not an event to go unreported, and Commander (S) 6th Flotilla, Alexander Quicke, was fully versed regarding the encounter by the time *D3* once more made fast in Haslar Creek. It wasn't long before Maitland-Dougall found himself "on the carpet" in front of his one-time captain, to be reprimanded for failing to remain on the surface to carry out correct recognition procedures with the destroyers in accordance with Flotilla Standing Orders. The fledgling captain was invited to explain his actions to Their Lordships of the Admiralty, in writing.

At Berehaven there was some excitement when the first of the American submarines arrived. This was the USS *L10* and she was followed at intervals by six sister boats and the depot ship USS *Bushnell*. In order to avoid confusion with the new British L class, some of which were also destined to join the flotillas at Berehaven, the American boats were given AL pennant numbers. Upon visiting one, Johnson found these American Ls to be but enlarged versions of the original H-class boats.

Capable submariners though they undoubtedly were, the Americans lacked actual wartime experience. Once they had settled in, Captain Nasmith called a conference of all British and USN commanding officers. Gathered around the familiar round table in Captain (S)'s office, the assembly discussed how best to introduce the USN boats into active patrol work. In the end it was decided that each British submarine would take along an American officer, starting with the COs, who would carry out normal watchkeeping duties under the discreet guidance of the RN captain.

The scheme worked well, the Americans got in some good practice with a fully worked-up crew and, according to Barney Johnson, the British COs got their jigsaw puzzles done. The Americans were popular with the British crews. The RN officers found their USN counterparts to be well trained in technical subjects though understandably lacking in the operational expertise that they themselves had acquired in three years of warfare.

Back at *Dolphin*, *D3* was having her adventures, including a near tragedy toward the end of February. At that time destroyers were being fitted with hydrophones to help them detect and attack dived U-boats. One of these was HMS *Trusty*, an elderly member of one of the Portsmouth flotillas assigned to patrolling the boom across the western entrance of the Solent. To help *Trusty*'s crew practise their hydrophone detection procedures, *D3*, which was doing local patrols to get back into shape after a maintenance period, acted as the target. It was while lying on the bottom in fairly shallow water near the boom gate that she was run over by the surfaced incoming submarine HMS/M *N1*, a boat three times *D3*'s size.

It was a very scary experience for the *D3* and for *Trusty*, who watched it all happen without realizing the possible consequences until too late and feared for the worst. Fortunately the keel of the larger submarine cleared *D3* by several feet and didn't come in contact with any vital parts of Maitland-Dougall's command, except for the periscope through which her captain had been watching the calamity develop. Besides jangled nerves and smashed crockery the only real damage done to either boat was a badly bent periscope on *D3* and some chips out of the keel of *N1*.

Not so fortunate were two of the Montreal-built H-boats, which were lost during the early part of 1918. *H10* was the first. Still a Yarmouth boat, she was commanded by Lieutenant M.H. Collier and, like so many others, never returned from a routine patrol in the North Sea. She was posted as "Missing, presumed lost" on January 19. It is generally accepted that she hit a mine, and a post-war examination of German records found no mention of an attack on a submarine that would otherwise account for her loss.

The second to go was *H5* from *Vulcan*'s Flotilla, and her loss served to underline once again that insidious, ever-present danger that nagged in the far reaches of the minds of all experienced submariners: being mistaken for the enemy.

After sunset on March 2, *H5*, under the command of an experienced submariner, Lieutenant A.W. Forbes, DSO, had surfaced in her billet about 20 miles southwest of Holyhead for the nightly charge. Visibility was negligible; it was either moonless or completely overcast.

So far as the master of the blacked-out SS *Rutherglen* was concerned, the object spotted by the lookouts in the water ahead of his ship was a U-boat. It appears Forbes had some idea of what was coming and tried to manoeuvre his submarine clear of the knife-like stem of the steamer, but it was too late and the freighter sliced into the thin-skinned *H5*, sinking the submarine almost immediately with only minor damage to herself. As the *Rutherglen* passed through the scene of the collision, the crew on deck sighted men struggling in the icy cold, oil-covered sea and heard their cries for help, but the ship did not stop. Mercifully the survivors could not have lasted long in the cold March waters. Included among the 25 casualties of this wartime tragedy was an American, Ensign E.W.P. Childs, USN, who was making an instructional cruise aboard the ill-fated submarine.

It was openly admitted by Captain Nasmith, and generally accepted at the

Admiralty, that there was no practical solution to the problem of identification between merchant ships and submarines at night, particularly when it was very dark, and the risk had to be accepted. The captain of the *Rutherglen* was duly congratulated and decorated for his quick-thinking action in sinking an *enemy* submarine. In the meantime *H5* was posted as "Missing, presumed lost." The manner in which the unfortunate *H5* met her fate was revealed to dependents and relatives only upon the submission of a written request, and even then the name of the merchant ship and her captain were concealed until long after the surviving participants had passed to their eternal rewards.

These losses, like all others, were deeply felt at Berehaven and Harwich, for the boats had been with their respective flotillas for some time and both ships' companies were well known in their respective depots. For Barney Johnson, and particularly for Maitland-Dougall, who had spent many months in *H10*, this was particularly so. The two Canadians had known the two boats since Montreal days and both had close friends aboard them. Petty Officer Fred Wall, DSM, who had been decorated at the same time as Barney and had been aboard *H8* when she was mined, was numbered among those lost in *H5*.

Five days after *H5* went missing, *D3* put to sea for a channel patrol, having been fully restored after her rough encounter with *N1*. Following Mansfield's *C20*, *D3* cleared Haslar Creek and headed seaward into the waters of Spithead. Their first destination was St. Helen's Bay on the eastern side of the Isle of Wight, where they carried out a trim dive and came to anchor to await the sloop expected around midnight to escort them clear of the harbour traffic and defence zone. Arriving on schedule the *Magnolia* picked up her charges and escorted them Channel-ward on a southeast course until well clear of shipping, then turned about and headed back to Portsmouth, bidding the submariners "good hunting" on passing. By dawn *D3* was dived in her billet midway between Brighton and Le Havre in an area identified as the East Southern Area. *C20* had been allocated a billet to the north of *D3*'s area. Maitland-Dougall was scheduled to rendezvous with an escort off Brighton at 3 p.m. on March 14 for the return journey to Fort Blockhouse.

Four days later a Royal Naval Air Service airship flying an anti-U-boat patrol encountered a submarine on the surface roughly in *D3*'s billet. She successfully exchanged identities using the standard signal-grenade recognition procedures. It was the opinion of the airship commander that the submarine was changing position within her billet.

The following day, March 12, 1918, *D3* was patrolling her billet on the surface, heading in a westerly direction. The weather was fine but hazy, making it all but impossible to keep an effective periscope watch, and Maitland-Dougall had come to the surface. Trimmed down and ready to dive, the submarine had little to fear, as she could be fully submerged in a few short minutes. It is possible the tall, young Canadian was contemplating his return to *Dolphin* in two days time, as the date of their scheduled arrival marked his twenty-third birthday.

At about 2:30 p.m. the men on the bridge of *D3* spotted a large airship approaching from out of the sun about three miles distant off the port bow. Judging by his reactions Maitland-Dougall must have been pretty certain the airship was a "friendly" and probably a sister to the one he'd encountered the previous day. There was little chance of it being a Zeppelin so far away and on the wrong side of the German lines. In any case, it was too late to dive, especially with the seas so calm. Assuming then that it was an Allied ship, he obviously felt confident her crew would recognize the white circle on a black ground air-recognition mark painted on the grey fore-casing and expected them to respond to the signal-grenade challenge even then being prepared for firing by the lookout. Red was the colour of the day.

Five hundred metres above *D3* the men aboard the French airship *A.T.O.* from Le Havre air station were tense and eager, for they could not identify the surfaced submarine about two miles away and below them. She had first been spotted by Adjutant Gobert, the dirigible's pilot and navigator, who immediately informed the airship's commander, L'Ensign de Vaisseau St. Remy. They were already on a good interception course and had the sun and prevailing breeze behind them, so St. Remy called his crew to readiness and ordered full speed both motors. The crew of the airship could not make out any identifying marks that might give them a clue as to the boat's nationality. *A.T.O.* was closing rapidly when suddenly what appeared to be a series of rockets streaming red fire ascended from the back of the submarine's conning tower and headed directly toward the balloon's huge, vulnerable, gas bag and its contents of 2,000 cubic feet of volatile hydrogen.

Unsuspected by *D3* the Frenchmen in *A.T.O.* were completely ignorant of the method of exchanging identities by using signal grenades. It's likely, too, that the bright sun shining from ahead and above the submarine was being reflected off the west fore-casing and that all the Frenchmen saw was a glare which would have blotted out any painted markings. Had he known she was French, perhaps Maitland-Dougall would have used the obsolete flashing-light signal as recommended on the reverse of the standard message pad then in use, but he had never encountered a French airship before nor had he been warned to expect one.

The airship commander and his four-man crew, however, were all firmly under the impression that they had been attacked and no further attempt was made at establishing recognition as they manned their stations to attack the U-boat below. St. Remy ordered his wireless operator, who had been busy trying to transmit his ALLO (enemy submarine under attack report) to base, to man the twin-barrelled machine gun in the bow of the gondola and open fire when ready, while at the same time instructing the pilot to commence a descending bombing run.

Aboard the hapless *D3* her captain hit the klaxon alarm button as they cleared the bridge amidst the sudden barrage of machine-gun fire that erupted from the airship in reply to their recognition signal. The first burst fell short, but the second and subsequent fullisades were on target, and the Frenchmen were elated by the sight of the bright balls of tracer ricochetting off the pressure hull of the target. The submarine had just begun to submerge when St. Remy let go his first pair of 52-kilo bombs, which exploded harmlessly astern of the rapidly disappearing submarine.

The frustration and agony being experienced by Maitland-Dougall and his crew must have been utterly devastating. He had suppressed his war-bred instinct to dive at the first sign of the airship and, obeying orders, had remained on the surface to exchange identities, only to be shot at and then bombed. Had they fallen into a trap, or had someone made a monumental error?

Judging his first drop to have missed, the airship commander instructed the pilot to bring their 240-foot-long dirigible around on the right of the estimated track of their target and he soon sighted the wake of the plunging U-boat in the clear, calm waters below. Aiming off ahead of the blue-grey streak, he let go a second and then a third brace of 52-kilo bombs, whose detonations sent tall columns of dirty grey water into the afternoon sky. It was a set piece attack; he couldn't miss.

The airship, having expended all its bombs, the equivalent of 300 kilos of ballast, began to rise rapidly, and the pilot struggled to keep her head to the wind, adjust lift and maintain control. St. Remy left him to it, as he was happy with their efforts and felt sure his second pair of bombs had bracketed the target. The wireless operator was ordered back to his set to transmit the ALLO report to their base at Le Havre.

Whichever pair of bombs had done the damage, *D3* was mortally wounded. About three minutes after the last explosion the crew of the bucking airship observed a mass of air bubbles at about where they would have expected to sight their quarry, and this was followed by the submarine's conning tower breaking surface in a welter of foam. Having no bombs left and being too unstable to shoot with any accuracy, they positioned themselves so as to be able to keep an eye on developments below. The dirigible still had its head and didn't stop rising until reaching 1,200 metres, at which point the wireless operator announced that he couldn't raise Le Havre, the signal traffic was too heavy and his set had insufficient power to break through.

By the time the pilot regained control of his craft, the submarine had disappeared altogether. In the eddies that marked its submergence were four dark objects that aroused the curiosity of the airmen. Closing the position and spiralling down to 20 metres, the Frenchmen could see through their binoculars that there were four widely scattered men swimming in the cold March waters below. Levelling off as best they could over the position, the airmen noticed that one of the men was shouting, so they stopped the motors in order to hear him. The survivor in the water spoke in English and one phrase was clearly distinguished: "You got us!" With their ship barely under control and still pitching unpredictably, the airmen couldn't get close enough to the surface even to pass a line, but they did collect up their own Perrin lifebelts and tossed them to the swimmers before starting up the engines and heading for shore to get help.

Making landfall, St. Remy fixed his position and plotted the position of the submarine 20 miles north, 10 miles west of Fecamp, then headed southward along the coast in search of a ship to send to the rescue. The first two vessels he contacted could not leave their duties, but eventually the French torpedo-boat *Typhon* responded, and abandoning the fishing smack she had in tow set off for the position of the survivors preceded by the airship. Together they searched for the four men until dusk, when the onset of fog forced the airship commander to abandon the mission and return to base before his landmarks were blotted out and they were left stranded. The *Typhon* continued searching, but it was obvious there was no hope for the submariners.

D3, her Canadian captain and his gallant crew were gone; there were no survivors. As darkness descended a cold, damp shroud of fog settled over the scene. After a while the torpedo-boat too departed.

Immediately upon landing, St. Remy reported the circumstances of the attack and his doubts concerning the nationality of the submarine to his commanding officer, Capitaine de Frigate Agnes. Agnes, realizing the gravity of the situation, passed a verbal report to his superior, and by late evening an account of the day's events had reached the senior British naval officer at Le Havre. A telegram was drafted for the Commander in Chief, Portsmouth, which was received by him the following morning and passed to *Dolphin* by way of Whitehall and Commodore Hall.

At *Dolphin* there was little doubt that *D3* was the victim of the attack, for there had been no word from her for over 24 hours. This was confirmed the following day when she failed to make the rendezvous off Brighton for the return to Portsmouth. On March 15, *D3* was officially, and regretfully, posted as "Missing, presumed lost." The events surrounding her sinking, however, were never made public. She became another submarine lost from unknown causes, one among many in that war.

The ripples of grief soon spread out from Whitehall as black-edged telegrams were dispatched to the 29 next of kin. Early the following morning in Bristol, birthplace and home of Able Seaman Henry William Powell, his young wife, three months pregnant, bought a workman's day return railway ticket for nearby Avonmouth, where she journeyed to the home of Petty Officer Lister's widow, Laura, to share their mutual grief and give what comfort she could. Such were the bonds of comradeship in a submarine's crew.

Most of *D3*'s crew had known no other submarine and many, like her captain, had been with the boat for a year or more. Her coxswain, William Osborn, a six-year submarine veteran, had been aboard when Johnson took command, which was also when 18-year-old Ordinary Telegraphist George Sanger had joined the boat. Chief ERA Turbett, whose home was in Dundee, had joined her straight from his submarine course in *Dolphin* in October 1916. One ERA had been loaned just for the one trip, and a few of the stokers had been aboard for less than a month. It had been a tightly knit ship's company.

Every officer and man in the Services was required to nominate a next-of-kin, a responsible person to look after their affairs and for notification in the event he were wounded or killed. Maitland-Dougall had nominated his maiden aunt, Mary Catherine, who had moved to Edinburgh after the disposal of Scotscraig. It was to Aunt Mary that the Admiralty telegram was directed and it was upon her shoulders the burden fell of informing his parents in faraway British Columbia.

The devastation of James and Winnifred Maitland-Dougall was complete. Both sons had now been killed. For the parents the world about them ceased to have meaning, all they had loved and cherished, had striven to build for, the reasons for their very existence, had been rent from them, swallowed up in the insane violence of the war in Europe. It was, perhaps, of some consolation that the boys had died bravely and as they had chosen. After a while the grief would ease and they would both pick up what was left of their lives, but there could be no more children, no more future.

It was left to Alexander Quicke to perform the final act in the oft-repeated routine that accompanied the loss of one of His Majesty's submarines. The reasons for the sinking had to be determined, if at all possible, for the safety of the remainder of the flotilla. What had gone wrong?

Fortunately young St. Remy had documented the entire drama the night he landed at Le Havre, a sleepless night for him no doubt. This report was forwarded, translated and, ironically, provided Quicke with the answers he needed.

As so often happens among allies, their methods of communication were not standard, each having his own procedures and codes. Where areas of responsibility overlapped, a sensible person would expect both sides to agree to using one or the other method so as to avoid confusion and misidentification, but this was not the case. Both Quicke and Maitland-Dougall had failed to appreciate that a problem might develop, neither had considered the possibility of *D3* encountering a French airship during that patrol. There had been a procedure laid down for such an occasion and it involved using a flashing-light signal, something every submarine was equipped to do. This method of exchanging identities, however, was obsolete and its use had recently been cancelled in British service. Even the small print on the back of the Admiralty signal form admitted the French had no knowledge of the signal grenade method. This effectively left no recognized way in which to exchange identities with the French airship.

In his case, Quicke concluded, Maitland-Dougall had followed correct, but futile, signalling procedures and had probably assumed it was a British airship, as he had no reason to think otherwise. For this, the Commander blamed himself. He also pointed out that even if the young Canadian captain had recognized the airship as being French, he had no valid method of exchanging identities at his disposal other than using the signal grenades and so could not have averted the tragedy.

That the French were completely unaware of the presence of a British submarine in that particular area and ignorant of the British method of identification using signal grenades identifies a lamentable breakdown of communications between allies. The authorities at Le Havre air station admitted to having no knowledge of the disposition of British submarines nor of British signalling methods, which is not surprising, it having been British policy not to tell the French.

Although he would not have been aware of it, the onus of identification fell entirely on the shoulders of the French airship commander, for he had no way of knowing the British could not communicate with him in a manner he could understand. That St. Remy and his four-man crew did not see, or failed to recognize, the identification mark on *D3*'s fore-casing is unfortunate and may indicate a lack of alertness on their part. It is true that the sun would have been shining directly onto the wet casing, but with the constantly changing angle of the deck caused by the boat moving through the water the white-on-black bull's-eye should have been visible for at least some of the time.

The fact that St. Remy did not attempt to signal the submarine is also unexplained. Had he done so using the flashing lamp, it is probable the submarine would have replied by the same method. The airship was in no danger and had all the time necessary to establish the identity of the submarine, although, had it been a U-boat, the time spent in trying to raise the boat with the signal lamp might have provided an opportunity for an enemy to slip away. Better an escaped U-boat than what did transpire.

Once the recognition grenades had been fired, the French crew, perhaps understandably, only had thoughts for attacking the submarine. Even so, it seems remarkable they did not attempt to communicate in any way nor see the bull's-eye air-recognition marking.

In the summary to his report Alexander Quicke states:

> In conclusion I desire to take this opportunity of placing on record that Lieutenant Maitland-Dougall, who entered the R.N. Submarine Service as a midshipman under me, was, in my opinion, in the very front rank of the younger Submarine captains, a most thorough, conscientious, and resourceful officer. His decision to dive just as the first two bombs were dropped after having complied with the only instructions available for making recognition signals under the circumstances was, in my opinion, the only course open to him; the odds were in favour of his escaping the effects of the light bombs once he was under water, and the airship had shown every indication of pressing home his attacks if he remained on the surface.

D3 was the only British submarine to be sunk at sea by air-dropped bombs during the Great War.

H15 at Grassy Bay, Bermuda, in November 1918. This was Johnson's last operational submarine command. – Vancouver City Archives

12 WAR'S END

At 11 a.m. on November 11, 1918, the guns of the Western Front fell silent and the war to end all wars was over. It was an armistice, not a peace treaty, not just then, but it brought an end to the killing and that was good enough for the men in the trenches — on both sides. More than four years of brutal slaughter and destruction had ended.

As soon as the signing of the document was announced, the Allied home front went wild with delight. In most Canadian communities there were parades and speeches throughout the day and in the evening great bonfires were lit to mark the victory and ward off the seasonal chill while the populace gathered in the streets, in each other's homes, and in churches and halls to give thanks, speculate and, most of all, to rejoice. The thoughts of most were directed to the future as hundreds of thousands celebrated the victory and eagerly looked forward to the homecoming of their menfolk and the resumption of their lives in a world at peace.

On the Front, in the bivouacs behind the silent, near empty trenches and on the shattered battlefields littered with the paraphernalia of the recent fighting, the event was followed by a few days of inertia while the soldiers, winners and losers alike, adjusted themselves to the idea of their own personal survival and thoughts of what peace held for them. Celebrations were of a more subdued character among the front-line soldiery, for them the real party could wait until they got home. Although it would not become apparent for some months, getting home was going to take far too long for many of the Canadians in Europe.

The end caught Barney Johnson at sea and it wasn't until the next day that he found out it was all over. While the Allied and German generals were signing the armistice documents, he was battling huge seas on his way to the United Kingdom by way of Bermuda, in command of the newly commissioned HMS/M *H15* and accompanied by the *H14*.

Both submarines had been built in the Fore River shipyard at Quincy, Massachusetts, as part of the original 20-boat contract that had seen him commission *H8* at Montreal three long years before. All ten Fore River-built boats were finished by March 1916, after which they were laid up pending the entry of the United States into the war. Six of these submarines were ceded to Chile early in 1917 as compensation for the ships taken over by the British government at the beginning of the war. At the end of 1917 it had been planned that the four remaining boats would depart for the United Kingdom at the beginning of the following March. During December *H15* suffered the ignominy of being accidentally sunk at her berth in 30 feet of water while fitting out. Plans for commissioning had to be deferred for six months. March 29, *H14*, *H11* and *H12* got under way as planned, but *H14* was forced to return to Boston and pay off with serious defects.

At Bermuda *H14* and *H15* put in alongside the *Shearwater* in the dockyard at Ireland Island. The old sloop, still under the command of Bertram Jones, had been fitted with a few guns and assigned to Atlantic patrols. It was then the submariners learned of the momentous news from the Western Front. Orders soon followed to keep the two submarines at Bermuda until arrangements could be completed for their disposal. The Royal Navy would have no further need of them and it was intended to offer them to the RCN, as Churchill had once suggested.

For Barney Johnson it had been a long and roundabout journey that landed him in Bermuda that rainy morning. A few weeks after Maitland-Dougall's death and the loss of *D3*, Nasmith's *Ambrose* Flotilla, including Barney's new boat, the *E54*, was ordered to Portsmouth. Here, he was joined by Roy Beech, who was first lieutenant in the brand-new *L8*, which joined the flotilla in mid-April straight from the Vickers yard at Barrow. *Ambrose*'s boats had been brought home to reinforce the Bay of Biscay patrol.

Before leaving Berehaven some significant changes were made to *E54*'s officer complement. When he had taken the boat over, Barney had inherited her first lieutenant and third hand, the former a regular RN officer and the latter from the RNR, a not uncommon situation at that time. In January Andy Barlow rejoined him from *D3* as third officer and in March the first lieutenant, Lieutenant G.W. Hoare-Smith, was relieved by Acting Lieutenant Arthur G. Madan, DSC, RNR. A long-time veteran of the Irish flotilla, this officer was well known to both Johnson and Barlow. That all three of *E54*'s officers were Royal Naval Reservists was a most unusual turn of events. It was a distinguished wardroom, too, for the captain had a DSO and his first officer the DSC. At that time only one other submarine, the *F2*, a non-operational boat in the *Thames* training flotilla, could boast an all-RNR wardroom, and she only had a two officer complement. Even near the end of the war, when the Submarine Service was at its wartime zenith and resources were stretched to the limits, an all-RNR wardroom was a rarity.

Shortly after their arrival at Portsmouth the commanding officers of the submarines were summoned to the office of the Commander in Chief, Portsmouth. Following "a most courteous reception," to quote Johnson's recollection of the event, the Admiral presented a brief sketch of the progress of the land war and outlined the near future as he saw it. The Commander-in-Chief confirmed that the war had definitely turned in their favour and that the Allied armies had reversed the Germans' drive for Paris and the Channel ports. It was his belief, and that of the Admiralty, that the German battleships might attempt a final sortie across the North Sea, and indeed, he hoped they would, and that all patrols were being strengthened until the crisis was resolved. Before leaving, the submarine captains were handed patrol orders to be implemented upon returning to their boats.

The operation soon came to an end. The High Seas Fleet was in no condition to leave harbour let alone engage in battle with the Grand Fleet. Except for the destroyer flotillas and U-boats, Germany's navy was completely immobilized in its ports, the bulk of the crews in a state of open civil rebellion. The Kaiser's capital ships would never again put to sea on active operations.

Patrol activity soon fell off for *Ambrose*'s boats. Only the ever-necessary anti-U-boat and routine blockade patrols were being maintained, and these were assigned to the new L-class boats, leaving Johnson's *E54*, the last of her kind in the flotilla, with little to do. It was something of a reprieve when the boat was selected for experimental underwater wireless reception duties.

In preparation for the experiments the bridge was fitted out with two flat aerial coils mounted at right angles to one another. About ten days later they embarked a group of senior officers, all signalling specialists, and set off for the Solent. Once in position Barney dived the boat and settled her on the bottom at 60 feet. The wireless reception experiment began while the officers sat down to an excellent lunch specially prepared in honour of the occasion. Throughout the meal the boat's wireless rating kept passing in long messages transmitted from a radio station in Wales, over a hundred miles away. The first trial was considered a great success. A series of tests were scheduled to follow. The next was to be held in the Firth of Forth with another at Scapa Flow.

Cap' Johnson, however, was destined to miss that trip. Early in the last week of May he was forced to report himself to sick bay, suffering from stomach pains and chest discomfort. After nearly four years of eating patrol rations and breathing stale air, battery gas and diesel exhaust fumes, his constitution had taken more abuse than any reasonable person his age could expect to get away with without incurring some kind of problem. A medical examination revealed that he had an ulcerated stomach, that the upper lobes of both lungs had collapsed, and that he was still suffering from the effects of the gassing he'd experienced during the summer of 1916. Although not laid up, he was a sick man and needed a good rest and care. With the war winding down it was decided he could be spared to recuperate at home, and he was sent off on indefinite sick leave.

A day or two later Barney took a train up to London, where he booked passage to New York aboard the Royal Mail Ship *Orduna*. While in London he paid a courtesy call on Commodore Hall. During their conversation the Commodore suddenly, and perhaps all too casually, recalled that there were two new H-boats outfitting at Boston that would be ready to make the crossing in a couple of months. Would he consider bringing them back to the UK? Seizing the opportunity, Barney gave his assent and was instructed to contact the RN Engineer Commander looking after the boats when he arrived at New York. He was given command of one of the submarines and was told he would be known as "Senior Officer H-Boats, USA."

Considerably buoyed by his new assignment Barney decided to treat himself to an early lunch at a good restaurant on The Strand. When ordering dessert he was disgusted at being charged two shillings and sixpence for a half a dozen strawberries, quite a sum even in those hard times, and at being required to produce his ration card before he could get a little sugar to sprinkle on them.

Wasting no time he went to Euston station, took the first available train to Liverpool, and by tea time was aboard the *Orduna* anchored in the Mersey. For the first time in many months he was able to enjoy the simple luxuries of white bread and fresh cream and could forget about ration cards. *Orduna* sailed that same evening and Barney Johnson turned in early to get a good night's rest.

At around 7 a.m. the following morning he paid a visit to the lower bridge, just to check on the weather and see what kind of a day it was going to be, as would any conscientious sea captain. According to his observations it was calm with a low-lying mist and the ship was making about 16 knots. No sooner had he completed his assessment when he heard the lookout in the masthead crow's nest report, "Lifeboat with survivors dead ahead." To Johnson, however, the object protruding through the mist was far more sinister: it was the conning tower of a U-boat with half a dozen men scrambling to get below.

Orduna's master, Captain T.M. Williams-Taylor, had realized their danger even quicker than had Barney, and already he could feel the heel of the big ship as her captain ordered the helm over so as to give his stern-mounted 6-inch gun a field of fire. As they neared the U-boat, which was manoeuvring for a firing position and obviously preparing to dive, Johnson heard the German captain shout out for them to surrender or he would sink them. To this Williams-Taylor responded with an appropriate seamanlike reply. By this time the Royal Navy crew manning the gun had opened fire and appeared to score a direct hit on the U-boat's conning tower, after which the submarine disappeared beneath the surface. The liner could not risk stopping to confirm a kill, or otherwise, and continued on her zigzag course for New York. Barney recounted that it was the smartest surface action he'd ever witnessed and was delighted that *Orduna*'s gunners had given the Huns a good strafing. As no U-boats were lost at that time, however, their target must have survived the attack despite appearances to the contrary.

Upon reaching New York six days later Johnson telephoned Engineer Commander Nibbs at Boston and learned that the two boats would be ready for commissioning in about six weeks and Nibbs promised to let him know in good time. By June 12 he was passing through Montreal, from where he cabled Ottawa informing Naval Service Headquarters of his circumstances. A few days later he was reunited with his family after an absence of 37 long months.

Two weeks later Barney reported himself fit for duty, but the British authorities in Washington told him to stay put. There was no hurry. He had plenty of time in which to relax, play golf, indulge his love of sailing, enjoy the love and attention of his family and the companionship of his friends. There was no better place for his convalescence than his own home.

It was another five weeks before Commander Nibbs telegraphed to say the crews were due to arrive at Boston in a fortnight's time. Needing no further urging, Barney left the comfort of his home and family and headed for Boston, where he arrived well in advance of the two ships' companies. Following instructions, he reported to Commander Nibbs, and to Captain Rush, USN, Commandant of the Boston Navy Yard. Completing his business with these officers, he went to Washington to pay a call on the British Commander-in-Chief.

It was a typical hot, still August day when Barney paid his courtesy call on the Admiral, who had his offices aboard a yacht moored in the Potomac. He was particularly anxious to make a good impression, as he intended to put forward a daring proposal for the two submarines. German U-boat cruisers armed with 5.9-inch guns were wreaking havoc among merchant ships passing through the Azores and Canary Islands, and he wanted permission to bring his boats in from the southwest and carry out an anti-U-boat patrol before continuing on to England.

Undress whites was the rig for the occasion. On dressing for his interview Barney had debated whether or not to wear an undershirt because of the heat. Modesty won the day and he put one on anyway — better safe than sorry.

He arrived at Vice-Admiral Sir William Lowther Grant's headquarters on schedule, where he was met by an immaculately dressed flag officer, who greeted him cordially and escorted him to the Admiral's office. Upon entering, Barney was startled to find a grim-looking elderly gentleman, clad only in his shorts and undershirt, seated in front of a 50-pound block of ice sitting in a pan on the desk in front of him with an electric fan positioned behind and angled to direct the chilled air in just the right direction. "Take off that damned coat," the Admiral shouted. Without a moment's hesitation Barney stripped off his tunic and, grateful for his decision earlier that morning to wear an undershirt, happily shared the Admiral's air conditioning while he presented his plan. Reassured by Johnson's knowledge and past experiences with the H-boats, the C-in-C gave his approval for the plan in principle but ordered a further visit for confirmation before his departure for England.

By the end of August both boats had commissioned, *H14* on the 15th under Lieutenant C.V. Powel, RN, and *H15* on the 23rd under Barney Johnson, Senior Officer H-Boats, USA. Whether it was by design or by accident, Johnson's officers were again all RNR, not as distinguished a group perhaps as in *E54*, but certainly all Merchant Navy types. Defects delayed both submarines during trials and they were not ready to sail until early November. The young officers and sailors didn't mind the delays. New England was enjoying a delightful Indian summer and the ladies' skirts then in vogue were very short, especially around the artists' colony at Providence, near where they were doing trials. Barney's men found it somewhat difficult to keep their minds on the job and he sympathized with their distraction. The free-and-easy conditions they found in America were in startling contrast to the austerities of wartime England.

While the boats were lying alongside Pier "G" at New London waiting to sail for England, Johnson went ashore for his final orders. With the war nearly over, his plan for a patrol met with strong opposition and in the end he was ordered to proceed as far as Bermuda, where he would be issued further instructions. On November 9 the two boats sailed in company with the USN tug *Arapahoe*, which was to guide them through the busy, and sensitive, New York traffic zone. With the onset of rough weather that evening, the tug asked to be allowed to return to port and Barney let it go. By midnight the submarines were well on their way but encountering very high seas and a heavy swell.

It was so rough that *H15*'s gyro toppled, while aboard *H14* a petty officer broke an arm in a bad fall. Early on the afternoon of November 12 the islands of Bermuda came in sight through the nearly continuous curtain of rain, and the submarines prepared to enter harbour completely unaware of the momentous happenings in Europe. Within a short time the boats had made fast in the dockyard at Ireland's Island alongside the *Shearwater*, and Barney was soon busy renewing old friendships among her ship's company.

When the armistice was signed there were seven Canadian submariners serving in the Royal Navy Submarine Service. Strange to relate, the Canadians were the only other nationality to appear on the Nominal Lists for the Royal Navy Submarine Service throughout the entire war. This is a little-known fact rarely recognized on either side of the Atlantic, and certainly a unique distinction for the fledgling RCN.

At Portsmouth William Beech was first lieutenant in *L8*; Jock Edwards, after 14 months as first lieutenant in *E55*, was doing his Periscope Course; and a proudly successful Ronald Watson was in command of the *V3*, a *Thames* boat, completing his probationary period as a new CO following completion of his "Perisher." Jock Edwards would take command of *C18* at *Dolphin* a week later. Rupert Wainman Wood was first lieutenant aboard *E38*, still attached to *Platypus* at Campbeltown. A recent arrival, Sub-Lieutenant Valentine S. Godfrey, was also aboard *Platypus* waiting for his first boat, while the last wartime Canadian submariner, Lieutenant Richard H. Oland, was on course in *Dolphin*.

Prior to his "Perisher" Watson had spent the first seven months of 1918 in the Mediterranean and Aegean as first lieutenant in *E11*. Much of the time was spent in patrolling off the Dardenelles in anticipation of the Germans attempting another breakout into the Aegean, such as they had made in January. On that occasion the battlecruiser *Goeben* and the cruiser *Breslau* had sunk two British monitors at Kusu Bay on the Island of Imbros while on their way to attack the Allied base of operations in the harbour of Mudros on the nearby island of Lemnos. As the only ships powerful enough to stop them were absent, the Germans could have created havoc had they not run into a minefield, which ultimately sank the *Breslau* and damaged the battlecruiser sufficiently to cause her to beat a hasty retreat back up the straits.

Submarine officers aboard Platypus *at Cambeltown, June 14, 1918. Left to right: Lt. Rupert W. Wood, RCN; S-Lt. Fredrick Bell, RN; Lt. H.G. Gorton, RN.*
– RN Submarine Museum

Part of the Mediterranean flotilla at Malta, late 1918. Left to right: H2, H4, E11, H1, H9, *and an* E*-class boat (probably* E2*). Note the difference between the "Atlantic" treatment of the enclosed bridge, as shown by* H9, *and the "Mediterranean" style, as fitted to the other three* H*-boats. Also note that the periscope fairwater on* H2 *has been shortened.* H9, *along with* H7, *joined the flotilla in August 1918.*
– RN Submarine Museum

It was dull, repetitious work and the boat made two patrols a month, each of six to seven days duration, working out of Mudros, where *Adamant* was based. Watson had originally been posted back to *Dolphin* during April, but that had been deferred when he was asked to remain aboard *E11* for a further three months. It was not until August that he reached England.

Prior to his move to Portsmouth, Edwards had seen plenty of enemy activity during the summer months of 1918 in the North Sea aboard the *E55*. On one day alone, June 19, while patrolling off the southern tip of Dogger Bank, German submarines were encountered on three separate occasions. They were only able to get within range of one of these U-boats, at which they fired two torpedoes but both missed. *E55* went into a much-needed refit in October and her first lieutenant was posted to *Dolphin*, where he arrived a week before the armistice.

The so-called Spanish influenza epidemic was sweeping the United Kingdom when the war ended and it was probably this that sent Rupert Wainman Wood ashore for medical treatment during November. By that time he had been first lieutenant aboard *E38* for 11 months and he would return to his boat later in the month. At the end of June 1918, this submarine was completely knocked out by the first wave of the epidemic, and at one point there were only three fit men in the entire crew. In order to quarantine the submarine, it was anchored out, like many another infected ship, and visited periodically by medical personnel. Those who were well enough were allowed ashore for short recreation periods only, otherwise everyone was confined aboard.

Wood too had seen plenty of action against U-boats during the early summer months. While on patrol at the end of May they had sighted four U-boats in one day, and despite getting in two attacks were unsuccessful.

His captain in *E38* was Lieutenant Paul L. Eddis, a man with an interesting story but who was destined for a tragic death after the war. This officer had survived the shelling of the stranded *E13* in August 1915 when, while attempting to enter the Baltic Sea, she went aground on Saltholm Island, neutral Danish territory in The Sound, that narrow neck of water joining the North Sea via the Skagerrak and Kattegat to the Baltic. The Germans, who maintained a permanent patrol in the area, were attracted by the activity of the Danish ships and discovered the immobilized E-boat. Long before the expiration of the internationally recognized 24-hour grace period, the time allowed a combatant to depart from neutral territory, and almost without warning, they shelled the helpless submarine, killing many of the crew and causing considerable damage before the Danes could intervene.

The survivors were eventually taken off and interned in Denmark. Eddis and his captain both broke parole and made their separate ways back to England. After his return Paul Eddis attended one of the early Periscope Courses and was given command of *E38*. In 1924 he was in command of the *L24*, which broke surface directly in front of the oncoming battleship HMS *Resolution*. Unable to avoid the collision, the huge ship ran over the unfortunate submarine, sinking her with all hands.

The two new RCN officers who joined the RN Submarine Service just before the war ended were both RNCC graduates, but neither had any previous submarine experience. A third officer a contemporary of the other pair, Sub-Lieutenant F.L. Houghton, had been scheduled for the course beginning November 7, 1918, but his name was withdrawn before commencement.

The first of the new arrivals was Sub-Lieutenant Valentine Stuart Godfrey. Born in England in 1898, his family had immigrated to Canada when he was still a youngster. Prior to entering the Navy he had attended Ashbury College in Ottawa and began his training at the RNCC in January 1913. In 1916 Midshipman Godfrey was posted to the battleship HMS *Barham* in the Grand Fleet. It was while he was in *Barham* that he volunteered. Upon being accepted for submarines he attended the course which commenced on August 8, 1918. Godfrey celebrated his twentieth birthday six days into the course, which ended on November 1.

Godfrey, who was not noted for scholarly achievement as a cadet, failed to pass the course by a few marks but, as junior submarine officers were in demand and as he was keen and showed some promise, he was given an opportunity to prove his worth. In the short time he spent in *Dolphin* he gained a reputation for being more than usually high spirited and was noted as being shabbily dressed, even by submariner standards. By the 5th of the month he had been posted to HMS *Platypus* at Campbeltown. Whether he actually went there at that time is not known. The records show he was posted to HMS *Maidstone* at Chatham ten days later for a month in a C-class boat, after which he probably continued on to Campbeltown. He was not sent to a boat straight away and spent a month kicking his heels as a spare officer, on his best behaviour and under his new CO's observation.

Twenty-one-year-old Acting Lieutenant Richard H. "Dick" Oland started his basic submarine course only four days before the armistice. A native of Dartmouth, Nova Scotia, and member of a prominent Maritimes brewery family, he was an RNCC classmate of Frank Houghton and Valentine Godfrey and had also been serving aboard HMS *Barham*. His submarine course would finish near the end of January. The outgoing, burly, young Canadian was popular with his instructors and course-mates alike. He made a good pass and was posted to *Ambrose* Flotilla.

On November 21, 1918, the German High Seas Fleet surrendered according to the terms of the armistice and sailed to internment at Scapa Flow under the escort of the ships of the Grand Fleet, whose crews stood by their battle stations throughout the short voyage. For the Royal Navy it was the last act of the war and signalled a return to peacetime routine and the beginning of a period of massive reductions. The huge navy that had evolved in the war was to be reduced as rapidly as possible until a manageable peacetime establishment was reached. The first stage of the process would take until 1921, the year of the Washington Conference.

After the armistice and the shift to peacetime routines had taken place, Cap' Johnson was ordered to put the *H14* and *H15* into reserve at Bermuda. While waiting he requested his release, in the hopes of returning to Canada aboard the *Shearwater*, but this was refused. The Admiralty still had need of his services. On December 13 Johnson and his men embarked aboard the cruiser HMS *Cornwall* for the return trip to England, arriving at Devonport on the 22nd and the following day at *Dolphin*, where he spent Christmas.

Early in the new year Johnson was given the task of looking after a dozen or so surrendered U-boats that had been collected at Portland, Dorset. These had been selected for presentation to the Allied nations as trophies of war, for technical evaluation and for service in their navies. He was given command of the *U-164*, one of the last large U-type German submarines completed. It was a paper command only, the submarine had no crew and was not seaworthy, but it did allow the Admiralty to continue paying him command and submarine allowances in recompense for his extended service and additional duties.

Late in January Barney Johnson was promoted to Commander and on April 24, 1919, he was finally demobilized. Returning to Vancouver in June, he found he'd been relegated to the "doghouse" by both family and Pilotage Service, each convinced he had been swinging the lead in England since the war ended. Within a short time, however, a fully reinstated Captain Johnson was back in the Pilotage Service trying to pick up where he'd left off four years and ten months previously.

At Halifax the CC-boats, along with most of the miscellaneous collection of small vessels that had been pressed into service during the war, were hastily paid off and the crews released. The two old cruisers had long ago been relegated to depot and accommodation-ship duties and both were immobile on their respective coasts. The *Shearwater* went into reserve in June 1919 and was sold into mercantile service five years later. The Admiralty ceded the two H-boats at Bermuda to Canada without cost and these were, with some reluctance, accepted by the Canadian government. They reached Halifax in the spring of 1919 and were placed in reserve until the composition of the post-war Navy could be decided upon.

At the end of December 1918, Commander Bertram Jones retired once again and, with his wife, Gwendolen, returned to the West Coast. Despite his requests, he had been denied the opportunity to serve overseas throughout the war, his services to the RCN being considered too important to permit his being employed elsewhere.

Lieutenant Hanson, RN, who had commanded *CC1* almost continuously since October 1914, returned to the Royal Navy early in 1919. He attempted to continue his career in submarines but was not successful. Returning to General Service he went aboard the battleship *Renown*, where he served for many years. His name disappears from the Navy Lists in the early 1930s.

Lieutenant Godfrey Lake, RNCVR, who had commanded the *CC2*, died quite suddenly and unexpectedly on October 25, a victim of pneumonia. He was only 37 years old but, like so many that autumn, he had contracted influenza, a serious malady in those days. He was a popular officer who had been with the submarines since the beginning, and his passing was mourned by all the submariners.

Lieutenant A.C.S. Pitts, who had joined the boats in late 1914, was demobilized at the end of December and returned to his home in British Columbia. Along with G.H.S. Edwardes he was one of the pioneer RNCVR officers and was the first person to be given a commission in that organization.

Chief Artificer Engineer Arthur J.S. Hunting was retained by the RCN to look after the CC-boats and the *H14* and *H15* when they were placed in reserve at Halifax. In September 1921, after eight years in Canada, he returned to service with the Royal Navy at Chatham, accompanied by his wife, Emma, and their three Canadian-born children. In accordance with prevailing regulations he was obliged to revert to his pre-war rank of chief ERA2.

Gunner (T) George Briscoe and Torpedo Coxswain Addison both returned to the West Coast, as did many of the men who had been engaged for the war only. ERA Dickie Pearson, who had helped out with the H-boat trials at Montreal in 1915, had been promoted to Artificer Engineer. After serving aboard the yacht-cum-destroyer HMCS *Grilse* and in the maintenance party for ships in reserve at Halifax, he was given the option of remaining in the Navy with reduction in rank or of taking a civil service job at NSHQ in Ottawa. He opted for Ottawa and held various positions in his department until retiring in 1963.

Another successful demobbed West Coast submariner who headed home that December was Fred Crickard. Fred had joined the submarines as an AB shortly after their arrival at Esquimalt. He came east with the boats as a leading seaman, was rated petty officer shortly afterward, and by the end of the war had been commissioned as a mate and was in command of a patrol boat, the *TR29*.

Crew of CC1 circa September 1918. Rear: third from left is Sig. M.S. Astwood, others unknown. Centre, left to right: CERA Stone, Ch. Art. Eng. Hunting, Lt. Hanson (CO), GNR (T) Geo. Briscoe, Torp. Cox'n Addison, ERA Turner, ERA Jones. Front: second from right is PO ST Riley, others unknown.
– Provincial Archives of BC

S-Lt. Valentine Godfrey and fellow officers in his Submarine Training Class, October 1918.
– RN Submarine Museum

Lt. W.J.R. Beech aboard HMS Titania *en route to China, 1919.*
– RN Submarine Museum

Crew of CC2 circa September 1918. Rear: LH man is Stkr. Sutherland, others unknown. Centre: Ch. Yeo. H. Reading, CERA Hawley, Ch. Art. Eng. Hunting, Lt. A.C.S. Pitts (CO), GNR(T) Briscoe, PO GL3 Woolet, Cox'n, unknown ERA. Front: unknown Stkr., LS ST Stapley, PO LTO Payne, unknown ERA, unknown ERA, PO TGM Marsden, PO LTO Porteous.
– Provincial Archives of BC

Dick Oland when he was Naval Control Officer at Halifax in 1940. – PAC 104481

Lieutenant John Grant Edwards, RCN, and his bride, Nora Helena (Richardson), on the occasion of their wedding reception at Potto Hall, Yorkshire, on October 15, 1919.

– courtesy John and Patricia (Edwards) Lansdell

The last of the RNCVR officers remaining in the Canadian Submarine Service at the end of the war, Lieutenant George H.S. Edwardes, was delegated to bring the two H-boats from Bermuda to Halifax in the spring of 1919 and to stand by them in reserve. Following the decision of March 1920 to release all but the RNCC-trained officers, Edwardes was retained until he could be relieved, and upon being released in July he too returned to Victoria. Shortly afterward he applied for command of the Victoria RNCVR Division, for which he was highly recommended on the basis of his long service and experience. Ottawa, however, was looking for a younger image for its post-war naval reserve and refused his request because of his age.

With the paying off of the CC-boats and the dispersal of their crews, the Canadian Navy's first experience with submarines came to an end. In that it proved the fledgling force could man and operate the craft, albeit with some indirect help from the Royal Navy, the effort was a success. Though never in action, the CC-boats had certainly proved their worth during the first few months of the war. They had been worked up in a remarkably short time and had kept the patrols for which they had been purchased. The boats and their crews had been ready, willing and capable of engaging the enemy, which, after all is said and done, was their only purpose. To assess their value on any other basis would be false. That they also proved a fertile training ground for active-service submariners was an unexpected bonus.

When the large German "Omnibus" U-boats appeared off the coast of Nova Scotia in the summer of 1918, both Canadian subs were in refit, recovering from their Odyssey from the West Coast. It was perhaps as well, for they were greatly overmatched by the German boats, which could outperform them in every way. Had the Canadian government acquired a pair of H-boats at the time Canadian Vickers made their offer, and equipped them properly, there may well have been some contest, but the CC-boats were long past their prime by that point.

Churchill, it will be remembered, had decreed that enemy naval forces would never appear off the North American coasts and the government had chosen to support this concept. Ignoring the military possibilities was certainly the least expensive alternative. When the East Coast patrol, a rag-tag collection of converted yachts, steamers and wooden patrol boats hastily assembled to counter the U-boat menace, did encounter one of the German intruders, the *U-156*, the intercepting vessel, instead of attacking as it should have done, put about to consult with the senior ship astern, giving rise to the first court-martial for "failing to engage the enemy" in the history of the RCN. Lacking experience in the use of hydrophones and without modern depth charges, there was little the RCN ships could have done once the U-boats dived in any case.

AFTER THE WAR

Except for Barney Johnson, who was released at the end of April 1919 and returned to Vancouver, all of the Canadian submariners serving overseas were regular RCN "straight stripers," as opposed to being members of the reservist forces which were demobilized immediately after the war. Of these, only Jock Edwards was not assured of a future with the Canadian Navy. After the armistice all of the remaining Canadians, including Jock, remained in service with the RN for the time being, and by June 1919 they had settled into new positions and were becoming accustomed to the regular routine.

Edwards was given command of the *R1*, one of the sleek little anti-submarine submarines, and was stationed at Fort Blockhouse. Ronald Watson had the *R2*, his second R-boat, which he'd taken over after five months in the *R8*, to which he'd been appointed after completing his probationary period in the *Thames* Flotilla.

Ronald Watson's R2, *his second command.* – RN Submarine Museum

Roy Beech had gone home to Victoria on a month's leave during February 1919, and shortly after his return to the UK he went aboard the *L1* as first lieutenant. This submarine was one of those selected for service on the China station, where the flotilla, which had been placed in reserve during the war, was being reformed. He was scheduled to sail for the Far East in September after a refit at Barrow.

Rupert Wood remained in *E38* as first lieutenant and was going to set a record, later to be broken several times, for the length of time spent in one submarine by a Canadian. His boat was now attached to *Maidstone* at Rosyth.

The long-suffering Royal Navy, with centuries of experience in the management of its personnel, had finally found a niche for Valentine Godfrey, in a K-boat. His new boat, the *K9*, was attached to *Platypus*, also at Rosyth. Although generally disliked and considered by some to be dangerous to serve in, the K-boats had large, comfortable wardrooms and as long as they weren't pressed too hard were tolerable to live in, for the officers that is, though certainly not for the men. *K9*'s unofficial ship's badge was unusual, though perhaps predictable. It consisted of one word, "GARM," the name of the dog of the underworld in Norse mythology and of a real dog belonging to King George V.

On completing his basic submarine course in April, Dick Oland was given the position of first lieutenant aboard the *R8* and took up his duties a month before Ronald Watson left for his second R-boat. He was born for the job and shouldered his new responsibilities easily and professionally. Except for Godfrey, who continued to draw critical remarks from his seniors, the new Canadians were settling in very well.

Big reductions were in the offing for the Submarine Service and these began to affect the Canadian group in the autumn of 1919. It was at this time that the Royal Navy began to lay up large numbers of obsolescent submarines, including all of those fitted with 18-inch torpedo tubes, as it had been decided to standardize on the more effective 21-inch torpedo throughout the Navy. Both Edwards' *R1* and Watson's *R2* were placed in reserve and the two Canadians were put in charge of their respective reserve groups, where they supervised the care of the laid-up submarines.

Prior to this depressing event there was a happy occasion to be celebrated when, on October 15, Jock Edwards married Nora Helena Richardson, daughter of Edwin Backhouse Richardson, a Yorkshire shipbuilder. The wedding was held in the Village Church, Swainby, and the reception at Potto Hall, the Richardson home. The new Mrs. Edwards, however, would not spend long as the wife of a Canadian naval officer.

In accordance with Kingsmill's instructions regarding officers not trained at the RNCC, Jock Edwards was obliged to relinquish his temporary commission in the RCN and his resignation took effect on May 1, 1920. He remained in England and settled down to family life. The young Edwards couple would bring three children into the world, two girls and a boy. Their youngest daughter would one day marry a Canadian businessman and settle in Vancouver. During the late 1920s Jock acquired a substantial home at Flixton, near Scarborough, in Yorkshire, where he and his family would reside until the mid-1950s.

E38 was another veteran destined for the breakers and Rupert Wood was transferred to the newer *H27*, again as first lieutenant. Shortly after taking up his new post, however, he fell ill and was hospitalized. Thinking to give another Canadian an opportunity, the authorities at Blockhouse posted Valentine Godfrey into Wood's vacant position for a six-month tryout as first lieutenant in a small submarine. Upon his release from hospital Wood was posted into one of the reserve groups at Portsmouth to give him a bit of a break. During the summer of 1920 he took three months accumulated war leave at home on Vancouver Island. Upon his return to England in September he was sent to

HMS/M L1 *at Hong Kong.*
– RN Submarine Museum

HMS/M M2 – RN Submarine Museum

HMS *Royal Arthur*, the depot at Rosyth. In October he would find himself posted aboard the *K8* as first lieutenant.

Godfrey's tenure as a first lieutenant was not a great success. Perhaps at 21 he was not yet ready for the responsibilities involved, or maybe, as his seniors noted, he was having too good a time ashore. In any event, after an adverse report in his new capacity, he was posted back to the big submarines to gain more experience and maturity, this time to HMS/M *M2* at Rosyth. She was one of the three 1,900-ton (dived displacement) "mutton boats," so called because of the resemblance of the big 12-inch gun and its gunhouse to a leg of lamb. At least, that's how the sailors who manned them saw it. These boats had been provided with reasonable accommodation for all hands, were impressive to look at, and possessed a certain public appeal. As a result they were often sent on long goodwill cruises to major Mediterranean and European ports and were frequently to be found in the company of battleships. No further complaints were registered concerning young Lieutenant Godfrey. After three months he was posted to the *M1*, where he would remain until leaving Royal Navy submarines in July 1921, when he returned to Canada for service in Canadian submarines.

Dick Oland, who had shifted to *H30* after *R8* was laid up in October 1919, remained in his new boat for ten months, transferred to *H51* for a few months, and then settled down aboard *H34*, where he was to remain for the following two years. She was a *Maidstone* submarine and the flotilla was under the command of the very distinguished submariner Captain Max (much later, Sir Max) K. Horton. He was succeeded by Captain Geoffrey Layton, who had been Eddis's captain in the ill-fated *E13*. Dick Oland was always regarded as a capable and likable young officer who obviously enjoyed being in submarines. He had been highly recommended for a command when he was forced to leave them for good in August 1922.

Beech arrived on the China station in November 1919, after a two-month voyage halfway around the world, and he would remain in the Far East as first lieutenant of the *L1* until he left submarines to return to Canada in May 1921, bettering Wood's record of 19 months in one boat by one month. He had been given command of the *L1* while she was in refit and was being considered for his "Perisher" when he was appointed to the RNCC, which had moved to Esquimalt after the Halifax explosion. He was reluctant to abandon the advantages he had won in the Submarine Service, but there was really no option, he had to consider his career in terms of what was required of him by the RCN. Beech would return to the submarine world for a short period much later in his career.

There was to be one last new submariner before the Canadian government closed the chapter on submarines and submariners for good in mid-1922. The lone peacetime volunteer was a graduate of the term of 1914, the fourth class to pass through the RNCC. After nearly four years aboard British capital ships Sub-Lieutenant Colin Degge Donald was accepted into the Submarine Service.

The big, athletic, 22-year-old Canadian hailed from Chemainus, a community on Vancouver Island in the same general area from which had come Maitland-Dougall, Wood and Beech. Like the others, Colin had been a student at Mr. Skrimshire's Preparatory School and was in the junior term when Godfrey and Oland graduated from the Naval College at Halifax. Colin was very good at sports and had undoubted potential as a boxer but was not noted for his sharpness of intellect. Nevertheless, he made a good pass in his basic submarine course and toward the end of July 1920 was posted to *K22* at Rosyth, where he joined Valentine Godfrey and would later be joined by Rupert Wood.

The war was now long over and all the remaining RCN submarine officers were busy pursuing their peacetime careers. At home in Canada, however, changes were in the wind, for the government and for the much-maligned Naval Service of Canada.

13   THE CANADIAN H-BOATS

In December 1918, Ottawa agreed to accept the two British H-boats offered free of charge to Canada by the Imperial government. Maybe it was too good a bargain to pass up, especially when, in 1915, the First Lord had expected the Canadians to pay the going price. By then, however, Churchill was long gone from the Admiralty and a different attitude prevailed at Whitehall. It is also highly likely that the Colonial Office had advised the Admiralty that the offer of the boats would serve as an appeasement to the Canadians, whose feathers were still a trifle ruffled by the Admiralty's arrogant handling of the original Canadian Vickers construction contract.

The optimists reasoned that the submarines were being given to Canada as replacements for the CC-boats which had been worn out in Admiralty service. This is a likely hypothesis. The Naval Service itself had shown little concern for submarines after the disappointments of 1915, and keeping the CC-boats going had been entirely a political decision predicated on the needs of the Admiralty. Canada certainly had no need of the boats after December 1914. The cynics took the view that, as all the surviving North American-built British H-class were destined for the scrap heap anyway, it was perhaps just a way of getting rid of two of them without incurring further expense to the Crown.

After considerable prodding by the Admiralty, who were anxious to get them off their hands, the two vessels made the short voyage to Halifax during May. There they were laid up in the dockyard while the debate dragged on as to what the composition of Canada's post-war navy was to be. At the time the subs were placed under the care of Lieutenant G.H.S. Edwardes, who had been given the task of bringing them to Halifax. Edwardes had a small crew of maintainers, headed by Chief Artificer Engineer Arthur Hunting, who looked after the retired CC-boats as well as the two new H-boats.

It was April 1920 before the decision was made to refit and commission the two new submarines into the RCN. They were to be known simply and unimaginatively as *CH14* and *CH15*. All work needed to bring them into operation was to be done as cheaply as possible: the Navy had little money to spare and the sort of wastage condoned during the recent war was severely frowned upon by the peacetime accountants.

As Lieutenant Edwardes was overdue for release, a new SO Subs had to be found. Ronald Watson was the senior serving RCN submariner and it was decided to bring him home to take command of the little flotilla. Other RCN officers serving in British submarines would be repatriated when the time came to fill out the rest of the officer complement. To man the boats a cadre of experienced petty officers and men would be recruited from the Royal Navy, not borrowed as had been done in wartime, while the bulk of the crews were to be volunteers from within the RCN itself.

H14 *and* H15 *at dock in Halifax, 1920.* - PAC HS-22592

Watson had commissioned the brand-new *H44* at Vickers, Barrow, in February 1920, completed her trials and joined the flotilla at Blockhouse when word reached him that he was going home. After nearly four years abroad, mostly in the Adriatic, Aegean and Mediterranean, he was on his way back to Halifax to take command of the new flotilla.

He was at once elated and disappointed. Returning to Canada to found a submarine branch in the peacetime navy was very gratifying but he and Aimee, his sweetheart from Malta days, had been planning to "tie the knot" that August. These plans were hurriedly pushed forward. Watson and his bride sailed for Canada on April 23, 1920, aboard the S.S. *Scotian*. He had two months war leave coming to him and on arrival reported to Commander Hose at headquarters in Halifax before heading for Edmonton to visit with his parents.

When he returned to assume his new duties, Ronald Watson found he had his work cut out for him. Two long winters had passed since the boats were laid up and little maintenance had been done beyond heating them, pumping out the bilges and keeping them dry. The batteries had been landed for safe storage and would have to be put back aboard. Both boats needed docking. He had no budget of his own and precious little in the way of facilities or manpower. As there was no money he was going to have to rely on ingenuity and common sense, which fortunately for him was something most submariners are amply blessed with. Arthur Hunting was going to prove invaluable, as were his ERAs. There was no hurry, however; they at least had time on their side.

By December conditions in the flotilla had improved considerably. A shore base was set up in one of the dockyard buildings, what had been the Patrol Base workshops and stores, with space to accommodate two crews, offices and workshops. A minimum base establishment had been approved, including a petty officer to take charge, a writer, a victualling PO, a PO cook, a junior cook, messmen for the senior rates' messes, messdeck sweepers and a modest working party.

When considering the make-up of the little base, which leaned rather heavily on the domestic side, it must be remembered that in those days all hands were expected to live and eat in the barracks or ship to which they belonged. Unless it was in the interests of the service and only when absolutely necessary, personnel, whether married or single, lived ashore entirely at their own expense, and sleeping and eating on board made good economic sense.

Although the flotilla was not allowed to take any crewmen on strength until the submarines were operational, manning levels for the two boats and a spare crew were under discussion, a roster of volunteers was being maintained, and Lieutenant Rupert Wood was being brought back to help out and eventually to command the other boat.

After a fact-finding visit to Canada by Viscount Jellicoe of Scapa, much debate in the House of Commons and the consideration of many permutations of types and numbers, the size and composition of Canada's post-war navy was tentatively decided upon in mid-1920. The reconstituted peacetime navy was to consist of cruiser, a pair of destroyers and the two submarines. The surface ships were to be purchased from the Admiralty; there was neither the time nor the capacity available to build in Canadian yards and, in any case, Canadian-built ships were much more expensive. It was an interim decision, the outcome of the Imperial Conference on Defence scheduled for 1921 would, hopefully, determine the future of the RCN in concert with that of the Royal Navy and those of the other Dominions. The new ships, the cruiser *Aurora* and the destroyers *Patrician* and *Patriot*, arrived at Halifax on December 21, 1920.

Admiral Sir Charles E. Kingsmill, as he had become, had hoped for a somewhat larger two-coast force and continued to do his best to educate members of Parliament in

In commission at last. CH14 *and* CH15 *"dressed overall."* – author's collection

Colin Donald aboard one of the CH-boats in 1921.
– DND photo PMR 85-683

what a navy was and how it worked, but he was pleading with a crowd of philistines, most of whom could not see past the dollar figures involved. What did a navy matter now that the war to end all wars was over? Disarmament was in the air and it had great public appeal. There were political advantages to be gained from diverting funds into social programs instead of a large and supposedly useless navy.

For Watson the arrival of the cruiser and new destroyers that December was something of a boon, as it provided him with a sympathetic base from which to draw a small number of experienced men when the time came. The ships' companies of the new ships were composed mostly of ex-Royal Navy personnel, at least some of whom had seen service in submarines at one time or another during the war. Being a cruiser, the *Aurora* was authorized to provide examination services for ratings wishing to compete for promotion in rank or to improve their trade qualifications, which allowed Watson to make the best possible use of the few trained men he did have. The presence of the ships also occasioned more activity in the dockyard and inspired a renewal of local interest in the Navy, from which the little submarine base could only benefit.

Service in the reconstituted RCN was an attractive proposition for the one-time British sailors. For the most part they kept their rank and standing in their trades, were better paid than in the post-war RN and provided with better accommodation both in barracks and aboard ship.

Both boats had been officially put into self-refit during April 1920, and it was decided they would commission 12 months later. Rupert Wood arrived in January, probably happy to have escaped from his K-boat and happier still to be back in Canada with the prospect of his own command. He had already taken his 87 days war leave during the summer of 1920, when he and his brother Maurice, at that time a sub-lieutenant attached to HMS *Stoneaxe*, had come home together. Both officers were thoroughly familiar with the task at hand, having attended several refits between them during the war, and work proceeded smoothly under the expert technical guidance of Arthur Hunting.

On April 1, 1921, *CH14* and *CH15* were officially commissioned, at which time the volunteers were entered on the submarine flotilla's books and the organization became self-contained. At first the flotilla could only muster enough men for one complete crew, that was sufficient to get things started. Training had been progressing while the boats were in refit, both in the classroom and on board, where the students were set to work. Once they were seaworthy the submarines were taken up to Bedford Basin one at a time for drills and exercises reminiscent of the antics of the CC-boats off Esquimalt during September 1914, but without the handicap of an unsound design.

By the end of December there were 50 men in the flotilla. Seven had come directly from the RN, a few had seen service in the CC-boats toward the end of the war, a further group was drawn from the *Aurora*, while the bulk came from the ranks of the post-war RCN. It was remarked that several came from inland and a number were from Quebec. The RCN volunteers were very green. Most had never been to sea in their lives, never mind served aboard submarines, but they were willing and it was worth it too.

In 1921 a junior rate's submarine allowance was 50 cents a day for every day actually spent aboard a boat, plus 25 cents a day hard lying money. The latter was received in recognition of the uncomfortable living conditions and reduced scale of rations that was part of small-craft life in those days. There were few bunks for the hands in the CH-boats, most slept on the deck when at sea. As had been usual during the war, food came from tins or jars and it was impossible to keep fresh foods edible for more than a day or so. The boats, however, were not expected to spend extended periods at sea.

For an Able Seaman, whose basic pay amounted to $1.90 a day, the extra 75 cents in allowances represented a significant increase in income. Chief petty officers and ERAs received 60 cents a day in submarine allowance, while petty officers received 30 cents; both groups were entitled to a hard-lyers' allowance of 25 and 30 cents a day respectively. Although their special allowances were slightly less than in the Imperial service, the basic rates of pay were higher in all cases, as a result of which all ratings in Canadian service received more pay than their Royal Navy counterparts.

Officers, on the other hand, fared less well. Their submarine allowance was a dollar a day, but they were not entitled to hard-lyers'. This was something of a sore point with the Canadians because their contemporaries serving with the RN and in the RN itself were entitled to the hard-lyers' allowance. Their complaint was that Canadians overseas and their equivalents in the RN all received the same pay, and this left the Canadians serving at home aboard Canadian subs 75 cents a day out of pocket. The NSC, however, remained adamant and the officers never did get the hard-lyers' in Canadian service.

By mid-August both submarines were operational and it was then that Valentine Godfrey and Colin Donald arrived to act as first lieutenants to Watson and Wood aboard *CH15* and *CH14*. That summer and fall the boats made courtesy visits around the Maritime provinces, calling in at Sydney, Cape Breton Island, Charlottetown, Prince Edward Island, and St. John, New Brunswick, as well as a stopover at Boston, Massachusetts. Six years after they had first been requested and three years after the end of the war, Halifax had its submarines.

The Canadian winter was hard on ships, and keeping them heated was expensive. It was decided to send the submarines to Bermuda for the winter months along with the rest of the tiny fleet. It was there, early in February 1922, that Rupert Wood married Marjorie Johns Burril of Yarmouth, Nova Scotia. The happy event took place in the Bermuda Cathedral and was no doubt well attended by officers and men from the submarines and ships in harbour.

The deployment to Bermuda that winter was something of a swan song for the submariners, and indeed for the rest of the Canadian Navy. When Mackenzie King's Liberals took office on December 29, 1921, even the much-reduced RCN became a target for financial cutbacks, and at the first opportunity its budget of $2,500,000 was arbitrarily slashed to $1,500,000. This in effect sounded the death knell of Canada's regular navy and by June 1922 the dismemberment of the force was complete. The cruiser went, as also did the two submarines, and while the destroyers and some trawlers were retained, these were split between the east and west coasts as training vessels. Although a large reserve force would eventually be created, for all practical purposes the professional RCN had ceased to exist.

When the dust had settled, Ronald Watson found himself back in the UK taking a long Physical and Recreation Training officers' course, from which he was to emerge almost a year later. Rupert Wood remained in the Navy and began the usual peacetime pattern of serving in various positions in Canada and the UK, as also did Valentine Godfrey.

Throughout this period Dick Oland had continued in his duties as first lieutenant aboard *H34*. With the reductions of 1922, however, he was reverted to General Service as of mid-September. He had enjoyed his time in boats and was highly recommended for a command, but as Canada had paid off its submarines, there was no future for him in that branch.

Colin Donald returned to the British Submarine Service and was appointed to *K6*, where he resumed his position of navigator. During the spring of 1923 he won the heavyweight boxing championship of the Atlantic Fleet and his CO, Lieutenant-

K6 *entering harbour and passing the battleship HMS* Queen Elizabeth. – DND photo E68-948

Commander O.E. Hallifax, who was well acquainted with the Canadians, remarked that he had "a cheerful temperament; keeps himself fit and is keen on games and exercise." In August he too returned to General Service to pursue a career in surface ships.

With Colin Donald's return to General Service, all of the Canadians had left submarines. Although most continued their naval careers, none was to return to actually serve aboard a submarine, although one did make a brief appearance later on.

In 1935 William Beech, by then a commander, was appointed to the position of Staff Officer, Operations, 1st Submarine Flotilla, under Captain (S) D'Oyly Hughes, DSO, DSC. The flotilla was based in the Mediterranean on the old depot ship *Cyclops* and his appointment was for one year. Beech was the last Canadian to participate in submarine operations until after the outbreak of World War II.

Most of the submariners followed the normal career pattern of the times, and with one exception all were still around when the next war erupted. That exception was Ronald Watson, who met a tragic and dramatic death one summer's eve in 1924.

Having returned from his P & RT course, Watson was appointed to HMCS *Naden*, the naval barracks at Esquimalt, as first lieutenant. A physically active man, he enjoyed sailing, and in order to combine this with his duties of base P & RT officer, he often took a whaler out sailing on the weekends with a crew of junior seamen.

On the afternoon of Saturday, July 12, 1924, Lieutenant Ronald Watson, his wife, Aimee, and three boy seamen, all in their late teens, set out from Esquimalt on a sail-training cruise in a standard 27-foot naval whaler. Around 7:30 that evening the boat was seen proceeding under sail in the direction of Foul Bay, and that was the last time they were sighted. When the whaler failed to return to base by sunset, a search party was organized and a search begun.

The light of dawn revealed the overturned, waterlogged, stripped and dismasted remains of the whaler in the cold waters of Foul Bay, where it was retrieved by a man who lived near the shore. When he realized what it was he'd found, he informed the authorities, who then began the sad task of searching for bodies, it being presumed there would be no survivors because of the low water temperature and thick beds of kelp. Only the remains of Aimee Watson were ever found. It was evident that efforts had been made by her companions to save her life but without success.

Driven into the shallows by adverse winds and treacherous currents, the boat had fouled her drop-keel and capsized amidst thick beds of kelp. Around 10 p.m. cries that could have been made by the survivors were heard by residents living near the shoreline but were taken for the squawkings of seagulls, their significance not being appreciated until the following day.

The Watsons left two infant children: a son, Gordon Calloway, age three, and a daughter, Barbara Fleury, only nine months old. The children were adopted by Watson's parents, who by that time had moved to Wichita, Kansas.

When World War II broke out, many of the remaining First World War submariners were either still in uniform or they returned to the Navy as the storm clouds gathered. In September 1939, Wood, Beech, Godfrey and Donald were all serving officers in the RCN, and Barney Johnson, who had already been involved in preparations for the coming conflict, soon had his uniform back on again.

Barney, who was 61 when his second war started, would see service both ashore and afloat. His first appointment was that of Officer in Charge of the Port of Vancouver, and he was later given command of the patrol-boat depot ship HMCS *Preserver*, which he took to Newfoundland waters. Barney later returned to Vancouver and finally accepted retirement from active service late in 1944. Toward the end of the war he was made a CBE for his valued services.

Commander B.L. Johnson, DSO, RNR, Belfast 1919.
– Vancouver City Archives

Wood, who was the CO of HMCS *Naden* that fateful September, would spend most of the war at Headquarters as Director of Ordnance, Mines and Torpedoes. Beech held various senior appointments at Halifax and later on the West Coast, where he relieved Wood as CO of *Naden*. His command was later expanded to include the dockyard and the entire Canadian Pacific Coast, for which he received a promotion to Commodore.

The "peppery" Godfrey would spend most of the war in command of one or other of the large converted B.C. ferries, HMCS *Prince David* and *Prince Henry*, aboard which he saw a fair amount of action. Colin Donald commanded two ships, HMCS *Annapolis* and HMCS *Ottawa*, and, like the others, held a variety of senior appointments ashore.

Jock Edwards tried to get a commission in the regular RCN but was refused and had to settle for the RNVR, where he served out the war. He was highly commended for his part in the planning of the Normandy invasion.

Robert Lawson, who had taken retirement in 1928 as a lieutenant commander, was reinstated and went to work at Headquarters in Montreal. Unfortunately he suffered from poor health and died in hospital toward the end of February 1941.

Dick Oland, who had left the Navy in 1930, was recalled to serve as the Naval Control Service Officer at Halifax, where he was instrumental in organizing the control of merchant shipping in that great wartime port. For his efforts he was made an OBE in the King's 1941 Birthday Honours list and was promoted to captain. Regrettably Dick Oland succumbed to a severe heart attack on the afternoon of September 15, 1941. Even in the midst of a deepening Battle of the Atlantic, senior seamen from both Canada and Britain took time to mourn the passing of a fine sailor and gentleman.

The RCN would own no more submarines until 1961, and although it emerged from World War II as the third-largest navy and one of the largest anti-submarine forces in the world, it would have no interest in submarine operations beyond those necessary for anti-submarine training. Canadian sailors, however, would still be fascinated by undersea craft. Although very few actually volunteered for submarines in the classic sense, about two dozen young RCNVR officers would serve for at least part of the war in British submarines, some with considerable distinction.

Looking forward. A D-class at sea in rough weather off Ireland.

– RN Submarine Museum

APPENDIX ONE

ROYAL NAVY SUBMARINES
IN WHICH CANADIAN OFFICERS SERVED
1914-1923

SUB	OFFICER	POS'N	FROM - TO		DEPOT-OPS NOTES
C18	J.G. Edwards	CO	1.12.18	1.1.19	Thames, Perisher
D1	W.M. M-Dougall	CO	12.9.17	10.11.18	Thames, OPS
D3	B.L. Johnson	CO	12.4.16	11.11.17	East Coast & Ireland
D3	W.M. M-Dougall	1st LT	5.5.16	11.9.17	East Coast & Ireland
D3	W.M. M-Dougall	CO	12.11.17	12.3.18	VI Flot. Channel (lost)
D4	R.W. Wood	3rd	1.2.17	1.1.18	Platypus, N. Atlantic
E2	R.C. Watson	1st LT	25.9.17	28.1.18	Adamant, Med & Adriatic
E11	R.C. Watson	1st LT	11.5.17	25.9.17	Adamant, Med & Adriatic
E11	R.C. Watson	1st LT	13.6.18	10.9.18	Adamant, Med & Aegean
E38	R.W. Wood	1st LT	1.4.18	1.10.19	Platypus, N. Atlantic
E54	B.L. Johnson	CO	22.11.17	27.5.18	Ambrose, N. Atlantic
E55	J.G. Edwards	1st LT	1.11.17	12.10.18	Maidstone, N. Sea
H2	R.C. Watson	1st LT	1.10.16	1.1.17	Med & Special Service
H8	B.L. Johnson	CO	7.5.15	26.3.16	N. Sea, mined, paid-off
H9	W.J.R. Beech	1st LT	1.2.17	1.3.18	Maidstone, N. Sea
H10	W.M. M-Dougall	3rd	24.6.15	4.5.16	Maidstone, N. Sea
H10	R.F. Lawson	1st LT	5.6.16	1.8.17	Maidstone, N. Sea
H15	B.L. Johnson	CO	Jul '18	Dec '18	USA, to Bermuda only
H27	R.W. Wood	1st LT	24.9.19	1.11.19	Dolphin
H27	V.S. Godfrey	1st LT	1.11.19	18.5.20	Dolphin
H30	R.H. Oland	1st LT	1.9.19	18.6.20	Vulcan
H34	R.H. Oland	1st LT	18.8.20	15.9.22	Maidstone
H44	R.C. Watson	CO	18.2.20	12.5.20	Rosyth
H51	R.H. Oland	1st LT	18.6.20	8.8.20	Vulcan
K6	C.D. Donald	4th	4.10.22	31.8.23	Rosyth
K9	V.S. Godfrey	4th	1.2.19	1.7.19	Rosyth
K22	C.D. Donald	4th	28.7.20	18.8.21	Rosyth
L1	W.J.R. Beech	1st LT	23.6.19	26.9.20	Titania, China Stn.
L1	W.J.R. Beech	A/CO	26.9.20	31.12.21	Titania, China Stn.
L7	J.G. Edwards	1st LT	1.1.19	1.6.19	Ambrose
L8	W.J.R. Beech	1st LT	1.3.18	1.3.19	Dolphin, Atlantic
M1	V.S. Godfrey	Jun.O	17.8.20	17.8.20	Inconstant, Rosyth
M2	V.S. Godfrey	Jun.O	18.5.20	17.8.20	Inconstant, Rosyth
R1	J.G. Edwards	CO	1.6.19	7.11.19	Dolphin
R2	R.C. Watson	CO	1.6.19	1.11.19	Dolphin
R8	R.C. Watson	1st LT	1.1.19	1.4.19	Dolphin
R8	R.H. Oland	1st LT	1.4.19	1.9.19	Dolphin
V3	R.C. Watson	CO	12.10.18	1.1.19	Thames, Perisher

APPENDIX TWO

Transcript of the article written by Jane Anderson following her visit with Cap' Johnson and *H8* at Chatham.

DAILY MAIL
May 21, 1916

SUBMARINE DRAMA

HOW A MINED BOAT
RETURNED HOME

SHATTERED VESSEL'S 300-MILE VOYAGE

In the annals of the Navy there is no more amazing story than that of a British submarine that was mined and sunk and yet made her way home safely and unaided. In a certain dockyard in England, writes Jane Anderson, telling the story, there is to be found a splendid tribute to the powers of British submarines and the skill of those who man them. It is one of the finest of His Majesty's undersea boats, which, with her bow twisted and bent as the result of a collision with an enemy mine in enemy waters, covered a distance of almost 300 miles under her own power, and arrived safely in a home port. Through the courtesy of the British Admiralty, I was permitted to see this submarine and talk with her officers, and her crew. She is in harbour, with her bow plating torn into strips and two of her torpedo tubes crushed. Her plates are crumpled; two of her bulkheads are broken away at the bow, but in her tubes are two unexploded torpedoes. The casing of the tubes is twisted and staved in, and the rear doors of them are jammed. But the quality of the high explosive in her torpedoes and the mechanism controlling it prevented an explosion, thus saving her from total destruction. She struck a mine head-on. The explosion smashed two of her bulkheads, broke all glass aboard her, and sent the crew sprawling to the floor of the compartments. But her torpedoes did not explode; her motors did not stop; her dials did not fail to register. She

DROPPED TO THE BOTTOM OF THE SEA,

and the water flooded in under the doors of the torpedo tubes. But within ten minutes after the collision she had been righted, had come to the surface, and turned her nose towards home. When I looked at her lying with her exposed tubes shining in the sunlight and her bulkheads in strips of rusty iron, it seemed incredible that she had been under the coast guns of the enemy, that she could have made in her damaged condition a journey of 300 miles, returning to a safe harbour with the information she had been sent to obtain. And, added to this, was the fact that she had made the voyage in a high sea, that for 20 hours, defenceless, she evaded the enemy patrols. I had heard stories of German

Johnson on the bridge bringing his battered command alongside HMS Maidstone at Harwich, March 23, 1916. – RN Submarine Museum

submarines sunk by a single shot, so I asked one of the officers how his boat had survived the tremendous shock of a mine explosion. "She held because of her strength," he said. "It broke her bow and it tore off two of her bulkheads. But the last one held. The efficiency of her pumps was not impaired. Within two minutes we had them working." He asked me if I would not come below and see the marks of the disaster. So I followed him across the gangway and on to the narrow deck which already was beginning to show red patches of rust. The hatch was open. Below I could see a white compartment with brass fittings. When I stood in this compartment I could see no traces whatsoever of the catastrophe. Directly in front of me were the rear doors of the torpedo tubes, painted a brilliant white: and to my right and left the great shining torpedoes were clamped in their racks. Only the wheel controlling the bow rudder was not true. The slender brass rod supporting it had suffered from the vibration. This was

THE ONLY MARK MADE BY THE MINE

of the enemy. Not that it was to be estimated as minor damage. For the rudders have their part to play in the rise and dive, and it was necessary to come up from the bottom of the sea. Not a simple matter with the rudders under control. "You see," one of the officers explained to me, "we didn't know what had happened — the water was spurting in and broken glass was everywhere. We didn't know how much of her was gone. We knew that every man aboard her had been knocked flat on his face, that the glass of the dials was rattling about underfoot. But we didn't know what was to become of us. We were as far down as we could be, and, as for getting up — well, it didn't look like much of a chance

. . . It was fine, you know, to see the crew. They got on their feet and at their stations before the commander had time to order them there. In two minutes the order to rise had gone through the engine room and the pumps were going. But whether we were going to rise or not remained to be seen. It was still enough, down there, after all the noise of the explosion. You could hear the motors turning — it's not much of a sound they make. But we were glad enough to hear it. And when we saw the bubble in the clinometer was registering, and the inclination was becoming less, we knew that matters were not as bad as they might have been. Then they reversed the motors. We waited. That was

A BAD MINUTE.

Then the broken glass began to rattle about again. We were moving. We weren't long in getting up. At any time there's nothing like coming up into the air and sunlight after you've been under for a hit. But this was different. Yes, this was a bit different. We came up. In the silence room there was the noise of the wireless sparking. The operator was testing it. At any rate we were floating. So we started looking her over for the damage." This was how he told it to me — the story of that black interval when these officers and the men of the crew waited at 100 feet below water level, not knowing whether or not their bulkheads were destroyed, whether their instruments were irreparably damaged, whether or not they would ever come up again into the sunlight. It was his ship he seemed to think of above all other things. "We found out what we'd come into," he said, "knew that there was no mistake about the mine. Things didn't look particularly promising. But it all came down to whether we could make port alone. Or whether we couldn't. The wireless was working. That is, we could send; we couldn't receive. We took a look at the bow plating and at the bulkheads. They looked pretty bad, hanging loose in strips. But we decided we could make it. The engines were right, nothing broken there. The periscope was true. It was only her bow and her rudder that were gone. So we started back. We drove along under our own power. It was a bit of a sea, but we made it. The waves broke over the bridge and pounded on the one bulkhead we had left forward. And so," he said, and smiled, "we came home." Then he took me over his ship, and explained its mysteries to me. He took me through four compartments, each one resplendent with white paint and polished brass. He showed me the periscope, lowered it, and revealed to me the grey horizon with the ships ranged against it. When I marvelled at this, he turned the periscope, and there flashed up before me, in a little clear image

A MINUTE PICTURE OF MEN

walking amidships of one of those distant vessels. Then he explained the fine mechanism of the control-room to me, and pointed out places for the men who have certain stations in this vital compartment. I do not think that I have ever seen such delicacy of construction as I saw in this immaculate little room and such evidence of efficiency and concentration. This was the heart of the ship; beyond the great water-tight doors there was the engine room with the breathing pipes and white intakes overhead, and beyond another white door was the battery room. But the control room was the centre of the source of power.

When I came up on the deck I remembered this room above all the others. But the officer who was with me would not admit that one part of his ship was finer than another.

I could not blame him for this. For I looked again at her smashed bow and torn bulkheads and I remembered that she had come some three hundred miles with the heavy seas pounding her. That she had dodged the patrols; that she had sent no message asking for help. She had come back broken, battered, helpless. But the work she had been sent to do she had done.

APPENDIX THREE

Text of Johnson's letter to Petty Officer Fred Wall, written sometime during the first two weeks of May 1916.

H. M. Submarine "D3"
% G. P.O.

H.M.S. MAIDSTONE,

SUBMARINE DEPÔT.

Dear Wall,

I regret to hear that the original plan of sending the crew to "Alecto" has not been carried out. As I am strange to this type of boat, the responsibility of taking everybody with me would be too great, so I shall endeavour to fill every vacancy *as it occurs* from my old crew. I have already applied for Fletcher and for Prior.

Will you do your best to keep track of all hands so that in event of there being a "H 12" we might be once more a crew.

Will you please convey my thanks to all hands for the gallant way in which they behaved on our last "stunt". I'm sorry that my influence was not sufficient to secure them the substantial reward which you all so thoroughly earned.

I hope that you will let me know which boat you get and I have every hope that we shall soon be shipmates again

Yours sincerely

B. L. Johnson

BIBLIOGRAPHY

During the five years spent researching this volume I have been privileged to be able to conduct my inquiries at or through the auspices of a variety of institutions where I have examined a considerable quantity of original source material. These include:

Public Archives Canada
The Public Archives of British Columbia
The Public Record Office, Kew
The Directorate of History, NDHQ Ottawa
The Royal Navy Submarine Museum Archives, Gosport
The General Register and Record Office of Shipping and Seamen, Cardiff

Unpublished Sources:

Johnson, B.L. "Naval Events 1914-1918." Vancouver City Archives, Add. MS 581.

Moth, Oscar. "Diary of a Submarine Coxswain." RN Submarine Museum, Gosport, Hants, UK.

Admiralty Publications:

OU 5528 (Previously CB 917) *Naval Staff Monographs (Historical)*. Admiralty, London.

BR 3043 *The Development of HM Submarines 1901-1930*. Ministry of Defence, London, 1979.

Submarines, 1914-1920. D.N.C. Department, Admiralty.

The Navy List. H.M. Stationery Office, London.

Published Sources: (a selection)

Compton-Hall, Commander Richard. *Submarine Boats*. Conway Maritime Press, London, 1983.

Edwards, Lt. Cdr. Kenneth. *We Dive at Dawn*. The Reilly & Lee Co., Chicago, 1941.

Halpern, Paul G. *The Naval War in the Mediterranean 1914-1918*. Naval Institute Press, Annapolis, 1987.

Hacking, Norman. *The Two Barneys*. Vancouver, 1984.

Hough, Richard. *The Great War at Sea 1914-1918*. Oxford University Press, 1983.

Jameson, William. *The Most Formidable Thing*. Rupert Hart-Davis, London, 1965.

Kemp, Lt. Cdr. P.K. *H.M. Submarines*. Herbert Jenkins, London, 1952.

Kipling, Rudyard. *Sea Warfare*. MacMillan and Co. Ltd., London, 1916.

"Klaxon," Commander J.G. Bower, RN. *The Story of Our Submarines*. William Blackwood and Sons, Edinburgh, 1919.

Liddle, Peter H. *The Sailors' War 1914-1918*. Blandford Press Ltd., 1985.

Newbolt, Sir Henry. *Submarine and Anti-Submarine*. Longmans, Green and Co., London, 1919.

Smith, Gaddis. *Britain's Clandestine Submarines, 1914-1915*. Yale University Press, 1964.

Tucker, Gilbert Norman. *The Naval Service of Canada*. King's Printer, Ottawa, 1952.

INDEX

trials, 71-72; replaces prop, 73, 77

H2 crew to Canada, 69; to Quebec, 71; crew to Canada, 69; to Quebec, 71, 75; to Gibraltar, has problems, 76; Watson 1st Lt., refit at Venice, 149, 151

H3, 75; sunk at Cattaro, 167

H4 crew to Canada, 69; launched by Mrs. Pirie, to Quebec, 71; at Rose Blanche Bay, 74-75; arrives St. John's, 76

(H5-H10 - see also 2nd Group)

H5 crew arrives Canada, 73, 78, 84, 87; new battery, 95; to Harwich, 97; makes patrol to Kattegat, 98-99, 121; Lowestoft raid, 136-138; joins Vulcan Flotilla on Adventure patrol, 153; lost, 180

H6 crew arrives Montreal, 73, 84; to Yarmouth, 97; operation ARH, 100; aground, 102; to Dutch, 103, 128

H7 crew arrives Montreal, 73; lends men to H10, 82, 84; to Yarmouth, 97; operation ARH, 100-104; Lowestoft raid, 136-138

H8 does trials with borrowed crew, 82, 92; operation ARH, 100-104; tractor seat, 103; into refit, 104; new battery, experiment in the Solent, 123; on patrol off Dutch coast, hits mine, 124-125; surfaces, damage assessed, 126-127; swings compass, encounters mines, 127; heads for home, has bearing and Nav O problems, prepares to dive, safe arrival, 128-130; extent of damage, 131; to Chatham, inspected by lady journalist, surveyed and paid-off, 132-133; crew and captain commended, 135, 139

H9, 145

H10 diving trials at Murray Bay, 82, 92; new battery, 79, 82, 95; first Lieut. late arriving, 84; M-Dougall rejoins, 90; battery problems, 95; first patrol, 98; operation ARH, 100-104; into refit, 104; Lowestoft raid, 136-138; attacked by aircraft, 138; Lawson joins, 139, 166; lost, 180

H11 sailed for UK, 188

H12 sailed for UK, 188

H14 to UK, forced to return USA, to be recommissioned, 187; wardroom all RNR, Johnson CO, to Bermuda, 191; into reserve, 194; ceded to Canada, 195, 204

H15, 186; to be commissioned, 187; accidentally sunk, 187; recommissioned, to Bermuda, 191; into reserve, 194; ceded to Canada, 195, 204

H30, 202

H34, 202

H51, 202

Haldane, Dr. J.S., FRS investigates illness in D3, 142-143

Hall, Alfred A., Lt. RNR joins D3, 179; killed, 183

Hall, Sydney S., Commodore (S), 82, 93, 132, 189

Hallifax, O.E., Cdr. assesses Donald, 210

Hampshire, HMS, 17

Hanson, Francis B., Lt. RNCVR capable CO, 104; CO of CC1, 168; died, 195

Halifax (Nova Scotia) sub crews arrive at, 70, 87; Dockyard, 16, 52; shore base for subs, 205

Hapsburgs, 15

Harcourt, Lewis - Colonial Secretary in London telegraphs Canadian PM and Gov Gen, 64

Harwich - sub HQ, 97, 139

Haslar Creek (berth for subs), 97

Haulbowlines, shipyard at Cork D3 into refit, 155; D4 into refit, 157

Hazen, J.D. - Minister of the Naval Service - wants to build SMs, 63; covers yardarm, 68

Herbert, Godfrey, DSO, Cdr. submariner, CO of Sea King, 160

High Seas Fleet, 97; Jutland, 140; immobilized, 188

Hiorns Reef, 97

Hizen, IJNS reinforces NA West Coast, 55

Holland Boat Company, 23, 33, 70

Hose, Commander Walter, 25; to sea in Rainbow, 44, 205

Hotel Place Viger, Quicke stays at, 73; Johnson stays at, 80

Houghton, Frank, Lt. volunteers for subs, withdraws, 193

Hughes, Colonel Sam, 21

Hughes, D'Oyly, DSO, DSC, Capt 1st Flot, 210

Hunting, Arthur J.S., Articifer Engineer, Flotilla Engineer for CC-boats, commended, 171, 205; cares for laid-up subs, returns UK, 195, 203

Imperial Conference on Defence, 205

Inflexible, HMS at Falklands, 55, 57

Influenza, Spanish flu epidemic, E38 knocked out, 193

Invincible, HMS flagship at Falklands, 55, 57

Iroquois, steamer, 29

Italy, 15, 139

Japan, 16, 18, 20; delays declaration of war, 44; Russo-Japanese war, 59

Japanese, in BC, 20; Imperial Navy, 18

Jellicoe, Viscount, 205

Jerram, Vice Admiral Sir Martyn commands W. Pacific force, 17; searches Java Sea, 50

Jenkins, G.E., Lt. CO H3, killed, 167

Johnson, Bernard Leitch, early recruit, 43; SM training, 45; released by Pilotage Commissioners, 50; accepts commission RNCVR, 51; friendship with Keyes, 57; appointed in command H8, 79; pleased to join H-boats, to RNVR, attached HMSDolphin, 80; experienced, 81; encounters Smith, 82; and RN officers, 85; has encounter with Little, 89-90; 92, transfers to RNR, 93; accepted in "The Trade", becomes "Cap", 94, 109, 123; mined in Akkepolle Gat, 124-131, 134; on leave, joins D3, 135; on patrol, 140; gassing problems, 142; refit and recuperation, 143; to Immingham, 145; finds Keyes again, overseas

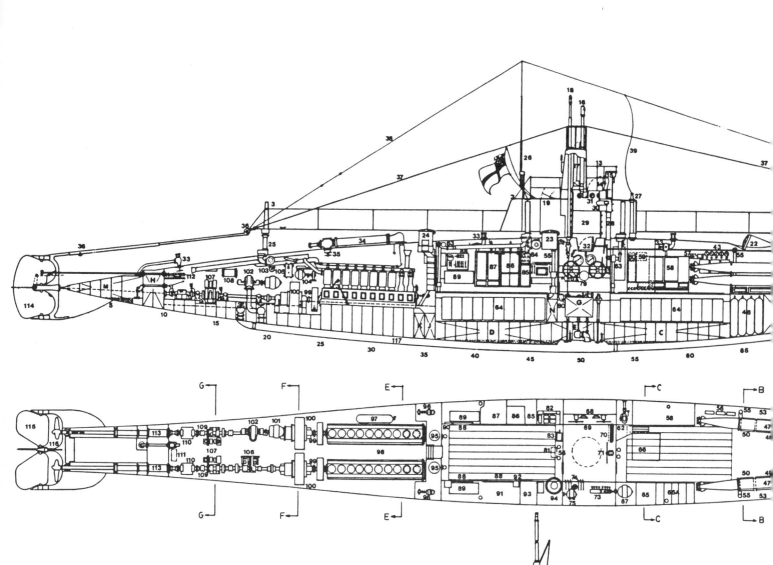

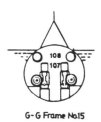

G-G Frame No.15

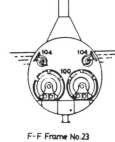

F-F Frame No.23

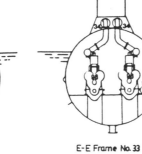

E-E Frame No.33

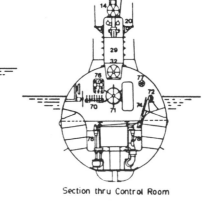

Section thru Control Room

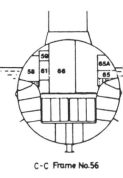

C-C Frame No.56

GENERAL ARRANGEMENT

ROYAL NAVY "H" CLASS SUBMARINES
H1 - H10

BUILT 1915, CANADIAN VICKERS LTD., MONTREAL, QUEBEC
ELECTRIC BOAT COMPANY DESIGN 602-E

DEPICTED AS RUNNING IN HOME WATERS, MARCH 1916
FROM AN ORIGINAL ELECTRIC BOAT CO. DRAWING DATED APRIL, 1915

TANKS

TANK	DESCRIPTION	CAPACITY (IMP GAL)	NOTES
A	NO.1 MAIN BALLAST	1,588	
B	FORWARD TRIM	1,158	
C	NO.2 MAIN BALLAST	6,504	
D	NO.3 MAIN BALLAST	5,937	
E	AUXILIARY BALLAST	2,080	MAIN COMPENSATING TANK
F	FUEL TANKS F1.	772	NORMALLY EMPTY ON PATROL
	F2.	903	
	F3.	1,190	
	F4.	1,482	
G	BUOYANCY TANK	218	AMIDSHIPS TRIM TANK
H	AFTER TRIM	535	
J	LUBRICATING OIL	675	
K	SUMP (APPROX)	85	
M	NO.4 MAIN BALLAST	816	AUXILIARY FUEL TANK
N	FRESH WATER	250	

MAIN BALLAS
AUXILIARY B
ALL TESTED
ALL FUEL TA
BUOYANCY TA

LUB OIL AND
FUEL TANK B
WATERTIGHT
HULL TESTED